PARTY POLITICS IN RU

Party Politics in Russia and Ukraine

Electoral System Change in Diverging Regimes

Bryon Moraski

NEW YORK UNIVERSITY PRESS
New York

NEW YORK UNIVERSITY PRESS
New York
www.nyupress.org

References to Internet websites (URLs) were accurate at the time of writing. Neither the author nor New York University Press is responsible for URLs that may have expired or changed since the manuscript was prepared.

Library of Congress Cataloging-in-Publication Data
Names: Moraski, Bryon, author.
Title: Party politics in Russia and Ukraine : electoral system change in diverging regimes / Bryon Moraski.
Description: New York : New York University Press, 2022. |
Includes bibliographical references and index.
Identifiers: LCCN 2021039778 | ISBN 9781479807758 (hardback) |
ISBN 9781479807765 (paperback) | ISBN 9781479807789 (ebook) |
ISBN 9781479807796 (ebook other)
Subjects: LCSH: Political parties—Russia (Federation) | Political parties—Ukraine. |
Proportional representation—Russia (Federation) | Proportional representation—
Ukraine. | Elections—Russia (Federation) | Elections—Ukraine. | Authoritarianism—
Russia (Federation) | Democratization—Ukraine. | Russia (Federation)—Politics and
government—1991– | Ukraine—Politics and government—1991–
Classification: LCC JN6699.A795 M67 2022 | DDC 324.20947—dc23/eng/20220118
LC record available at https://lccn.loc.gov/2021039778

New York University Press books are printed on acid-free paper, and their binding materials are chosen for strength and durability. We strive to use environmentally responsible suppliers and materials to the greatest extent possible in publishing our books.

Manufactured in the United States of America

10 9 8 7 6 5 4 3 2 1

Also available as an ebook

CONTENTS

Introduction

In February 2014, revolution shook politics in Ukraine for the second time in ten years. Like the 2004 Orange Revolution, Ukraine's 2014 Euromaidan, or Revolution of Dignity, does not qualify as a great revolution such as those that guided the academic contributions of Barrington Moore (1966) and Theda Skocpol (1979). However, among domestic participants and international observers, the moniker "revolution" circulated freely, and in both cases the politicians controlling Ukraine's executive branch lost power. Despite this similarity, much differentiates the two events. For one, the Orange Revolution was a response to electoral fraud. Following the second round of the 2004 presidential election, both sides levied accusations of malfeasance while supporters of the opposition candidate and former prime minister, Viktor Yushchenko, rallied and set up tents in Kyiv's Independence Square. In 2004, the conflict was resolved peacefully as the ruling of Ukraine's Supreme Court to repeat the second round of voting paved the way for Yushchenko's electoral victory over the outgoing president's hand-picked successor, Viktor Yanukovych. In the years following the Orange Revolution, Yanukovych would continue as a major player in Ukrainian politics, eventually emerging victorious in Ukraine's 2010 presidential election. However, unlike the events that kept him from office in 2004, President Yanukovych's political demise in 2014 was marked by violence and occurred in the absence of elections.

While Yanukovych presented himself as a moderate democrat seeking to heal past divisions during the 2010 election, Motyl (2010, 126) contends that Yanukovych, upon assuming office, undermined Ukrainian democracy, neglected the country's broken economy, and began realigning the country with Russia. In 2011, Freedom House downgraded Ukraine from "free" to "partly free."[1] The organization justified the shift by citing "deteriorating media freedom, secret service pressure on universities to keep students from participating in protests, government hostility toward opposition gatherings and foreign nongovernmental organizations, and an increase in presidential influence over the judiciary" ("Ukraine, Freedom in the World 2011," https://freedomhouse.org). In 2012, Ukraine's rating would fall lower as Freedom House criticized the regime's politicization of courts, crackdown on free media, and forceful dispersals of demonstrators.

President Yanukovych's actions appeared to take a more promising turn in 2013, thanks to talks with the European Union (EU) about a possible Ukrainian association agreement. However, tensions between the regime and its opponents came to a head on November 21, 2013, as a few hundred protesters took to the streets of Kyiv when Yanukovych announced his decision to reverse plans to sign an EU association agreement. While the demonstrations began as a dispute over policy, the tenor soon changed. In the early hours of November 30, Ukraine's riot police violently disbanded a pro-Europe rally, injuring hundreds of demonstrators. Although President Yanukovych subsequently condemned the use of force, an estimated 10,000 protesters gathered outside Kyiv's Mikhailovsky Cathedral, which had given sanctuary to the injured. By this point, the regime's use of force had become a rallying call for those challenging its legitimacy. As tents and barricades were once again erected on Independence Square, opposition politicians used the incident to call for an early presidential election.

An adequate account of the dramatic events between the initial protests and President Yanukovych's February 2014 departure from Kyiv, which was interpreted by Ukraine's legislature as a decision to vacate office, merits more treatment than what is necessary here.[2] However, one notable conclusion that could be drawn from the events is that they illustrated a need to strengthen the institutional framework for holding Ukrainian politicians accountable. Shveda (2014, 20), for example, contends that the Revolution of Dignity constituted a continuation of the Orange Revolution, which was successful but incomplete. Specifically, he identifies low levels of public confidence in governmental institutions in Ukraine as well as economic and social conditions that are "complicated by total corruption" (21).

While political scientists have sought to determine whether different institutional arrangements might be correlated with higher levels of public satisfaction than others (Pharr et al. 2000; Warren 1999), with the rules that govern legislative elections attracting particular attention (Aarts and Thomassen 2008; Anderson and Guillory 1997; Bernauer and Vatter 2012; Wagner et al. 2009), Ukraine has been no stranger to changes in how its national legislature is elected. Prior to the Orange Revolution, Ukraine elected its legislature using a mixed-member system that combined party-list, proportional representation (PR) in a single national district as well as single-member-district (SMD) mandates allocated on the basis of plurality rule.[3] In the two legislative elections that followed the Orange Revolution, a closed-list PR-only system was used. By 2012, the electoral system was changed once more, this time back to a mixed-member system. In other words, between 2002 and 2014, Ukrainian politics was characterized by two dramatic transitions of executive power as well as substantial changes to its legislative electoral system.

These developments make Ukraine an inherently interesting case for examining the effects of major electoral system changes on party politics. Specifically, a study of Ukrainian elections and parties during this time period offers an opportunity to develop new insight into how parties and legislators in a political regime characterized by competitive, even hotly contested elections navigate the implementation of newly adopted electoral rules. To better understand how parties and legislators navigate the operation of newly adopted electoral rules in a less competitive political environment, I examine an increasingly authoritarian regime where the legislative electoral system also moved from a mixed-member system to a PR-only system and back: the Russian Federation.

While the history of electoral system change in Russia in some ways parallels the Ukrainian experience, Russian politics has been characterized by a significant amount of political continuity in the executive branch, with Vladimir Putin serving as president or prime minister since August 1999. In 2003, Russia's legislative elections, like Ukraine's 2002 legislative elections, allocated half of the mandates using party-list proportional representation in a single national district and the other half using single-member-district plurality rule. In 2007 and 2011, a closed-list PR-only system governed Russia's legislative elections. During this period, President Putin was not only elected to a second term in office (in 2004); he also turned the presidency—though not necessarily executive power, as Putin became prime minister—over to a handpicked successor, Dmitri Medvedev (in 2008). In 2011, Russia's legislative election results were roundly denounced as fraudulent, leading to protests against the ruling party, United Russia, and against the anticipated return of Putin to the presidency. While dramatic, the popular protests failed to alter the outcome of the 2012 presidential election: Vladimir Putin returned to power for a third term and, in 2018, was reelected to a fourth term.

Based on this brief overview, one might conclude that Russia's and Ukraine's experiences with electoral system changes simply highlight the insignificance of electoral rules in the two countries. After all, Ukrainian politics has witnessed political instability, regardless of the electoral system in place, while Putin's regime appears to have consolidated itself while alternating electoral systems. Worse yet, we see two different sets of political outcomes despite what appear to be similar electoral system changes.

Although these observations are true, their veracity does not mean that the electoral system changes in Russia and Ukraine did not matter. Rather, I submit that these developments represent an opportunity to examine the extent to which the various opportunities and constraints associated with different regime types may influence party politics and legislator behavior. Specifically, I set aside more conventional questions about how electoral systems influence party systems, such as the number of parties contesting elections or represented in the legislature. Instead, I investigate how electoral systems affect the relationship between specific parties and individual legislators, with a particular emphasis on their implications for party development and party discipline. In other words, this book analyzes the consequences of Russia's and Ukraine's experimentations with PR-only systems by asking the following questions. First, how do parties respond to electoral rule changes, such as the institution of closed-list PR, that give them sole control over the nomination process? Second, how might authoritarian regimes, in particular, combine the use of PR with other institutional changes to consolidate power? And, finally, to what extent does answering these questions help explain the brevity of closed-list PR in these particular cases?

Electoral System Change in an Era of Electoral Authoritarianism

Although electoral system change had been depicted as a rare event (Dunleavy and Margetts 1995), the situation has changed since the end of the Cold War. Lundell (2010, 77–78), for example, finds that electoral system change in democracies became more common after 1991 and included several prominent cases, such as substantial electoral system changes in Italy, Japan, and New Zealand. As the developments in these established democracies raised new questions about the assumed durability of electoral institutions (Cox 1997, 18), transitions from communist rule provided fertile ground for examining the relationship between regime change and institutional choice (e.g., Bielasiak 2006; Birch et al. 2002; Crawford and Lijphart 1995; Luong 2002; Shvetsova 2003).

One consequence of these developments has been the shift from the study of how electoral systems shape party systems to one about why parties alter electoral systems. The prevailing consensus is that electoral systems and party systems have mutual effects (Benoit 2007, 364) and that self-interest largely determines the electoral system preferences of politicians and parties. Drawing on interviews with politicians in four established democracies, Bowler et al. (2006), for example, find that while politicians' ideological positions and attitudes about democracy structured their views of electoral system change, the effects of these considerations were less systematic and less influential than the effects of self-interest with those elected under an existing system less inclined to change it (see also Remington and Smith 1996). Such findings support Lijphart and Grofman's (1984, 11–12) contention that, although electoral system reform is possible, it is not probable.

Of course, electoral systems are changed, leading scholars to suggest that such instances may be an artifact of extraordinary historical circumstances (Nohlen 1984, 222–23). Institutional design following the collapse of communism, for example, has been likened to a "rebuilding of the ship at sea" (Elster et al. 1998) in Eastern Europe. In interwar Europe, the electoral threat that ruling parties faced following dramatic expansions in suffrage proved to be a powerful driver of change (Boix 1999; Calvo 2009). In both contexts, a prevailing view is that, when politicians and parties were charged with reformulating electoral rules, prospective assessments of the new rules' effects given the deciding politicians' self-interests guided the final decisions. Those who believed that they were in a position to dominate electoral politics in the near future preferred more restrictive systems, such as SMD-plurality, that tend to favor larger, more established parties. By contrast, those whose electoral prospects were uncertain preferred more permissive electoral rules, such as party-list PR, that lower the threshold for representation and allow more parties to access parliament. A crucial sticking point in the literature, however, is how to determine the actors' self-interests.

Andrews and Jackman (2005) submit that, despite different temporal and regional contexts, electoral rule design (or redesign) in both postcommunist Europe and interwar Europe operated under conditions of extreme uncertainty and that the levels undermined the ability of political actors to accurately predict future benefits from specific electoral rules. As they note, the ability of actors to confidently predict the effect of electoral rules on election outcomes requires relatively accurate information on "1) the number of parties that will compete in future elections; 2) the preferences of voters over these parties; and 3) the effect of the electoral rules themselves, especially institutional details such as the district magnitude or electoral threshold" (Andrews and Jackman 2005, 67). Moreover, each of these pieces of information are interdependent. Thus, politicians cannot gauge voter preferences unless they know the number of parties competing. Likewise, the ability to anticipate the consequences of new electoral rules depends on the information one has about voter preferences and the number of parties. According to Andrews and Jackman, the absence of reliable information on one or more of these dimensions should lead politicians to evaluate proposed reforms from the perspective of how their parties performed under the current rules in the previous elections. One should expect the status quo (which was generally majoritarian rules for the cases that Andrews and Jackman investigate) where a set of political actors both dominated the previous elections and control the electoral system decision. By contrast, where electoral uncertainty is high and politicians have reasons to hedge their electoral bets, the more likely it is that a version of proportional representation will prevail (Andrews and Jackman 2005, 82).[4]

One lesson from the literature is that electoral system change may be unlikely in the absence of larger historical developments that threaten the electoral position of the party or parties in power. However, Barzachka (2014) submits that electoral system changes may be an artifact of threats that are not necessarily electoral in nature. Specifically, she submits that, during democratic transitions in particular, a powerful ruling party more concerned about the stability of the regime than about electoral outcomes may accept a tactical loss of legislative seats in exchange for gains in another arena, such as policy, that can influence the regime's transition. Similarly, Bodian (2016) views extra-institutional threats of mass protests, civil unrest, and political violence by the opposition as driving cases of "imposed electoral reform"—that is, electoral system changes under single-party and dominant-party rule in West Africa. Together these works outline incentives beyond seat maximization that may lead rulers in nondemocratic states to engage in electoral system reform.

However, we still know fairly little about when and why authoritarian regimes alter the electoral systems governing their legislatures. One explanation for this gap may be that scholars have traditionally assumed that legislatures and elections in authoritarian regimes are of little significance. For example, Gasiorowski (1995, 883) questioned the relevance of institutional variation in authoritarian regimes. While he notes that Huntington's (1968) emphasis on political institutionalization matters to authoritarian regimes, Gasiorowski observes that questions about "consociationalism, party system structure, electoral rules, and the type of executive are largely irrelevant" in these regimes. Scholars have subsequently challenged this position (Blaydes 2010; Gandhi 2008).

There are reasons to expect a bias in favor of preserving the existing electoral system to prevail in authoritarian regimes where elections are the primary means of legitimizing political power. As Schedler (2013, 21) emphasizes, those governing electoral authoritarian regimes must continually work to preserve their hold on power and can never be confident in their ability to detect, let alone prevent or contain, threats. These dangers may elevate the level of risk aversion that incumbents have when it comes to altering the institutions that brought them to power. At the same time, those governing authoritarian regimes enjoy a large "menu of manipulation" at their disposal (Schedler 2002); as a result, the possibility of unintended consequences may lead authoritarian incumbents to see electoral system changes as more dangerous, or even too transparent, than other, subtler kinds of manipulation that can influence electoral outcomes (e.g., relying on patronage or dispensing rents). Ultimately, though, how authoritarian incumbents evaluate the trade-offs between changing electoral systems and relying on other tactics that influence legislative representation is an empirical question, and the final decision will likely depend on the perceived benefits of different electoral system options given the political context at the time.

Taken together, the literature suggests that electoral system change in authoritarian regimes may be rare events, as those who succeed under the rules in place will be reluctant to alter them. While this risk aversion also exists in democratic contexts, the twin uncertainties prevalent in electoral authoritarian regimes, as well as the forms of electoral manipulation at these incumbents' disposal, may make electoral system change even more unlikely. To the extent that electoral system change does occur in authoritarian settings, it will most likely occur when those in power are responding to electoral or extra-institutional threats. Indeed, if a challenge threatens the legitimacy of authoritarian regimes by piercing their image of electoral invincibility (Magaloni 2006), authoritarian incumbents may react swiftly and decisively.

Although the nature of electoral system change likely depends on the particular context and specific nature of the threat, extant literature suggests that autocrats should prefer majoritarian electoral systems, such as single-member-district plurality, over more proportional options. For example, Birch (2007) contends that electoral fraud and manipulation are both more likely and more efficient in SMD contests than in PR systems because: "Candidates in SMD systems have more to gain from individual efforts to manipulate elections, relative to their expected losses, than is the case for candidates in PR systems, and the number of votes that must be altered to change the outcome of the election is typically smaller under SMD than under PR" (1540). In other words, those interested in electoral falsification should prefer majoritarian elections arranged in low-magnitude elections (i.e., one to two seats per district) to more proportional rules that govern the allocation of seats in districts with large magnitudes. Schedler (2013, 234–40), moreover, finds that SMD-plurality systems are correlated with higher margins of victory, which buttress the image of electoral invincibility that authoritarian regimes value.

From this perspective, the adoption of nominally more proportional rules, such as the use of closed party-list PR, in authoritarian regimes appears exceptional. Indeed, according to McFaul (2000, 30), early in President Vladimir Putin's tenure, Putin's advisers spoke openly about eliminating Russia's PR mandates, a move that McFaul interpreted as one that could help "resurrect a system dominated by a single 'party of power.'" Turovsky (2011, 203) notes that it was odd to see the adoption of proportional representation in large post-Soviet states—not only in Russia and Ukraine but also in Kazakhstan and Kyrgyzstan—given the Soviet-era history of district contests, the prevalence of personalist politics in the region, and the territorial size of the countries in question. Stroh (2010), however, finds that the use of PR rules in Rwanda assisted the regime's centralization of power by undermining local accountability and by reinforcing a democratic façade that undermines the people's will. Stroh's work suggests that PR rules may complement authoritarian rule, just in different ways than majoritarian rules.

With this discussion in mind, I submit that the adoption of closed-list PR systems in Russia and Ukraine was a critical opportunity to develop greater party institutionalization, regardless of regime trajectory, because the new rules dramatically altered the politics of candidate selection by giving parties monopoly control over who could run for legislative office. This matters because control over the candidates who compete in elections is a function that conventionally defines political parties. Norris and Lovenduski (1995), for example, depict parties as the gatekeepers of elected office. Hazan and Rahat (2006b, 368), meanwhile, note that "a party's candidates will help define its characteristics—demographically, geographically, and ideologically—more than its organisation or even its manifesto. Candidate selection determines not only the choices before voters . . . but also the composition of the parties in the legislature, and, through them, the government and the opposition."

Electoral Systems and Party Institutionalization

While citizens may view political parties with suspicion, parties are central to the structuring of elections and the organization of modern governments. Apter (1965, 186), for example, observes that political parties generate, mobilize, and direct power, while Weiner and La Palombara (1966, 410) emphasize that political parties "have been an important and on the whole successful instrument for establishing legitimate national authority." As a result, scholars interested in democracy and democratization have dedicated a significant amount of attention to investigating the evolution and institutionalization of political parties (e.g., Aldrich 1995; Levitsky 1998; Randall and Svåsand 2002) as well as the role that a developed party system plays in facilitating democratic consolidation (e.g., Mainwaring 1999; Mainwaring and Torcal 2006; Morlino 1998; Weghorst and Bernhard 2014).

According to Bernhard and Karakoç (2011, 2), studies of party volatility—that is, the extent to which vote or seat shares fluctuate across parties from one election to the next—dominate the party institutionalization literature (see, e.g., Bogaards 2008; Kreuzer and Pettai 2003; Mozaffar and Scarritt 2005; Roberts and Wibbels 1999; Tavits 2008). Since institutionalized party systems are commonly conceptualized as instances where interparty competition is stable and parties have roots deeply anchored in society (Mainwaring and Scully 1995), this approach makes sense. However, since a party system is also a composite of the individual parties that make it up, scholars of party institutionalization also investigate how voters become attached to certain parties (Mainwaring and Zoco 2007; Manning 2005) and the degree to which individual parties employ programmatic appeals to win votes (Kitschelt et al. 1999; Kitschelt et al. 2010; Van de Walle 2003). Such works illustrate how the evolution of specific parties shape the operation of party systems. Randall and Svåsand (2002), in particular, contend that a failure to differentiate between the institutionalization of individual parties and the institutionalization of a party system actually runs the risk of overlooking key aspects of how politics operates in the developing world that may not conform to Western experiences.[5] As chapters 1 and 2 outline in greater detail, this book takes Randall and Svåsand's (2002) concerns to heart. Since parties in Russia and Ukraine are not mass-based organizations whose leaders are constrained by decades of democratic practice, one cannot assume that the operation of party politics there will conform to Western experiences. In the pages to come I investigate how specific parties in Russia and Ukraine responded to similar electoral system changes—the adoption of solely closed-list PR rules—that gave political parties monopoly control over the nomination of legislative candidates.

Although PR systems are generally described as preferable for developing democracies, closed-list PR systems that elect all their representatives via a single national district have their detractors. According to Barkan (1995, 108), for example:

> Democratization hinges on the simultaneous development of two different relationships: 1) *representation* of citizens by their chosen leaders,

a relationship characterized by dialogue and accountability; and 2) *tolerance, bargaining,* and *compromise* among rival political groups. The former links elites and nonelites who have a common political interest, and constitutes the "vertical" dimension of democracy. The latter obtains mainly between leaders of opposing interests, and constitutes the "horizontal" dimension of democracy. (italics in the original)

Thus, in his debate with Reynolds (1995) about the most appropriate electoral system for plural societies, Barkan (1995) encourages scholars to give questions of representation as much consideration as they do to consensus-building.[6] He notes that, especially in agrarian societies, "most people define their interests and differentiate themselves from one another on the basis of where they live, rather than what they do" (107). According to Barkan, rural residents view elections through a lens that focuses primarily on the needs of their local communities, from access to health care, schools, or even an adequate supply of water. As a result, rural voters often support the same parties and candidates because they are evaluating those parties and candidates on the basis of their potential or existing record of constituency service.

In Barkan's opinion, a closed-list PR system can systematically frustrate voter expectations because, where party leaders determine the composition of their party's list of candidates, which in turn influences the candidates' electoral chances, the political careers of existing or aspiring members of parliament hinge on satisfying their party's leadership. Service to specific geographic constituencies matter only to the extent that the party leadership chooses to prioritize it. Where such prioritization is absent, PR rules risk developing a suspended state, one "that is disconnected from the population and eventually loses its authority and its ability to govern" (108).

It is important to note that Reynolds's (1995) reply to Barkan emphasizes the plethora of systems subsumed under the moniker of "proportional representation." Thus, Reynolds contends that institutional designers "can retain one of the underpinnings of consociational government (a proportionally constituted parliament) while avoiding the main drawback of PR: the detachment and lack of accountability of representatives elected from party lists" (117). Among the potential remedies that Reynolds offers is to adopt a PR system that reduces the size of the multimember districts employed. Using multimember districts, which elect five to twelve members each, allows voters to elect deputies who will represent specific geographic constituencies while still allocating seats among contending parties in a fashion that would create the kind of inclusive legislatures considered desirable. More notable, however, is the second option that Reynolds identifies: mixed-member electoral systems—that is, systems that elect some representatives from single-member-districts and others from multimember districts using party lists.

I summarize this debate not only because Barkan identifies the lack of vertical accountability as a specific problem associated with PR systems that use closed party lists but also because Reynolds appears to accept this criticism for closed-list PR systems with large district magnitudes, such as those that elect all representatives via a single national district. The agreement is notable because it reveals how the electoral system changes that are the focus of this book are, by both accounts, in the wrong direction if one wants to strike a balance between horizontal and vertical accountability. In both Russia and Ukraine, politicians chose to replace mixed-member systems with closed-list PR systems that elected all representatives in a single national district. Equally important is the fact that scholars would not expect aspiring autocrats to move in this direction either. As already noted, extant literature expects autocrats to prefer majoritarian electoral systems, such as single-member-district plurality, over more proportional options.[7] Equally important is the fact that scholars would not expect aspiring autocrats to move in this direction either. As already noted, extant literature expects autocrats to prefer majoritarian electoral systems, such as single-member-district plurality, over more proportional options. These developments illustrate how electoral system changes in general may deviate from scholarly prescriptions and emphasize the extent to which the changes under investigation defy expectations and merit investigation.

I contend, however, that electoral system change offers autocrats more than just a tool for controlling election outcomes; it may also function as a means for promoting party institutionalization. In fact, to the extent that effective governance and political stability contribute to regime legitimacy, I submit that it is reasonable to expect autocrats in countries characterized by weakly institutionalized parties to consider changing the legislative electoral system in a direction that promotes party development. As such, authoritarian regimes seeking to advance party institutionalization may find more proportional rules appealing. More specifically, I agree with Meleshevich (2007), who submits that party control over candidate nominations is a largely underappreciated, albeit crucial, first step toward party institutionalization. While this underappreciation likely reflects the degree to which the extant literature is grounded in the experiences of established democracies, especially West European examples, a widening of the analytical lens to include post-Soviet cases in particular challenges the assumption that parties by and large control who competes in elections for national office. Removing this assumption thus creates new opportunities for examining the political consequences of adopting a closed-list PR electoral system. For example, previously independent legislators must receive a party nomination if they hope to extend their time in office, while political parties must decide whether they wish to pursue these proven, if more independent-minded, individuals as candidates—and at what cost. Chapter 1 develops these considerations further, while chapter 2 presents initial cross-party analyses for both Russia and Ukraine that lay the groundwork for the more rigorous investigations presented in chapters 3, 4, and 5.

Why Russia and Ukraine?

The relationship between electoral systems and party politics in Russia and, to a lesser extent, Ukraine has attracted scholarly attention not only because of the country's geopolitical importance but also because of the exceptional nature of the relationship. Moser (2001), in particular, uses the deviant case of Russian politics in the 1990s to illustrate how conventional expectations from the literature on electoral systems, including Duverger's Law,[8] fall short in contexts where political parties are weakly institutionalized. Moser then extends the analysis beyond Russia to similar cases—including other postcommunist cases such as Ukraine, as well as other countries employing mixed-member electoral systems—to probe the limits of his theory. Like Moser (2001), my work on Russia's electoral system began with an interest in seemingly deviant behavior: the regime's adoption of a more proportional electoral system despite its move in an authoritarian direction (Moraski 2007). As noted, conventional wisdom on legislative electoral systems would expect that more restrictive rules, such as SMD plurality, to prevail in authoritarian contexts rather than party-list PR, since the former facilitate electoral fraud (Birch 2007) and are correlated with higher margins of victory (Schedler 2013, 234–40). Indeed, Remington (2006, 5) depicts Russia's adoption of PR as particularly puzzling given both President Putin's "domination over parliament" and its expected impact of increasing the number of opposition members in the Duma. On the latter point, Remington notes that Vladislav Surkov, a Putin aide and liaison with parliament, emphasized how United Russia's 300-seat majority following the 2003 Duma elections relied on 80 percent of the SMD deputies joining the party after the elections. Thus, under a PR-only system, United Russia would have had a 239-seat majority (Remington 2006, 27).[9]

Although Russia's move toward closed-list PR has received substantial scholarly attention (discussed below), its consequences remain largely understudied. That being said, my interest is not to determine whether the Russian experience has been replicated in other authoritarian countries. Rather, I am interested in comparing and contrasting how parties and politicians across regime types respond to instances of electoral system change. From this perspective, the best option is to pair Russia with a case that experienced a similar electoral system change, despite a different regime trajectory, and that is also as similar to Russia as possible in terms of other potentially important variables. Ukraine fits this bill better than any other option available.

First, pairing an analysis of Russia with one of Ukraine helps control for historical and cultural legacies, thereby reducing the likelihood that observed cross-national differences in how the parties and politicians under investigation adapted to closed-list PR rules can be attributed to attitudes and behaviors rooted in the ancien régime. For seventy years, one-party rule and a nominally parliamentary system of government defined politics in Russia and Ukraine. The Soviet state used elections to control citizens, with universal participation serving as a means to socialize and manipulate the public (Birch 2007, 1541). While the nature of Soviet elections varied over time,[10] Herron (2009, 27) contends that elections across post-Soviet countries are likely to exhibit similar features due to their shared electoral experiences, including the

Communist Party's control over candidate nominations and a Soviet-era reliance on SMD majority rules. Hale (2014, 58–59) casts an even wider net, submitting that one important political continuity from the Russian Empire through the Soviet era—one that has shaped politics in contemporary Russia and Ukraine—is the legacy of patronalism, defined as "a social equilibrium in which individuals organize their political and economic pursuits primarily around the personalized exchange of concrete rewards and punishments" (20).[11]

Although shared histories may control for differences that might frustrate other cross-national comparisons (such as the amount of experience with multiparty elections or the prevalence of elite interactions grounded in patronage), Russia's and Ukraine's post-Soviet paths have diverged in meaningful ways. Arguably, the most notable distinction between the two countries that one might expect to influence party politics is the difference in presidential turnover. Despite similar executive-legislative arrangements,[12] Russia has experienced the transfer of presidential power from one handpicked successor (Putin, who was Boris Yeltsin's) to another handpicked successor (Medvedev, who was Putin's) and back (with Putin's 2012 return to the presidency). In Ukraine, by contrast, fiercely fought elections and popular protests have contributed to genuine instances of presidential turnover. Seven different presidents have led Ukraine so far: Kravchuk (1991–1994), Kuchma (1994–2005), Yushchenko (2005–2010), Yanukovych (2010–2014), Turchynov (February–June 2014, as acting president), Poroshenko (2014–2019), and Zelenskiy (2019-).

Differences in presidential turnover matter because presidential change often leads to the formation of new pro-presidential parties and thus to a transformation of the party system (Turovsky 2011, 198). Way (2016), for example, submits that political pluralism has prevailed in Ukraine precisely because Ukraine's presidents, as well as its oligarchs and former members of the *nomenklatura* who back them, have failed to centralize political control in a manner that would facilitate authoritarian rule and that this includes an inability to establish a well-organized and durable ruling party. The opposite, meanwhile, appears to hold true for Russia. In fact, the differences in presidential turnover are often used to indicate that Russia and Ukraine have experienced different regime trajectories. Brudny and Finkel (2011, 814), in particular, contend that while Ukraine under Kravchuk (1991–1994) and Kuchma (1994–2004) may have resembled Russia's hybrid regime during roughly the same period, the 2004 Orange Revolution—which brought a Western-leaning president to power following massive street protests over election fraud—signaled that part of Ukrainian society had rejected the Russian path of creeping authoritarianism. In their view, Ukraine's post-2004 trajectory more closely resembles those of countries in Central Europe than Russia's, thanks in part to the number of free and fair parliamentary and presidential elections that have been held since.[13] To explain this outcome, Brudny and Finkel focus on differences in the evolution of two countries' national identities.[14] They contend that Russia's liberals failed to develop a democratic alternative to an authoritarian national identity rooted in Russian imperialism while the same antiimperial attitudes that contributed to Ukraine's independence have impeded the emergence of a hegemonic, nondemocratic national identity in Ukraine (Brudny and Finkel 2011, 828–29).[15]

Given these developments, it is plausible that, for some scholars, the differences between Russia and Ukraine may challenge the premise that the two countries can be compared to one another. Yet comparisons matter most when they allow us to identify differences between the objects under investigation that may shape our expectations and understanding. Thus, I submit that, for certain questions such as party development and legislator behavior following instances of electoral system change, there are not only enough similarities but also enough meaningful differences to make a comparison of Russia and Ukraine intellectually fruitful.

Russian and Ukrainian Paths to Closed-List PR

The Russian Federation stands out as a valuable case for those interested in the rise of electorally dominant ruling parties because the current ruling party, United Russia, emerged in reaction to the country's experimentation with competitive (if not democratic) elections. From December 1993 through December 2003, the Russian Duma was elected using an unlinked, mixed-member electoral system: Half of its 450 seats were distributed via 225 SMD plurality elections; the other half were distributed through party-list PR with a 5 percent threshold. Although

Russia's election laws experienced some tinkering during this period (see Brudny 2001), the main features of its parliamentary electoral system were viewed as relatively stable (McFaul and Petrov 2004, 20–21).

Like many other postcommunist countries, Russia also lacked an institutionalized party system throughout the 1990s and early 2000s. Meleshevich (2007, 30), for example, observes that Russian parties failed to establish full control over legislative nominations, let alone act as political gatekeepers. In fact, other political organizations—from regional political machines associated with incumbent governors to politicized financial-industrial groups–emerged as party substitutes (Golosov 2004; Hale 2006). According to Smyth (2006, 103), Russia's mixed-member system offered aspiring legislators an option not available to legislative candidates elsewhere: whether to even affiliate with a party. More notable, perhaps, is that Russia also lacked a stable governing party for the early part of its post-Soviet history. During the Yeltsin era, the Kremlin seemed either unwilling or unable to establish a viable ruling party, moving from Russia's Choice to Our Home Is Russia to Unity over the course of three elections. Indeed, to the extent that United Russia emerged in 2001—after Unity joined with its toughest competitor in 1999, Fatherland–All Russia—the Kremlin offered the population a different pro-presidential party—commonly called the "party of power" in Russian politics—for every election through 2003.[16] According to Chaisty (2005), the emergence of a parliamentary majority under President Putin during the Third Duma (1999–2003) did little to improve the quantity of partisan legislation. While Russia's executive played a definitive role in fostering party cohesion, deputies belonging to legislative factions largely composed of regional politicians elected via the single-member districts (i.e., Russia's Regions and People's Deputy) still proved appreciably less disciplined than other members of the governing coalition (Chaisty 2005, 314–15).

Despite a number of institutional reforms that followed the March 2000 presidential election of Vladimir Putin, the core components of Russia's electoral system remained largely intact for the 2003 Duma elections (see Moraski 2006; Remington 2006). Indeed, the existing system seemed to work to the Kremlin's advantage: By the time the dust settled from the 2003 Duma elections, Russia's latest party of power, United Russia, had established a legislative status that no other party had previously attained in Russia: it enjoyed a constitutional majority of seats, thanks in large part to a postelection bandwagon effect (Clark 2005).

With substantial legislative support now at his disposal, President Putin moved to further consolidate power after his March 2004 reelection. Arguably, the most dramatic turning point came in the wake of the September 2004 Beslan hostage crisis, in which a group of terrorists occupied a school in a southern Russian town in the republic of North Ossetia and took more than a thousand children, parents, and teachers hostage.[17] Following these events, Putin called for a series of institutional changes that were designed to enhance the regime's ability to respond to challenges to state power. He identified two goals in particular: the establishment of a single system of authority, with key officials in Russia's regions more accountable to the president; and the strengthening of national parties. To accomplish the former, a system of presidential appointees would replace the popularly elected regional chief executives. The latter was to be accomplished by moving Duma elections to an entirely proportional representation system ("Vladimir Putin vystupil . . ." 2004).[18]

Drawing on a series of interviews with 17 "highly placed officials, politicians, or *eksperty*" directly involved in the reforms, White and Kryshtanovskaya (2011, 559) use the electoral system reform to peek "inside the black box" of political decision-making in post-Soviet Russia.[19] The interviews reveal that the primary goal of the reforms was to eliminate sources of unpredictability within the Duma or any elements that allowed regional politicians an opportunity to exert influence in a way that might undermine the stability and manageability of the country's system of government (White and Kryshtanovskaya 2011, 576). According to a senior member in the presidential administration, a proportional system "would on the whole be 'more transparent. I mean, transparent for us. For the Centre. Simpler to control'" (563). One reason this assessment prevailed among the interviewees was the shared belief that SMD deputies were "controlled by the regional authorities," making the elimination of these mandates "an 'action against regional influence'" (563). Thus, according to White and Kryshtanovskaya (2011, 563), although United Russia itself might possibly win fewer seats with the move to an entirely proportional system, the outcome was seen as a reasonable price to pay for a more easily managed Duma.

To a large degree, explanations from regime insiders complement existing scholarly explanations that depict the move to closed-list PR as part of a larger effort to consolidate United Russia's position as a hegemonic party (Smyth et al. 2007), or at least a "lasting" party of power (Moraski 2007), and to increase Kremlin control over the Duma (Remington 2006). Or, as Turovsky (2011, 203) puts it, while PR systems are typically associated with higher levels of political competition, some former Soviet states have adopted these electoral rules as a way to consolidate the elite and create pro-presidential legislative majorities by incorporating smaller pragmatic groups into ruling parties.[20]

According to White and Kryshtanovskaya (2011, 558), the adoption of Putin's proposed reforms was almost a given due to the president's control over the government and the fact that a pro-Kremlin party dominated the Duma: while some Duma deputies expressed concern about "the loss of their links with a particular locality" or "the attenuation of their relative independence," there was "little need to explain the merits of legislative changes or persuade a majority of deputies to adopt them, even if (as in this case) there was some initial reluctance to do so." The interviews substantiate this position. According to one official, described as "an independent-minded deputy from the United Russia fraction," the party's delegation in the Duma was merely "an extension of the executive and nothing more than that, it simply ratifie[d] the decisions of the executive" (569). According to a "leading election specialist," meanwhile, "we know precisely that the president stated his position" and also that his position was "not simply more influential than other views, but decisive" (569). Thus, the abolition of SMDs was "quickly supported even by those who had always been passionate proponents of the majority system" (569).

While the move to presidentially appointed regional chief executives took effect in early 2005, Russia's first PR-only elections occurred in 2007—that is, during the Duma elections that would set the stage for Russia's 2008 presidential election. Despite President Putin's repeated statements that he intended to obey the Russian constitution and step down in accordance with the mandated two consecutive term limit, the March 2008 presidential election itself proved uneventful. Indeed, the decision to change Russia's legislative electoral system from a mixed-member system to a closed-list PR system, and the 2002 decision to raise the legal threshold from 5 percent to 7 percent, have been interpreted as helping to reduce the uncertainty that might have been associated with Putin leaving the presidency (see, e.g., Moraski 2007). Indeed, according to at least one of White and Kryshtanovskaya's (2011, 560) respondents, the 2007 Duma elections were seen as the "main" event from the perspective that "[i]f we won, a victory in March 2008 would be inevitable."

Ukraine's first post-Soviet legislative elections were governed by a single-member-district majoritarian (or double ballot) system. Harasymiw (2005, 193) describes the incremental changes to Ukraine's electoral laws as a "slow and clumsy process, marked by much politics and considerably less imagination." Not only did Ukrainian political parties lack a monopoly on access to elected office; a proliferation of parties and the success of independent candidates largely defined Ukraine's first elections. In fact, due to the majoritarian requirement, only 49 deputies won mandates on Election Day despite a turnout of nearly 75 percent. A second round of voting was held over two weekends in April, with only 338 of a possible 450 deputies chosen by the middle of the month. Of these representatives, less than half (168) were affiliated with political parties (Harasymiw 2005, 196). The presence of so many independent deputies fragmented the parliament and impeded the formation of a stable majority (D'Anieri 2007, 155–57). Thus, from Harasymiw's (2005, 197) perspective, Ukraine's 1993 electoral law "did a very good job of inhibiting rather than facilitating" the initiation of competitive electoral democracy.

Although an entirely PR system would have been an effective means of dealing with independents, Ukrainian politicians instead opted for an unlinked, mixed-member electoral system that resembled the one governing Russian Duma elections at the time: Half of the assembly's 450 seats were allocated in a single national district using closed-list PR, and the other half were distributed via 225 SMD plurality contests. A main difference between the two countries' systems was that, in Russia, the threshold for representation in the PR tier was 5 percent, while in Ukraine it was set at 4 percent. Despite the lower threshold, the anticipated consequences of the two electoral systems were similar. As in Russia, the PR component of Ukraine's mixed-member system was expected to advance the cause of party-building, while the SMD-plurality component was expected to motivate the kinds of strategic behavior from parties and voters that would promote party consolidation (Birch 2000, 104). In other words, combining these two types of electoral tiers into a single system was viewed as an attempt to encourage both representation and accountability (Harasymiw 2005, 198).

The results of Ukraine's 1998 elections failed to meet expectations, however. While some party consolidation occurred under the new system, it was not much more than one might expect through the learning process that follows founding elections. The number of independents dropped from 163 to only 114 (D'Anieri 2007, 161), even though the number of seats available to independents was reduced by half. Meanwhile, despite a decline in the number of party factions gaining access in parliament (from 11 to eight) through the PR tier, 22 different parties or blocs gained access via the plurality tier (Birch 2003, 525). Ukraine's mixed-member electoral system thus preserved (if not contributed to) party proliferation in the country.

Ukraine utilized a mixed-member electoral system again in its March 2002 elections. The 2002 Verkhovna Rada elections are particularly noteworthy because they provided Ukrainian elites and voters a lay of the land leading into the country's upcoming presidential election, scheduled for 2004 (Kuzio 2003) while also showing modest signs of coalescence in the party system. In the PR half, the number of parties passing the 4 percent threshold dropped from eight to six, while the percentage of the vote for parties that failed to pass the threshold went from 34 percent to 19 percent (D'Anieri 2007, 160–61). In the SMD half, meanwhile, the number of independents declined to 93. Although larger parties in Ukraine began to see district mandates as impediments to legislative majorities (Birch 2003, 525), the results of the 2002 elections alone were insufficient to motivate Ukraine's move to a pure PR system. Instead, the change reflected additional shifts in the political landscape and, as in Russia, an attempt to gain greater control over the presidential succession process.

Ukraine's 2002 Rada elections operated in an altered political context. According to Kuzio (2003), in the 1990s issues of statehood, sovereignty, and territorial integrity had bred an uneasy alliance between oligarchic centrists and national democrats who sought to stave off domestic (i.e., communist) and foreign (i.e., Russian) challenges. Leading into 2002, however, Ukraine's borders were uncontested, and the primary issue on the political agenda was the country's political trajectory. Although Ukraine's more ideological parties, on the left and the right, were divided over economic reform, they supported deeper democratization. President Leonid Kuchma's administration and a ruling class of oligarchs, by contrast, favored a more authoritarian, corporatist regime (Kuzio 2003, 26). The lengths to which incumbent interests would go to maintain power became evident when secretly recorded audiotapes linked Kuchma and his inner circle to strong-arm tactics during the 1999 presidential election and other illegal actions, including the death of the journalist Heorhiy Gongadze (Herron 2009, 44).

According to Herron (2009, 45), the growing popularity of antipresidential politicians and the fact that the upcoming 2004 presidential election would determine Kuchma's successor were two critical factors stimulating the presidential administration's interest in institutional reforms. Kortukov (2019), in particular, observes that, while President Kuchma did secure a parliamentary majority following the 2002 elections, it was not particularly reliable and largely reflected the inability of four opposition parties, who were just five seats short of a majority, to agree on the distribution of leadership posts. Having failed in an attempt to create a dominant ruling party and with approval ratings at record low levels, Kuchma pursued an "exit strategy" that centered on constitutional changes and electoral reform (Kortukov 2019, 494).

In an effort to pass constitutional changes that would weaken his successor and strengthen parliament, Kuchma packaged them with changes to the electoral system that he hoped would help garner the necessary support. According to Kortukov (2019), although opposition parties were divided with regard to the proposed constitutional changes, they were united behind the move to a PR system. In fact, two opposition groups—Our Ukraine and the Tymoshenko Bloc—had spent two years promoting such a change. Despite this, however, both legislative factions abstained from the final vote, presumably because they questioned Kuchma's intentions. One Our Ukraine deputy, Jaroslav Kendzyor, for example, depicted the electoral system proposal as an attempt to bribe Communist Party and Socialist Party deputies: "We support this system [PR] . . . but not as bait for a constitutional coup" (quoted in and insertion by Kortukov 2019, 494). In the end, though, the proposed electoral system change passed—following an amendment to lower the legal threshold from 4 percent to 3 percent—with 255 deputies voting in favor.[21] The constitutional reform proposals, meanwhile, failed to secure the required 300-deputy supermajority for adoption (Kortukov 2019, 494), thus rendering moot the concerns of Our Ukraine and the Tymoshenko Bloc.

As this discussion highlights, the use of mixed-member electoral systems impeded party institutionalization in Russia and Ukraine as the different halves worked to the advantage of different types of candidates and parties. The plurality contests, in particular, allowed small parties and independents to circumvent the legal thresholds governing the PR ballot.[22] While the adoption of closed-list PR systems emerged as an obvious response to this situation, the option became viable not only when incumbent presidents could marshal the legislative support for such a change but also when they felt that such a change was politically expedient.

Despite these similarities, the first closed-list PR elections in Russia and Ukraine took place in countries with two very different regime trajectories. While the trajectory of the Russian regime at the time of its electoral system change was in an authoritarian direction and followed the ruling party's overwhelming victory in recent legislative elections (Gel'man 2006),[23] Ukraine's political trajectory at the time of its first PR-only elections were widely seen as moving in a more democratic direction, thanks in part to its 2004 presidential election and the Orange Revolution that helped bring a pro-Western politician, Viktor Yushchenko, to power (see, e.g., Hesli 2007).[24]

Figure 1.1 provides a sense of Russia's and Ukraine's regime trajectories from 1992 through 2015 according to the Electoral Democracy Index available in the Varieties of Democracy (V-Dem) dataset (Coppedge et al. 2018; Teorell et al. 2016). Teorell et al. (2016) utilize a global sample of 173 countries, starting in 1900, to address deficiencies that they identify in extant measures of electoral democracy, such as scores from Freedom House (https://freedomhouse.org) and The Polity Project (www.systemicpeace.org). Specifically, the V-Dem data rely on more than 2,600 country experts from around the world to score countries with regard to elected officials, the degree of free and fair elections, freedom of expression, associational autonomy, and inclusiveness of citizenship.

Similar to others, the scholars behind V-Dem ground these dimensions of electoral democracy in Dahl's (1971) work on polyarchy, and

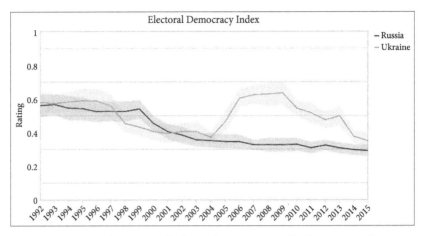

Figure I.1. Varieties of Democracy's Electoral Democracy Index for Russia and Ukraine, 1992–2015

as a result V-Dem's Electoral Democracy Index is strongly correlated with Freedom House and Polity measures. However, unlike those other indices, the V-Dem index also explicitly acknowledges the potential for measurement error and thus is accompanied by a measure of uncertainty (Teorell et al. 2016, 3). The corresponding confidence intervals that accompany V-Dem's Electoral Democracy Index therefore prove especially useful when comparing countries at similar levels of democracy because it helps scholars rein in the temptation to draw false distinctions. In figure I.1, for example, the shading that accompanies the lines reflects the uncertainty associated with the corresponding point estimates of electoral democracy and highlights the degree to which Russian and Ukrainian levels of electoral democracy overlapped from 1992 through 2004. Note, however, that the two countries diverged significantly from one another starting in 2005. Put differently, the two countries' regime paths clearly diverged in the years separating their last elections held under mixed-member electoral rules—2003 in Russia and 2002 in Ukraine—and the first elections held under closed-list PR—2007 in Russia and 2006 in Ukraine. During this period, the Electoral Democracy Index identifies Ukraine's regime as increasingly liberal and Russia's as increasingly authoritarian. While the two country's paths begin to converge again as the years progress, these data highlight how the adoption of fully proportional, closed-list systems in Russia and Ukraine constitutes a valuable (if fleeting) opportunity to explore how political parties in similar countries but different regimes respond to similar electoral system changes.

To conclude, politicians and parties in Russia and Ukraine witnessed changes in the rules that determined access to their national legislatures at roughly the same time in the two countries' post-Soviet transitions after years of district-based elections that undermined party institutionalization. In both cases, key questions that emerge are not only how political parties adapted to the new PR-only rules but also how district deputies, who were technically reformed out of office, navigated the changes. In chapter 2, I focus explicitly on district deputies as a way to assess the behavior of this crucial subset of prospective candidates—those who were presumably the primary target of the electoral system changes in both countries.

Plan of the Book

Chapter 1 begins with the observation that an expanded use of elections in authoritarian regimes offers new opportunities for those interested in seeking to investigate the relationship between electoral systems and party politics. Since scholars of regime transitions assert that party institutionalization shapes the consolidation of both authoritarian and democratic regimes, I review the extent to which weak party institutionalization characterized post-Soviet politics in Russia and Ukraine and describe how the countries' previous electoral systems operated in such contexts. This discussion lays the groundwork for the contention that prospective democrats and aspiring autocrats had reason to find closed-list PR electoral systems attractive, as well as for the assertion that the politics of candidate selection under these new systems offers a novel opportunity to analyze party development given that the new rules give parties control over who runs for office.

Since an important anticipated consequence associated with the move to closed-list PR systems in Russia and Ukraine entailed limiting the influence of more independently minded legislators, chapter 2 examines the degree to which different parties nominated those incumbents commonly identified as the most unruly: district deputies.

An investigation into the nomination of district deputies in the first PR-only elections offers insight into whether Russian and Ukrainian parties sought to maintain local ties, at least in the short term, as well as the degree to which the parties sought to reinforce existing elite bonds or build new ones. It turns out that Russia's ruling party, in particular, utilized list construction to co-opt previously unaffiliated district deputies, often preferring independents over other partisans.

While chapter 2 focuses on how multiple party organizations interact with a narrow set of incumbent deputies in an effort to better understand the factors that might attract similar candidates to different parties, chapters 3 and 4 limit the number of organizations and expand the range of candidate characteristics under investigation to examine which factors may have attracted parties to different candidates. These chapters consider each country in isolation, focusing in particular on the ruling party in Russia and the two Ukrainian parties with the largest number of deputies previously elected in district contests.

Chapter 3 uses Russia's closed-list PR system as an opportunity to investigate the development of United Russia. Specifically, chapter 3 analyzes whether the party's relationship with incumbent Duma deputies, as a pool of potential candidates, varied systematically on the basis of key characteristics such as previous party affiliations, the decision to bandwagon in United Russia's direction, legislative experience, and legislative mandates. The analysis yields several insights. For example, while United Russia appears to have preserved its relationship with deputies who had already committed to it, the party was also more likely to nominate district deputies than list deputies. The latter finding suggests that United Russia valued deputies with existing local ties. Just as important, chapter 3 presents evidence of party *system* institutionalization in Russia. It finds that United Russia was more likely to nominate independents and politicians from smaller parties than deputies previously nominated by the other major legislative parties: the Communists, the Liberal Democratic Party (LDPR), and Rodina. In fact, the variation uncovered corresponds closely to these parties' political origins and post-Soviet histories.

Following up the discussion in chapter 3, chapter 4 uses multivariate analyses to compare the range of factors that parties in Ukraine may have taken into consideration when nominating incumbent deputies following the move to a PR-only system. In contrast to chapter 3, however, chapter 4's focus on Ukraine widens the lens to examine the characteristics that helped or hindered the legislators' prospects of landing on one of two competing party lists. Chapter 4 finds that Ukraine's pro-presidential party, Our Ukraine, was more likely than the Party of Regions to co-opt previously unaffiliated deputies. In addition, the cross-party analysis reveals that, while Our Ukraine was more likely to nominate district deputies than list deputies, it did not systematically discriminate between mandates when ranking incumbent legislators. And while the Party of Regions did not discriminate among district and list deputies when selecting candidates for its 2006 list, it did tend to reward district deputies with better list ranks. Taken together, the results support the expectation that parties may use the move to PR rules to develop greater party organization by investing in candidates with existing ties to specific geographically defined constituencies, even though the mechanism—candidate selection or candidate ranking—may differ across parties.

Chapter 4 also reveals that, while co-optation levels varied across the two Ukrainian parties, both parties behaved in a way to suggest some concern for party unity following the 2006 elections. Specifically, both Our Ukraine and the Party of Regions were less likely to nominate deputies who had changed legislative factions more frequently in the preceding Rada. Since both parties pursued this practice, the results may be interpreted as reflecting a level of risk aversion among parties in weakly institutionalized, but still competitive, party systems.

In chapter 5, I pool legislators from Russia and Ukraine into the same analysis to compare the nominations by Russia's ruling party versus those made by the pro-presidential party and a primary opposition party in Ukraine. Chapter 5 finds that political parties—regardless of the regime in which they operate and their relationship with the executive—can be expected to navigate the move to PR-only rules by reinvesting in a core of seemingly loyal and experienced deputies. However, the analysis also suggests that prior party affiliation may mean different things to different organizations. For United Russia and the Party of Regions, prior party membership clearly mattered. The same cannot be said about Our Ukraine, for which a previous party nomination proved sufficient. In general, chapter 5 demonstrates how some party practices when navigating electoral system change may be common across regime type or party status (pro-presidential or not), while others may be party specific. Just as important, it reveals that, even if pro-presidential parties are more likely to invest in greater regional organization than other parties (see also chapter 2), the difference between that of a pro-presidential party in an authoritarian regime and that of a pro-presidential party in a more democratic regime may be far more than the difference between pro-presidential and opposition parties in a more competitive electoral environment.

The second part of the book changes tack, acknowledging that the conditions facilitating the comparisons made in chapter 5 were temporary due to the countries' evolving regimes. Chapter 6 investigates the Russian practice of placing regional governors on the ruling party's list. Building on prior research into reverse-coattail effects, the chapter contends that Russia's reliance on elections to legitimize the regime illustrates how electoral effects more commonly associated with democratic elections may prove relevant in authoritarian settings. While conventional wisdom holds that the expansion of "gubernatorial locomotives" between 2003 and 2007 bolstered the ruling party's regional vote shares, chapter 6 finds that United Russia also performed as well in regions where long-serving governors were left off United Russia's 2007 list as it did in regions where the locomotive practice was used. These results support a gubernatorial vulnerability hypothesis (developed in the chapter), which I contend reflects the Kremlin's leverage over all governors thanks to the system of presidential appointments in place at the time.

Chapter 6 also reveals that the effectiveness of locomotives in Russia varied not only across space but also across time thanks to the institutionalization of Russia's gubernatorial appointment system, which removed governors best positioned to deliver votes in the Kremlin's desired direction. In addition, this chapter contends that the proregime benefits of Russia's PR-only system did not depend solely on gubernatorial list placement, since under the new rules those regions that delivered more votes in the ruling party's direction were allocated more seats from United Russia's list. These rules incentivized the delivery of votes for United Russia in 2011 as a way for regional politicians to maximize levels of regional representation. Such behavior proves substantively important given the political circumstances in Russia at the time.

Chapter 7 turns attention back to politics in Ukraine. Although the chapter considers different indicators of party cohesion, the bulk of it focuses on the selection of the country's first prime minister following the implementation of Ukraine's PR-only electoral system. The vote is a critical moment in Ukrainian politics because it allowed the losing candidate in Ukraine's 2004 presidential election, Viktor Yanukovych, to reinsert himself into national politics as a legitimate and influential member of the executive branch. In fact, subsequent tension between Prime Minister Yanukovych and President Yushchenko was the catalyst for Ukraine's second PR-only elections, which were held in 2007. In general, the analysis presented in chapter 7 raises doubts about the ability of Ukraine's PR-only system to overcome the kinds of prior practices and elite behavior that had undermined the consolidation of the country's party system up to that point.

To conclude, the book summarizes the work's main findings and uses insights from the preceding chapters to evaluate the decisions to end Russia's and Ukraine's experimentations with PR-only rules. In general, the conclusion emphasizes the value of unpacking the institutional components of contemporary authoritarian regimes and calls for future comparisons of institutional changes across regime types as a way to better understand when, why, and to what extent similar institutions operate differently in diverse political settings.

1

Electoral Systems, Political Parties, and Candidate Selection

In many countries around the world, the expansion of multiparty competition since the end of the Cold War has not coincided with transitions to democracy (Carothers 2002) as much as transitions from authoritarian rule, with only the trappings of participation and representation, to other forms, in which rulers deploy popular elections as a way to attain greater legitimacy while still not releasing their grip on power. Levitsky and Way (2002; 2010), for example, identify regimes that base their legitimacy on multiparty elections where the playing field is heavily tilted in favor of existing rulers as "competitive authoritarian." Meanwhile, Schedler's (2006) concept of "electoral authoritarianism" emphasizes the centrality of elections to politics in many contemporary authoritarian regimes while challenging previous assertions that elections are instruments of democracy (e.g., Powell 2000).[1] In these regimes, election outcomes are depicted as the product of voter choices and regime manipulation (Schedler 2013, 239), meaning that victory depends on voter decisions (Claypool et al. 2018; Reisinger et al. 2017) as well as the means used by authoritarian incumbents to marginalize their opponents.

A fundamental premise of this book is that the expanded use of elections as vehicles for establishing legitimacy in authoritarian regimes provides new opportunities for examining the consequences of electoral systems. With this in mind, the work widens the analytical lens in two ways. First, while the majority of works examining electoral systems concentrates on countries that meet a minimum threshold of democracy, scholars in this tradition generally contend that their findings shed light on how democracy works. However, without examining electoral system consequences in authoritarian states, we cannot be confident that the dynamics uncovered from democratic cases tell us anything specific about democratic elections. If we see similar behaviors and consequences in authoritarian and democratic states, then it is problematic to assert that the outcomes reflect the democratic process. Instead, the behavior and consequences should be better understood as artifacts of electoral competition. The difference matters not only because it reminds scholars that democracy is more than the holding of elections but also because it illustrates how competition itself can lead actors to test, if not cross, established norms that set the rules of the game. In other words, from sports to politics, some people cheat. In fact, the higher the stakes of competition, the more incentive there is for actors to seek to win at any cost, and this may include changing the rules of the game themselves. In democracies, however, more actors abide by the rules more of the time, and the officiating, thanks to greater independence and impartiality, is better positioned to deter if not catch illicit behavior. Second, by closely investigating the effects of electoral system change in the same two countries over time, this book seeks to uncover the relative costs and benefits of the different electoral systems in each context. This effort highlights the degree to which similar outcomes in what may appear to be similar settings to the casual observer can stem from fundamentally different practices and developments.

To gain greater insight into how authoritarian regimes utilize electoral system changes relative to regimes with fairer and more competitive elections, I compare the operation of Russia's closed-list proportional representation (PR) electoral system to the operation of a similar system in Ukraine. By doing so, the work seeks to contribute to existing research on elections and legislatures in authoritarian regimes, research that unpacks how institutions commonly associated with democracy may serve authoritarian ends by operating as a means for co-opting elites (Boix and Svolik 2013), controlling existing party members (Magaloni 2006), and regulating state–society relations (Gandhi 2008; Gandhi and Przeworski 2006; Wright 2008). The work also reinforces the position of skeptics (e.g., Kaya and Bernhard 2013; McCoy and Hartlyn 2009) who question the claim that the process of holding elections improves democracy's prospects (e.g., Lindberg 2009); it does so by illustrating how any link between authoritarian elections and the prospects for democratization likely hinges on how successful autocrats are at using elections to serve their interests (Gandhi and Lust-Okar 2009, 215).

In this chapter, I discuss the issue of party institutionalization and highlight the degree to which its implications span regime types. For scholars of democratic consolidation and authoritarian consolidation, party institutionalization matters. In this context, I then review the degree to which weak party institutionalization characterized politics in many postcommunist states, including Russia and Ukraine, and consider the extent to which the electoral systems that were used preserved, if not contributed to, this situation. This discussion sets the foundation for understanding why democrats as well as aspiring autocrats might find closed-list PR rules attractive and how the politics of candidate selection may offer insight into the means by which political parties navigate this particular electoral system change.

The Importance of Party Institutionalization

Questions of party institutionalization have become foundational to the study of democracy. Mainwaring and Scully (1995), in particular, demonstrate how party systems in Latin America differ dramatically in terms of their levels of institutionalization; such variation has had important implications for the process of democratic consolidation in the region. More recent scholarship suggests that institutionalized party systems improve the ability of voters to make informed decisions (Moser and Scheiner 2012) and lead to stable policy-making (Flores-Macías 2012). Yet programmatic and ideological linkages between voters and parties have been weak in most third-wave transitions (Mainwaring and Torcal 2006, 204). For example, in an essay on the indispensability of political parties, Lipset (2000, 52) observes that two of the most important countries in Eastern Europe—Russia and Ukraine—suffered from unstable party systems throughout the 1990s. Meanwhile, in a global study of electoral rules and their effects on legislative representation and voting behavior, Norris (2004, 86) observes that Russian and Ukrainian experiences with mixed-member electoral systems proved exceptional: both had "fragmented multiparty systems despite using combined-independent electoral systems" due to "the existence of multiple social cleavages, and the election of many independents and small parties via the single-member districts."

While Norris's work is representative of a rich literature that emphasizes how legislative electoral systems structure democratic competition, party development, and voting patterns (e.g., Cox 1997; Cox and Katz 2002; Duverger 1954; Lijphart 1994; Rae 1967; Taagepera and Shugart 1989), the effects of electoral system change in illiberal contexts remains understudied. One reason for the discrepancy may be that, at first glance, it seems unlikely for formal institutions, particularly those governing elections, to matter much once political rights and civil liberties fall below a certain threshold. For example, Aldrich's (1995) assertion that mass enfranchisement provides incentives for politicians to invest in party-building might lead one to conclude that the relationship between legislative electoral systems and political parties matters little where voter preferences do not determine election outcomes.

Although an "equitable and open competition for votes between political parties" is a primary criterion for democracy (Huntington 1991, 26), party institutionalization is also widely considered "a necessary, though not sufficient" component of democratic consolidation (Meleshevich 2007, 11). The distinction between "necessary" versus "sufficient" is worth emphasizing, because scholars also present institutionalized parties as foundational to authoritarian stability. Huntington, for example, famously begins *Political Order in Changing Societies* with the claim that the "most important political distinction among countries concerns not their form of government but their degree of government" (1968, 1). He goes on not only to depict communist totalitarian and Western liberal states as examples of effective political systems but also to link this development to the presence of strong parties: "The modernizing countries which achieve high levels of actual and presumptive political stability possess at least one strong political party" (408). Recent scholarship corroborates the relationship between strong ruling parties and authoritarian stability (Brownlee 2007; Geddes 1999; Magaloni and Kricheli 2010; Smith 2005). Thus, scholarship on politics in both democratic and authoritarian regimes roundly associates party institutionalization with regime consolidation.

It is not surprising that scholars interested in the future of postcommunist Eastern Europe turned their sights to issues of party development (e.g., Grzymala-Busse 2002; Ishiyama 1999; Ishiyama and Kennedy 2001; Kitschelt et al. 1999; McFaul 1992). Since the communist regimes were examples of "elections without choice" (Pravda 1978), an association with a defunct ideology tainted the former ruling parties and contributed to a political vacuum across the region. As a result, many postcommunist states in Eastern Europe experienced high levels of electoral volatility (Tavits 2005; 2008), largely as an artifact of elite behavior. Zielinski and colleagues (2005, 365), for example, observe that politicians in Eastern Europe "frequently switch political parties either by creating new parties and abandoning their old ones or by moving from one existing party to another." They contend that such behavior bred weakly institutionalized parties with shallow societal roots and murky reputations (367). Russia's 1999 Duma elections poignantly illustrate this dynamic, with more than three-fifths of the proportional representation (PR) vote going to parties that had not competed four years earlier (Rose 2000, 54). Ukrainian elites, meanwhile, relied on what D'Anieri (2007) labels "disposable parties." For example, the two most successful competitors during the 2002 Rada elections were For a United Ukraine (FUU) and Our Ukraine, two electoral blocs that had not competed in the previous elections (D'Anieri 2007, 168–69).[2]

For Rose (2000), levels of party-system fluidity, such as those witnessed in Russia, impede democratic accountability. To the extent that different parties compete in every election, voters may be "tricked" into voting for politicians whom they would otherwise punish for their role in poor governance. Zielinski and colleagues (2005, 393) note that a strong electoral incentive to implement good policies emerges only when political parties have strong organizational cohesion. From this perspective, therefore, political parties must become lasting institutions if they are to play their proper roles in democratic societies (Aldrich 1995).

Complementing the studies of party institutionalization in democratic regimes is a rich tradition of scholarship investigating the consequences of legislative electoral systems (Duverger 1954; Lijphart 1994; Rae 1967; Taagepera and Shugart 1989). These works commonly depict voters as rational actors whose interests are defined in terms of their preferred party's electoral prospects, while electoral concerns are widely seen as driving the decisions of party leaders and party members about forming or joining new parties, which in turn determine the number and kinds of parties on offer. In other words, electoral motives help explain not only why parties emerge, persist, or fail under different electoral arrangements but also the variation in the number of political parties represented in different democratic legislatures around the globe. To the extent that government formation depends on the number of parties represented in these legislatures, this theorizing has also advanced our understanding of government stability (Dodd 1976; Laver and Schofield 1990) as well as (though more controversially) the congruence of policy with voter preferences (Golder and Lloyd 2014; Golder and Stramski 2010; Powell 2009).

For simplicity's sake, the effects of electoral systems on party systems in democracies are conventionally distinguished on the basis of two pure types: majoritarian and proportional. Since proportional systems generally grant more parties representation in parliament and increase the likelihood of coalition government, while majoritarian systems limit the range of representation and make stable, single-party governments more likely, scholars have depicted electoral system choice as a matter of taste. According to Lijphart (1994, 144), the choice depends on whether one values "minority representation and the principle of proportionality more highly than the two-party principle and government accountability, or the other way around." In practice, many features of proportional systems—from assembly size to electoral formulas to legal thresholds—can yield election results that more closely resemble majoritarian systems, while the use of the alternative vote or the double ballot can increase the probability that multiple parties—and the prospects for coalition governments—will persist under majoritarian rules. According to Gladdish (1993, 54), the range of options is "so elaborate as to make each set of national arrangements virtually *sui generis.*" It should not be surprising that political scientists have also dedicated significant energy toward considering which combinations of electoral rules may best facilitate democracy (Carey and Hix 2011; Hain 1986; Lakeman 1974; Norris 2004; Powell 2000), including in Russia (see Golosov 2012b).

Since PR and majoritarian systems have their respective tradeoffs, Lijphart (1994, 145) describes mixing electoral systems as a potentially fruitful endeavor for those interested in striking a balance between broader representation and greater accountability. Likewise, Shugart and Wattenberg (2001a) see electoral systems that combine PR and majoritarian mandates as providing an opportunity to balance the advantages and disadvantages of each system operating in isolation. They begin by dividing mixed electoral systems into two categories (Shugart and Wattenberg 2001b). In mixed-member majoritarian systems, voters cast two ballots: one to select a single candidate to represent a narrowly defined geographic district, and one to select a party usually offering a list of candidates to fill multiple seats representing a larger, possibly nationwide district. In mixed-member majoritarian systems, the two ballots are not linked to one another. In contrast, in mixed-member proportional systems, the two portions of the ballot are linked; as in German Bundestag elections, the party-based PR ballot determines the overall balance of seats with parties' share of seats elected via single-member districts subtracted from the share they receive in the PR tier. For Shugart and Wattenberg (2001a), the German case illustrates how mixed electoral systems can yield a stable, two-bloc party system. In a similar vein, Norris (2004) finds that the mean number of parties in mixed-member systems with many single-member-districts (SMDs) (e.g., Japan, South Korea, and Taiwan) fall closer to the mean number of parties found under majoritarian rules. Meanwhile, in mixed-member systems where the party-list share of the vote determines the overall distribution of seats (e.g., Hungary and New Zealand), the party systems tend to resemble those common to PR-only rules (see also Kostadinova 2002). However, Norris (2004, 93) also finds that Russian and Ukrainian experiences with mixed-member rules defy global patterns. According to Moser (2001), these exceptions reflect the degree to which the consequences commonly associated with electoral systems depend on the presence of well-institutionalized parties.

Like Shugart and Wattenberg (2001b), Moser (2001) emphasizes the difference between linked and unlinked mixed-member systems to explain why party politics in Russia and Ukraine in the 1990s, in particular, defied one of the most substantiated theories in political science: Duverger's Law, or the expectation for SMD-plurality (or first-past-the-post) electoral systems to produce two-party competition at the district level (Duverger 1954). Drawing on Western experiences and prevailing theory, Moser submits that, in unlinked systems such as Russia's, the mechanical effect of the SMD tier (i.e., its tendency to overrepresent larger parties when translating vote shares into seat shares) could be expected to have a greater effect on the final distribution of total legislative seats by adding disproportionality to the election results that would not be overridden by the PR tier (Moser 2001, 6–7). Conventional theorizing would expect such an outcome because elites and voters should behave strategically in the SMD contests: Like-minded parties would coordinate candidate nominations rather than risk exclusion, and voters would "satisfice" and support an acceptable candidate with a chance to win the election as opposed to a marginal candidate, since voting for the latter could increase the electoral prospects of an unacceptable alternative. In practice, however, Russia's SMD-plurality elections demonstrated high levels of candidate proliferation throughout the 1990s, and because Russian voters were in a poor position to identify prospective victors, sincere voting prevailed.

In the end, Moser (2001) submits that Russia's mixed-member electoral system produced more proportional results than Russian legislative elections would have witnessed had they been held under either set of rules in isolation. That is to say, nationally organized parties and loose coalitions that organized around nationally visible politicians performed well in the party-list PR tier, and parties with stronger regional organization and independent candidates performed well in the district elections (also see Moser 1995; 1997; Yargomskaia 1999). At the same time, Moser (2001) contends that these outcomes are not unique to Russia. He finds similar results in Ukraine's single-member-district (SMD) majoritarian contests before expanding his analysis to other postcommunist countries, as well as countries from other regions of the world, in an effort to demonstrate the degree to which his findings reflect variations in party institutionalization.[3] A particularly valuable conclusion from Moser's work is not only that a lack of institutionalized parties explains the unexpected outcomes he identifies but also that these outcomes—especially the proliferation of independent candidates competing in district contests—would continue in Russia as long as political parties failed to monopolize access to elected office (31).

Building on Moser's work as well as an emerging debate about interaction effects across electoral tiers (see Cox and Schoppa 2002; Ferrara and Herron 2005; Herron and Nishikawa 2001; Moser and Scheiner 2004), Bochsler (2009; 2010) questions the utility of mixing electoral tiers, submitting that the practice has inhibited the learning necessary to stabilize postcommunist party systems. Specifically, he contends that PR tiers lower entry costs for political parties, while majoritarian tiers produce just enough disproportionality to create unrepresented electoral niches that small parties seek to fill. Thus, by combining low thresholds in one tier and disproportionality in another, mixed-member systems contribute to a fluid configuration of party competition, high levels of party volatility, and relatively unpredictable electoral outcomes. From this perspective, Bochsler (2010, 756) submits that, at least in postcommunist states, mixed-member electoral systems more closely resemble Pandora's Box than the best of both worlds described by Shugart and Wattenberg (2001a).

Given these findings, one might reasonably interpret a decision to move from a mixed-member electoral system to a closed-list PR system as an institutional change with the potential to increase party institutionalization and, by extension, political stability. However, as noted from the outset, while party institutionalization and political stability may be critical to democracy's consolidation, they also contribute to the consolidation of authoritarian rule. Schedler (1995, 3), for example, proposes a curvilinear relationship between party institutionalization and the quality of democracy. In underinstitutionalized party systems, citizens fail to develop long-term attachments to parties, making their support transitory and election results contingent. While elections may still be used to hold politicians accountable, those elected to office may also undermine party institutionalization (e.g., by abandoning old parties and creating new ones) as a way to avoid such accountability. In overinstitutionalized party systems, meanwhile, voters are not only divided into captive markets with "given and fixed" preferences, but they also do not decide elections. Instead, "[c]andidates win elections by inheritance, and electoral results seem to be not only predictable but immutable" (Schedler 1995, 7). For aspiring autocrats, establishing an overinstitutionalized party system should prove more appealing than preserving an underinstitutionalized party system: Although either system may permit incumbents to legitimize their rule via elections while simultaneously avoiding electoral accountability, it is overinstitutionalized party systems that keep the electoral pendulum from swinging, which in turn makes a defeat at the ballot box possible but not probable.

Electoral System Change as a Catalyst for Party Change

In the electoral systems literature, proportional representation is commonly prescribed for developing democracies. PR systems not only have lower thresholds of representation that lead minority interests to form parties; they also allocate seats in a relatively inclusive manner, which should be appealing to plural societies (Andeweg 2000; Lijphart 2004). Electoral authoritarian regimes, in contrast, are believed to prefer more majoritarian systems because the corresponding disproportionality can convert small vote margins into decisive electoral victories, which in turn contribute to an image of regime invincibility (Schedler 2013, 234–40). Despite these generalizations, autocrats concerned about party institutionalization may have reason to find closed-list PR systems attractive. Way (2005a, 236), for example, contends that both informal ties and formal organizations such as parties serve to reduce elite defections that can threaten a regime: "[T]he absence or weakness of such organizations increases opportunism among allies, who are more likely to change sides when they perceive the incumbent to be vulnerable." Langston (2006, 57) agrees, noting that splits in the ruling party constitute one of the greatest dangers to electoral authoritarian regimes that rely on single-party governance.[4] Moreover, while Gandhi and Przeworski (2007) find that authoritarian regimes with durable institutions survive far longer than authoritarian regimes without them, Brownlee's work (2007, 2–3) emphasizes the importance of well-developed, cohesive ruling parties. Such observations suggest that authoritarian regimes interested in using political parties to consolidate their rule may therefore value closed-list PR thanks to a characteristic that has been observed in democratic contexts: the system's ability to "encourage the formation and maintenance of strong and cohesive political parties" (Lijphart 2004, 101). Work by Golosov (2016, 368) supports this position, submitting that authoritarian regimes may even draw on lessons from democracies about how electoral rules may produce desirable outcomes, such as party system nationalization. His analysis of 185 electoral democracies and authoritarian regimes reveals that electoral systems demonstrate similar effects. In both democracies and autocracies, electoral systems with high district magnitudes (i.e., proportional representation and mixed-member systems) facilitated greater party system nationalization while high legal thresholds impeded the ability of territorially based parties to win representation in the national assembly.

Although we still know relatively little about how legislative electoral systems operate in authoritarian regimes relative to democratic regimes (but see Golosov 2006; 2016; Lust-Okar and Jamal 2002; Stroh 2010), we do know that national elections can serve as focal points for popular protest (Tucker 2007) and therefore have the potential to destabilize authoritarian regimes. We also know that where state capacity is high—indicated by an ability to control the media and regional and local actors—autocrats are in a strong position to attain decisive victories at the ballot box (Seeberg 2021). From this perspective, holding elections may actually contribute to the long-term stability of authoritarian regimes as autocrats move beyond the short-term risks associated with elections and develop the tools of repression and co-optation needed for staying in power (Knutsen et al. 2017). In fact, legislatures and political parties have been identified as institutions that help authoritarian regimes co-opt and monitor elites (Boix and Svolik 2013; Magaloni 2006), regulate state–society relations (Gandhi 2008; Gandhi and Przeworski 2006; Wright 2008), and even reduce the chances for social protest (Reuter and Robertson 2015). Svolik (2012, 115), for example, finds that authoritarian regimes that employed legislatures and parties were significantly less likely to experience leadership change via coups or mass uprisings.

To the extent that legislative elections in authoritarian regimes function as exercises in "competitive clientelism" (Lust-Okar 2006),[5] it is reasonable to expect that authoritarian rulers may use electoral system change as a means to improve the electoral prospects of certain parties and even to alter the nature of existing patron–client relationships. As Stacher (2012, 31) notes: "Authoritarianism is not a stagnant governing approach. Political elites in Arab states [for example] constantly work to ensure that they remain in the regime and the system remains viable." With this in mind, studies of electoral system change in contemporary authoritarian regimes may provide new opportunities for understanding how such regimes use political parties and legislative elections to consolidate and maintain their hold on power.[6]

The idea that autocrats are adaptable and adapt in ways that are designed to keep them in power complements previous studies of party change and continuity in developed democracies. For example, both Panebianco (1988) and Harmel and Janda (1994) operate from the premise that political parties, although they are conservative organizations, can change when they have to. As Panebianco (1988, 242) notes, party changes may be responses to internal party politics (such as changes in leadership), external stimuli (such as an electoral threat), or both.

Harmel and Janda (1994) also remind us that parties are more than passive organizations. While parties may change in response to societal demands, party changes also may reflect internal party developments. In other words, internal party decisions and party-specific goals matter. At the same time, Harmel and Janda submit that perhaps the most powerful stimuli are those that challenge a party to reconsider its ability to effectively meet its primary goal, whether that goal is winning elections or something else (such as policy advocacy).

Taken together, the extant literature lays a foundation for the expectation that common concerns may lead different political parties operating in different types of regimes to pursue similar tactics if those parties are confronted by similar stimuli—whether internal or external—and are driven by similar motivations. For example, if an ability to deliver decisive electoral victories defines ruling parties in authoritarian regimes, then any stimulus that would make such an outcome appear less certain should yield a party response. Specifically, these parties can be expected to make internal party decisions that will reflect a desire to avoid changes in the status quo—that is, party decisions will be designed to help the ruling party preserve its electoral dominance. However, to the extent that a ruling party in a democratic regime is also motivated by a desire to preserve its electoral position, there is ample reason to expect similar party behavior despite the differences in regime type. Of course, regime differences may make some tactics (particularly, the use of coercion) more viable for the ruling party of an authoritarian system than for a ruling party in a democratic one (see, e.g., Frye et al. 2014, 2019).[7] In practice, the observed differences should reflect the different opportunities and constraints that the parties encounter given the regimes in which they operate rather than different party motivations.

In sum, if political parties have similar goals and concerns, then scholars should expect those organizations to respond to stimuli in similar ways, with ruling parties in particular pursuing tactics designed to preserve the status quo (i.e., their positions of power) and, more likely than not, opposition parties seeking ways to alter the status quo. While the ability of the parties to effectively reach these goals will vary from organization to organization as well as by regime type, parties and politicians operating in any regime where electoral victories determine access to the corridors of political power are likely to be motivated, at least in part, by what Mayhew (1974) identifies as the electoral motive.[8] As such, electoral system change may be a powerful catalyst for party change and, in turn, changes in legislative behavior.

Candidate Selection and Party Institutionalization

A central mechanism associated with closed-list PR electoral systems that facilitates strong and cohesive parties is the role that political parties play in nominating legislative candidates, including decisions about where to rank politicians on their lists of candidates, as these decisions directly impact those individuals' electoral prospects. Specifically, the likelihood that a specific candidate will be elected depends on her rank relative to the number of seats that her party wins. Typically, if a candidate holds the seventieth spot on a party list and the party only wins sixty-nine seats, then she will not be awarded a mandate.[9] Since party leaders generally use the power of list placement to promote party discipline and limit dissension (Andeweg 2000, 529), replacing an electoral system that employs single-member-district mandates with a solely closed-list PR system not only changes the institutional framework that governs candidate selection but also should promote party cohesion.

Ranney (1981, 75) defines candidate selection as "the predominantly extralegal process by which a political party decides which of the persons legally eligible to hold an elective public office will be designated on the ballot and in elections communication as its recommended and supported candidate or list of candidates." According to Rahat and Hazan (2001, 109), candidate selection is not only part of the larger process of political recruitment but also a defining function of political parties in a pluralist democracy, possibly even "*the* function that separates parties from other organizations" (Hazan and Rahat 2010, 6; emphasis in original). While candidate selection may be central to parties in advanced industrial democracies (Farrell and McAllister 1995; Katz 2001; Norris and Lovenduski 1993, 1995; Studlar and McAllister 1991), Meleshevich (2007) contends that the politics of candidate selection is better understood as an indicator of party institutionalization. Meleshevich's work complements Randall and Svåsand's (2002) contention that relying on a concept of party institutionalization that primarily reflects the context of Western industrialized democracies risks overlooking key aspects of politics in the developing world simply because they do not conform to that distinctive experience.

According to Meleshevich (2007, 30): "The existence of effective non-party, alternative ways of political recruitment for the legislative branch of government indicates a low level of party-system institutionalization." In these instances, the national legislature will generally consist of an unusually large number of independents or a large number of deputies who may be elected under a party label but who do not have especially strong links to the party nominating them.[10] In fact, for Meleshevich, post-Soviet party systems, as in Russia and Ukraine, are cases in point. In none of the elections to the lower house of Russia's Federal Assembly, the State Duma, held between 1993 and 2003 did Russian parties establish full control over legislative nominations or act as political gatekeepers. According to Smyth (2006, 128), an uncertainty about the value of party labels and the fact that Russian parties did not have monopoly control over electoral resources led to a proliferation of organizations designed to "suit the needs of different types of candidates." As a result, independents constituted large swaths of the country's national legislators, representing narrow business interests or politicized financial/industrial groups as well as regional political machines (Golosov 2004; Hale 2006; Zudin 1999). Moser and Scheiner (2004, 582) place the abundance of unaffiliated deputies in post-Soviet legislatures in comparative perspective:

> While independents win less than 10% of the vote in Japan, in Russia officially nonpartisan candidates took 58% of the vote in 1993, 38% in 1995, and 43% in 1999. Independents in Russia not only made up a large proportion of candidates competing for office, they also accounted for the largest proportion of the winners. Fifty-two percent of winners were independents in the 1993 Russian elections, 34% in 1995, and 46% in 1999. Ukraine and Armenia had similarly high levels of nonpartisanship in their SMD tiers with 48% of the SMD vote going to independents in Ukraine and 44% in Armenia.

For Moser and Scheiner (2004), the presence of party substitutes and the election of independent deputies in Russia and Ukraine resulted, at least in part, from the electoral rules in place at the time. The mixed-member systems in both countries provided aspiring legislators with a decision unavailable to legislative candidates elsewhere: whether to even affiliate with a party. As Smyth (2006, 138) notes, legislative candidates in Russia could decide the extent to which they wished to attach themselves to a party, which in turn had implications for whether they campaigned under a party label, expressed support for a particular party platform, or sought to cultivate a personal vote.[11] One particularly important aspect of the move to closed-list PR in Russia and Ukraine was that these changes granted political parties a monopoly over the nomination of legislative candidates (i.e., under closed-list PR, prospective legislators must be nominated by a party to compete as candidates for office) and tied the candidates' electoral chances to their nominating party's electoral performance.

Although monopoly control over candidate nominations should help institutionalize political parties, it does not guarantee party system institutionalization, let alone the institutionalization of any specific party.[12] As Meleshevich (2007, 30–31) points out, party institutionalization not only requires that ambitious politicians see parties as "the exclusive springboard to power"; for most of them, electoral success depends on a career within a party. In a similar vein, Svolik (2012, 164) contends that, for a ruling party to contribute to the survival of an authoritarian regime, politicians must not only become party members but also must see service to the party as a prerequisite for career advancement, which will in turn give them a vested interest in the regime's preservation. Only once these conditions are met does a party have the opportunity to experience what Levitsky (1998, 79–80) calls "value infusion"—the process by which politicians and voters come to value a party as an organization rather than simply seeing it as a means for winning elections and pursuing policy goals.[13] If one extends this expectation to cases of electoral system change, how a political party treats party insiders relative to other individuals seeking legislative office will offer insight not only into how that party has adapted to this stimulus but also into whether its tactics were conducive to its institutionalization, as individuals are less likely to become emotionally invested in an organization that treats its members poorly.

On the whole, the methods that parties use to select candidates are not only "nonstandardized and predominantly unregimented" (Hazan and Rahat 2010, 4); they are largely secretive, even in democracies (Gallagher and Marsh 1988). Since candidate selection is an internal party process, parties in most countries determine the rules governing the process and are free to change those rules largely as they see fit (Hazan and Rahat 2006b, 367–68). As a result, generalizing across parties (let alone across countries) is difficult. To overcome this obstacle, Hazan and Rahat (2006) recommend concentrating on the "selectorate" of a party (i.e., those who select the candidates), because the selectorate has "the most significant and far-reaching" consequences for legislative behavior. For example, the likelihood that legislative deputies will toe the party line is greater when party elites control nominations, since the party leadership is less likely to renominate deputies deemed disloyal. Meanwhile, legislators who are not dependent on any party organ for reselection put party cohesion at risk (Hazan and Rahat 2006b, 369).

Hazan and Rahat (2006b, 370) also submit that one might expect similar candidate selection methods to prevail in some cases: "First, every political system and political culture will generate norms that are likely to restrict the parties' choice of candidate selection to a more limited variety of 'legitimate' or acceptable methods. Second, parties tend to imitate one another." From this perspective, similar political cultures and shared experiences, such as a history of weak party development, as well as similar electoral systems can be expected to yield similar candidate selection methods. In fact, Russia's ruling party, United Russia, and the two main Ukrainian contenders under investigation, Our Ukraine and the Party of Regions, all convened party congresses to formally adopt their candidate lists prior to their countries' first closed-list PR elections. And, according to Hazan and Rahat (2006b, 370), party congresses reside in the middle of the selectorate spectrum. They are neither particularly inclusive nor particularly exclusive, which matters, since the authors also find that moving from a more exclusive selectorate to a more inclusive one influences the degree of party cohesion, the level of intraparty competition, and even the representativeness of the legislative delegation.

Media coverage of the closed-list PR election campaigns offers some insight into the "unregimented" nature of candidate selection in Russia and Ukraine, even with the parties' seemingly similar selectorates. Russian media, for example, reported that the list of candidates proposed by United Russia's party leaders at its 2007 party congress enjoyed wide support, with 476 delegates voting to adopt it, three opposing it, and two abstaining. Yet journalists also noted that President Putin appeared to play an influential role in the list's construction. The head of the party's central executive committee, Andrei Vorobyov, publicly acknowledged that the list was tweaked on the basis of recommendations from Putin, which included limiting the number of oligarchs on the list ("*S''ezd 'Edinoi Rossii' Utverdil Federal'nyi Spisok Partiii*" 2007). To the extent that one person—President Putin—may have determined the party's relationship with specific candidates, or a specific subset of candidates, United Russia's selectorate can be deemed as moving closer to the exclusive end of the spectrum. This dynamic contrasts sharply with other news reports that United Russia's party list would reflect results from internal party primaries. Ultimately, however, the primaries were neither public affairs (Petrov 2007) nor decisive. For example, among the governors on United Russia's 2007 party list, six were documented as not having participated in the primaries ("List of 'Snubbed' Governors" 2007, 11). However, since some attempt to take regional interests into account—regardless of whether the interests were those of the public or of regional elites—seems to have characterized United Russia's candidate selection process, it seems appropriate to locate United Russia's selectorate in the middle of the spectrum. It also offers a reason to expect that United Russia's 2007 list would include politicians with regional ties, such as deputies previously elected via district mandates.[14]

The potential for key individuals and internal party politics to play significant (if obscured) roles in the candidate selection process can also be seen in Ukraine. While members of the Party of Regions confirmed the list of candidates at its December 2005 party congress ("Partiya Regionov" n.d.), party leaders were responsible for compiling the list. In fact, Ukrainian media reported that it was the party's leader, Viktor Yanukovych, who asked an influential Ukrainian businessman, Rinat Akhmetov, to compete as a candidate for the party ("Rinat Akhmetov budet ballotirovat" 2005).[15] For Our Ukraine, meanwhile, its status as an electoral alliance introduces an additional dimension to the politics of candidate selection with interparty negotiations among the six parties' leaders shaping the process. In this case, while the core of the alliance— the People's Union Our Ukraine—adopted its list of candidates at a party congress ("Krome Yushchenko . . ." 2005), internal bloc politics limited the share of its candidates on the unified list to 65 percent ("V bloke Yushchenko . . ." 2005). Thus, unlike the cases of United Russia or the

Party of Regions, one should expect leaders from the different parties composing the electoral bloc of Our Ukraine to populate much of its 2006 list and that their positions may have come at the expense of less influential party figures, including incumbent deputies.

As this discussion suggests, an analysis of how party organizations in different regimes respond to similar electoral system changes must contend not only with potential confounders operating at the country level but also with party-level explanations associated with differences in the formal and informal politics of candidate selection. In other words, while the countries and timing in question permit substantial control over potentially important system-level variables while targeting regime differences as one potential explanation for diverging outcomes in how the closed-list PR systems operated, variations in party behavior also likely reflect party-specific differences. With this in mind, chapter 2 begins the empirical analysis by narrowing the pool of prospective candidates under investigation while allowing greater variation in the number and types of parties. Chapters 3–5 expand the number of prospective candidates under investigation and limit the number of parties.

Conclusion

In this chapter, I review literature on party institutionalization and electoral systems to contend that the politics of candidate selection in the aftermath of electoral system change may offer new insight into party development. In developing democracies as well as developing autocracies, closed-list PR systems may prove to be an appealing option for those concerned with party institutionalization. In fact, to the extent that effective governance and political stability contribute to regime legitimacy, I submit that it is reasonable to expect autocrats in countries characterized by weakly institutionalized parties to consider changing their countries' legislative electoral systems in the direction of those that promote party development. This discussion, however, raises a new question: How do parties in weakly institutionalized party systems balance the potential benefits of nominating politicians with proven electoral records and legislative experience against the risks to party discipline? I turn to this question in chapter 2.

2

Closed-List Proportional Representation and the Dynamics of Candidate Selection

In chapter 1, while discussing how Russia and Ukraine have suffered from weak party institutionalization, I emphasized the degree to which this matters to the consolidation of democratic as well as authoritarian regimes. Given the extent to which the electoral systems used in those countries had preserved, if not contributed, to this condition, I depict closed-list proportional representation (PR) rules as a potentially attractive reform option, as it gives political parties monopoly control over the nomination of candidates. In other words, such a step toward PR eliminates the opportunity for aspiring legislators in Russia and Ukraine to run for office as independents. The adoption of closed-list PR systems also moved the politics of candidate selection to center stage, turning list decisions into opportunities for observing how individual parties navigate major electoral system changes. In these cases, a primary question emerges: How did parties in Russia and Ukraine balance the potential benefits of nominating certain politicians—specifically, those with proven electoral records and legislative experience—against the risks to party discipline that these individuals might represent? Of course, one possibility is that parties might resolve this conundrum by simply avoiding potentially troublesome politicians in the first place.

This chapter represents an initial attempt to tackle this important question. I begin by justifying the decision to narrow the field of prospective candidates to incumbent legislators—that is, those prospective candidates with the most leverage vis-à-vis political parties. I focus on one meaningful subset of incumbent legislators: Russia's and Ukraine's district deputies. These politicians merit closer investigation because (1) they constitute the group of deputies who technically lost their mandates due to the electoral system changes under investigation; and (2) they still possessed characteristics that political parties may have found desirable, such as the ability to garner the support of a plurality of voters in geographically delineated districts.

Incumbents as Prospective Candidates

While the quantity and types of prospective candidates for any party are, in theory, limited only by the number and diversity of adults in society meeting the formal legal requirements for candidacy, the number and types of prospective parties with a chance of winning a substantial share of legislative seats are relatively small. The asymmetry of this many candidates/few parties scenario gives parties an advantage in the two-sided relationship of party list construction: prospective candidates have a relatively small number of potential mates, while parties enjoy a plethora of options. From this perspective, then, it is entirely plausible that parties could avoid nominating candidates whom they see as risky bets.

Despite the asymmetry that exists between candidates and parties, list construction decisions must still be mutual, and some politicians are simply more attractive candidates than others. In other words, some prospective candidates will, on average, have more leverage vis-à-vis potential nominating parties than others. With this in mind, in this chapter I concentrate on why incumbent deputies—that is, individuals presumably with more leverage and more options—affiliate with specific parties in the aftermath of electoral system change.

Incumbent legislators possess characteristics that are both politically meaningful and readily observable to political parties. In other words, they constitute a pool of prospective candidates who are, by and large, known quantities. Since these traits are also observable to scholars, analyzing a party's willingness to nominate certain sitting legislators and not others permits an opportunity to explore decisions within the "secret garden of politics" (Gallagher and Marsh 1988). At the same time, for a cross-national analysis, focusing on incumbent legislators helps to ensure that all of the individuals under investigation have met the necessary candidacy requirements, which can vary from country to country.

In chapters 3–5, I consider a range of the characteristics, including differences in legislative mandate and source of nomination, that may have influenced the party nominations of incumbent legislators during the first closed-list PR elections in Russia and Ukraine. This chapter examines a wider range of parties while narrowing the prospective candidates to those who were technically reformed out of office: district deputies. District deputies constitute a qualitatively important subset of potential candidates. Similar to other incumbent legislators, district deputies should have possessed more leverage vis-à-vis political parties than individuals who did not already hold national legislative office, thereby providing a better opportunity to examine the politics of list construction from the perspective of candidates with greater agency in the process. The ability of district deputies to win personalized contests and their positions representing geographically delineated constituencies should make many district deputies "free agents" with characteristics that parties find appealing. Indeed, some district deputies may have emerged as attractive candidates precisely because of their connections to the regional political machines or politicized financial-industrial groups that had allowed them to compete successfully as independents under the previous electoral system.[1]

The Parties

While political parties are central to scholarship in political science, political scientists do not always agree on what constitutes a party, since providing such a definition has normative implications (White 2006). Aldrich (1995, 283–84), for example, notes: "Political parties can be seen as coalitions of elites [seeking] to capture and use political office" and that a "major political party is an institutionalized coalition, one that has adopted rules, norms, and procedures." For current purposes, conceptualizing parties as coalitions of elites pursuing public office makes sense, but defining "major" political parties as those that are more institutionalized places the cart before the horse, since I am interested in how parties adapt to—if not capitalize on—electoral system changes that could help institutionalize them in the first place. With this in mind, I employ Sartori's (2005, 56) definition of a political party: "A party is any political group identified by an official label that presents at elections, and is capable of placing through elections (free or non-free), candidates for public office." One benefit of this definition is that it does not assume that parties are highly formalized organizations, but it permits the possibility that the "official label" in question could identify an electoral alliance of political organizations (i.e., an electoral bloc).[2] This approach complements how post-Soviet states regulate parties where electoral blocs are not necessarily subject to higher legal thresholds and where electoral legislation generally "defines parties as *voluntary citizen organizations designed to articulate citizen interests and to participate in politics*" (Herron 2009, 80; italics in original).

Another benefit of Sartori's definition is that it allows for the possibility that decision-making power operates via informal channels outside the party, including personal connections and patronage networks. This matters because informal relationships may influence key elements of party politics in developing states, including politicians' career paths (Freidenberg and Levitsky 2006, 179), as illustrated by the abundance of eponymous parties and blocs that have participated in elections across the former Soviet Union (Herron 2009, 83). Meanwhile, in this chapter and those to come, I use the phrase "major parties" to identify organizations winning enough district seat shares to facilitate comparison.

From Unity to United Russia: The Making of a Dominant Party

Although political parties are commonly depicted as foundational to the operation of modern democracy, they can also play important roles in totalitarian, authoritarian, and electoral authoritarian systems (see, among others, Duverger 1954; Huntington 1968; Levitsky and Way 2010; Schedler 2013). Political parties not only generate, mobilize, and direct power (Apter 1965, 186); they can also function as key instruments for national authority (Weiner and La Palombara 1966, 410). As more regimes have managed to consolidate power via elections but without other components necessary for democracy, including the rule of law, political science has witnessed a renewed interest in the rise of organized and cohesive parties as vehicles of governance in illiberal states (e.g., Gandhi 2008; Greene 2007; 2010; Magaloni 2006; Reuter 2017). According to Brownlee (2007, 2–3), for example, it is the presence of a well-developed, cohesive ruling party that separates durable authoritarian regimes from unstable ones (see also Geddes 1999). By his account, strong, cohesive ruling parties generate two self-reinforcing dynamics. The party's presence provides collective benefits that help maintain political unity. In addition, with this greater cohesion, the opposition is denied allies within the government, which keeps the opposition weak. With the establishment of a cohesive ruling party, therefore, elections in authoritarian states function like safety valves as those in power use elections to regulate societal discontent and relegate the opposition to the margins (Brownlee 2007, 8).

The Russian Federation stands out as a valuable case for those interested in the rise of electorally dominant parties because the ruling party during most of Putin's reign, United Russia, emerged in reaction to the country's experimentation with competitive, if not democratic, elections. Like many other postcommunist countries, Russia not only lacked an institutionalized party system throughout the 1990s (Golosov 2004; Hale 2006; Moser 2001); it also lacked a stable governing party. During Boris Yeltsin's presidency, the Kremlin seemed either unwilling or unable to establish a sustainable ruling party, moving from Russia's Choice to Our Home Is Russia to Unity over the course of three elections. Indeed, to the extent that United Russia emerged in 2001 after Unity joined with its toughest competitor in 1999, Fatherland–All Russia, the Kremlin actually offered the population a different pro-presidential party—commonly called the "party of power" in Russian politics[3]—for every set of elections through 2003.[4]

In the 2003 elections for the lower chamber of Russia's national legislature, United Russia won more than 49 percent of the vote and established a legislative majority. Going into the 2007 elections, United Russia amassed a membership of 1.66 million (Sakwa 2011, 23) and co-opted a majority of Russia's governors (Reuter 2010; 2017) while preserving its image as the party of President Putin (Ivanov 2008; Roberts 2012a). In fact, President Putin personally led United Russia's 2007 party list, a move that helped maximize United Russia's vote share while also making it the first pro-presidential party in post-Soviet Russia to win a majority of seats in two consecutive legislative elections (2003 and 2007).

Smyth (2006, 102) depicts United Russia's rise as "meteoric." Despite originating from an entity, Unity, that lacked structure and organization, it enjoyed substantial electoral success and legislative discipline, thanks in part to acts of "coercion and out-of-system behavior." In fact, United Russia's ascent is widely associated with a reversal of competitive electoral politics in Russia (e.g., Gel'man 2005; 2006; Laverty 2008; Wilson 2006).

In 2005, Freedom House, for example, changed its assessment of the Russian Federation from "partly free" to "not free" (www.freedomhouse.org).

Among scholars studying Russia, Reuter and Remington (2009, 503) tackle head-on United Russia's conversion into a "dominant" party, which they define "as a party that has the leading role in determining access to most political offices." They contend that in a dominant-party authoritarian regime, opposition forces may be allowed to compete, but they also are largely marginalized. Equally important, the dominant party, thanks to its determinative role as a successful supplier of benefits, "can reduce transaction costs for elites in bargaining over policy, give career opportunities to ambitious politicians, manage conflicts and succession struggles among elites, mitigate uncertainty for elites over whom to support, and coordinate electoral expectations on the part of elites and voters" (Reuter and Remington 2009, 503).

While Reuter and Remington (2009) depict Russia's ruling party, United Russia, as a dominant party following the 2007 Duma elections, others would not have been so quick to employ that moniker. Meleshevich (2007, 104), for example, notes that United Russia's longevity "remains to be seen." Sakwa (2011, 12) contends that United Russia's role as a "dominant party" was a limited one because political parties in Russia are essentially regime "accessories" (also see Roberts 2012a). Since executive power is paramount in Russia, Sakwa (2012, 311) suggests that Russia has a dominant *power* system as opposed to a dominant *party* system. Bogaards (2004, 175), meanwhile, operationalizes a dominant party as one that "has won a parliamentary majority plus the presidential elections, where present, in three consecutive multi-party elections." In subsequent work, he applies the "three elections" rule to authoritarian contexts—that is, those where dominance is preserved through extrademocratic means—as well as more democratic contexts (Bogaards 2008, 115).

With these considerations in mind, Reuter and Remington's (2009) work may be understood as investigating a dominant-party-in-the-making since—using Bogaards's (2004) indicator—United Russia did not qualify as a dominant party until after the 2011 Duma elections.[5] This matters because both the 2007 and 2011 elections were governed by closed-list PR rules, making the question of the electoral system that was in place as the party consolidated its electoral dominance particularly relevant. In fact, regardless of the nomenclature employed, Reuter and

Remington's (2009, 518) account highlights the degree to which United Russia's evolution depended not only on the public endorsement of the Kremlin but also on institutional reforms, such as changes to the Duma's electoral system. These changes helped United Russia overcome the commitment problem that plagued previous pro-presidential parties.[6]

While applying the literature on party development to aspiring dominant parties may allow us to better understand how such parties emerge, it is not entirely evident that the Kremlin would be motivated to invest much in a ruling party beyond what had been established with the 2001 merger of Unity and Fatherland–All Russia. Specifically, Smith's (2005) theory of the origins and durability of single-party rule contends that the fiscal and political conditions at a party's inception shape its long-term trajectory. According to Smith, authoritarian elites invest in party-building when they encounter "organized opposition in the form of highly institutionalized social groups such as mass-mobilizing parties or dedicated foreign or colonial armies" and when they "have little or no access to rent sources" (422). Rulers who do not face an organized opposition and have ample access to rents that can be allocated to constituencies have little incentive to build much in the way of party organization.

Although Russia's pro-presidential party during the 1999 Duma elections, Unity, did face a relatively organized challenger (for Russia at least) in the form of Fatherland–All Russia, the latter party did not qualify as a mass-mobilizing party. Rather, it was an electoral alliance of the Fatherland movement—which was created by Moscow's mayor at the time, Yuri Luzhkov, to promote his presidential ambitions—and what was essentially a club of a number of regional leaders (Brudny 2001, 158–59). More important, the Kremlin dealt with Fatherland–All Russia by bringing it into the fold: the former rivals merged into a single party—United Russia—in December 2001.

Much has also been made of the Putin regime's ability to capitalize on Russia's wealth of natural resources, especially oil and gas reserves (e.g., Jaffe and Manning 2001; Rutland 2008; Treisman 2010). McFaul and Stoner-Weiss (2008, 78), for example, point out that real disposable income in Russia increased by more than 10 percent relative to 2000, consumer spending skyrocketed, and unemployment fell appreciably to 6 percent in 2006 (from 12 percent in 1999). These gains are regularly linked to world oil prices, which increased during most of Putin's first two terms in office. Since Russia also occasionally surpassed Saudi Arabia during this period as the largest oil producer in the world and the state solidified its control over the Russian oil industry with the 2003 arrest of the oligarch Mikhail Khodorkovsky and seizure of the oil company Yukos, Russia's rulers had sufficient access to rents going into the 2007 Duma elections. Moreover, even if these benefits probably stemmed more from good fortune than from good policy (McFaul and Stoner-Weiss 2008), the average Russian appeared to reward both President Putin and United Russia. McAllister and White (2008, 950), for example, note that Putin's approval ratings not only started high, at around 76 percent in January 2001; they actually improved over time, reaching 87 percent by December 2007. More telling, though, is their finding that support for Putin was primarily tied to the country's economic performance as opposed to other factors, such as perceptions of Putin as a strong leader. Meanwhile, Rose and Mishler (2009, 130) find that Russians' approval of the economic system is the primary determinant of whether they endorse the existing regime and that this matters more than whether elections are free and fair.

While Smith's (2005) work implies that the Kremlin had little reason to invest in a ruling party beyond the investments it had made by the time of the 2003 Duma elections, Reuter and Remington (2009) point out that Smith's theory rests solely on incumbent incentives and that a full understanding of dominant-party emergence requires an investigation into the willingness of other elites to commit to the party. Specifically, do elites see the party as a primary vehicle for gaining access to the corridors of power? If they do, then the party's long-term prospects improve dramatically. However, this contention also suggests that political opportunism drove individuals to the ruling party, implying that a change in political winds could lead them away as well. To stem party defection, it is critical for those in the upper echelons of power to remain committed to the party and continue to invest in it over time. At least in the short term, a party's institutionalization depends on the incumbent rulers' commitment to it; however, this is another questionable piece of the puzzle for United Russia. Kryshtanovskaya and White (2009, 291), in particular, compare the party affiliations of different groups of Russian elites and find that the percentage of United Russia members declines as one moves from governors (81 percent) to Duma deputies (70 percent) to government ministers (7 percent) to Kremlin officials (3 percent). This finding indicates a commitment problem within the executive branch, where the true power lies. Moreover, as Reuter and Remington (2009) acknowledge, the process of party development itself may impose costs on those in power, since constructing a dominant party requires state leaders to cede some personal autonomy as well as some control over patronage and policy to the party.[7] In other words, investing too much in United Russia risks its emergence as an independent source of power and thus as a threat to presidential power (see Hale 2006, 207).[8]

Even if the Kremlin's commitment to United Russia's development at the time of Russia's first PR-only elections was far from assured, the timing of those elections should have worked in the party's favor. According to Weiner and La Palombara (1966, 410–11), leadership succession can be an important juncture in party system development. Brownlee (2007) likewise identifies periods of succession as critical moments in the life of authoritarian parties. In his cases, "[p]arties provided the bridge . . . from one leader to the next, revealing that regime persistence hinged not on one figure's preternatural political acumen but on the continual organizational infrastructure in which all were embedded" (205). From this perspective, one important aspect of the first PR elections in Russia is that they were also the legislative elections preceding the transferal of presidential power from President Putin to his handpicked successor, Dmitri Medvedev. Given the inherent uncertainty that accompanies any change in presidential leadership, the move to closed-list PR in Russia was likely an important step in the process of institutionalizing United Russia: The move not only granted parties sole control over the nomination of legislative candidates; United Russia's status as the party most closely associated with the Kremlin in general and Putin in particular could function as a source of organizational continuity during this period of succession (Moraski 2006; 2007).

Ukraine's Fragmented Party System

While the election of Ukraine's second president, Leonid Kuchma, initially benefited from a well-developed regional network in Dnipropetrovsk, Kuchma—like Yeltsin in Russia—relied on the support of a variety of political parties and oligarchs during his time in office

(1994–2004) (Way 2016, Chapter 3, "Authoritarian State Building . . .").[9] As a result, many of the hallmarks of post-Soviet party politics characterized Ukraine's 2002 elections—the mixed-member elections that preceded the country's move to closed-list PR. The party system was fragmented, patronage ties often defined party-building, and legislators regularly switched political party affiliations, with the parties and electoral blocs themselves changing names and in turn weakening their ties to the electorate (Semenova 2012, 29). In this context, a typical party's prospects often hinged on the fortunes of its leader, as political personalities mattered more than particular platforms or ideologies (Diuk and Gongadze 2002, 160). The electoral bloc of Viktor Yushchenko, Our Ukraine, is one such example.

After leading Ukraine's government as prime minister from 1999 through 2001, Yushchenko created Our Ukraine following an April vote of no confidence that removed him from office (Kuzio 2005, 29). The party's organization benefited from the support of Kuchma's official representative in the legislature, Roman Bessmertnyi, as well as that of Petro Poroshenko, the leader of the pro-presidential party, Solidarity. Poroshenko not only headed Our Ukraine's 2002 election campaign; he also helped Yushchenko win the backing of a powerful business network that included oligarchs from banking, energy, and food production (Way 2016, Chapter 3, "The Tapes Crisis . . ."). Among the masses, Yushchenko's leadership during a period of sustained economic growth made him a symbol of hope and a rallying point for those opposing President Kuchma (Diuk and Gongadze 2002, 159). Thus, by the start of Ukraine's 2002 election campaign, the locus of opposition had shifted away from the Communist Party of Ukraine and toward Our Ukraine as well as toward another electoral coalition, the Tymoshenko Bloc, founded by Yulia Tymoshenko, a former deputy prime minister for fuel and energy in Yushchenko's cabinet (Kuzio 2005, 29–32).

Since Ukraine's political system at the time, similar to others in the post-Soviet space, significantly concentrated political power in the executive branch, the 2002 legislative elections assumed particular importance because they set the stage for the country's 2004 presidential election. While Our Ukraine's electoral performance was expected to portend Yushchenko's presidential prospects, those interested in preserving the status quo backed the pro-Kuchma bloc, For a United Ukraine

(FUU).[10] One important similarity between Russia's and Ukraine's party systems prior to the adoption of closed-list PR rules was the creation and re-creation of parties dedicated to backing the president and defending a regime that invested significant power in the presidency (Diuk and Gongadze 2002, 162). In fact, Wilson (2002) contends that political technologists from Russia promised to deliver a Ukrainian version of Unity, which won more than 23 percent of the votes in the 1999 Duma elections despite not having existed just a few months before. While President Kuchma initially vetoed this option, preferring to divide and conquer his opponents, "the growing threat from former prime minister Viktor Yushchenko and his Our Ukraine bloc forced the authorities to launch the rival [FUU] project in the fall of 2001" (Wilson 2002, 92).

The FUU bloc consisted of five parties as well as several prominent unaffiliated political figures, such as the head of the presidential administration, Volodymyr Lytvyn, the railways minister, Heorhiy Kyrpa, and a renowned pole-vaulter, Serhiy Bubka (Meleshevich 2007, 47). Diuk and Gongadze (2002) depict the parties that composed For a United Ukraine as epitomizing the kinds of personality-driven organizations that characterized post-Soviet party systems at the time. The parties were led by "oligarchs or officials from the president's circle who mouthed reformist-sounding slogans but were clearly in the race to preserve the current opaque and impenetrable system that [had] enriched so many of those with access to power" (Diuk and Gongadze 2002, 160). According to Way (2016), For a United Ukraine was an artifact of the weak party structure that ultimately undermined President Kuchma's ability to consolidate authoritarian rule, one that not only encouraged defections but also limited Kuchma's choice of Viktor Yanukovych, the governor of Donetsk Oblast in eastern Ukraine, as a potential successor: "Yanukovych was the natural choice as successor not because he was the candidate most likely to appeal to the broadest number of Ukrainians but because he possessed the strongest and best-funded organization among the competing pro-Kuchma 'clans'" (Way 2016, Chapter 3, "National Divide . . .").

Two notable parties that were part of the For a United Ukraine bloc are the People's Democratic Party (NDP) and the Party of Regions. Founded in 1996, the People's Democratic Party was expected to help consolidate centrist forces behind President Kuchma. NDP members became head of the presidential administration (Yevhen Kushnaryov, 1996–1998) and prime minister (Valeriy Pustovoitenko, 1997–1999). Going into Ukraine's 1998 legislative elections, the NDP positioned itself as the moderate wing of the Kuchma regime and offered a gradualist approach to the economy that would prioritize market reforms while guaranteeing jobs, terminating wage arrears, and supplying adequate pensions (Zimmer and Haran 2008, 553). However, in Ukraine's 1998 elections, the NDP performed much better in the single-member-district (SMD) contests (picking up 71 seats) than it did nationally, where it received about 5 percent of the list vote, resulting in only 17 seats. Over the next four years, the NDP suffered from a lack of internal cohesion, and by the 2002 elections its legislative faction had been reduced to those 17 list deputies (Zimmer and Haran 2008, 554).

As the fortunes of the NDP waned, the Party of Regions became the electoral core of For a United Ukraine. Thanks to its status as the ruling party in the eastern region of Donetsk, the Party of Regions did not simply back Kuchma; it also proved to be especially effective at machine politics. In 2002, for example, the Party of Regions contributed significantly to the electoral success of FUU. While the bloc received only 11 percent of the national vote, it won almost 40 percent of the vote in Donetsk (Zimmer and Haran 2008, 554). According to D'Anieri (2019), the rise of the "Donetsk clan" and the electoral influence of the Party of Regions—especially in the SMD elections in eastern Ukraine— reshaped the balance of power among Ukraine's oligarchs. By 2002, Donetsk Oblast was more than the country's most populous region: Its primary oligarch, Rinat Akhmetov, emerged as Ukraine's wealthiest individual, and the Party of Regions proved "more adept than any other in the country at converting patronage into votes and party discipline" (D'Anieri 2019, 106).

International and domestic observers described Ukraine's 2002 elections as severely tarnished by government efforts to manipulate the vote. The Committee of Voters of Ukraine, for example, documented the use of state resources against opposition parties, while other nongovernmental organizations reported an uneven playing field with state- and oligarch-owned media openly promoting candidates who supported the regime (Diuk and Gongadze 2002, 160). Still, among the six parties or blocs to pass the 4 percent legal threshold governing the list vote in

2002, Yushchenko's Our Ukraine led the way with 24 percent. The Communist Party—also an opposition party—was second with a little less than 20 percent. The pro-presidential bloc, For a United Ukraine, came in a distant third with just under 12 percent. The Tymoshenko Bloc, the Socialist Party, and the Social Democratic Party (United) rounded out the field of successful list parties with single-digit performances (Official Website of Ukraine's Central Election Commission, available at www. cvk.gov.ua).

Despite a poor national showing in 2002, FUU still managed to assemble a faction of 175 deputies to start the new legislative session, thanks to victories in the single-member-district contests and decisions by many independent deputies to join the bloc in the elections' aftermath (Semenova 2012, 29).[11] Shortly after the elections, Viktor Yanukovych became Ukraine's new prime minister, and key government posts were awarded to the electoral parties that comprised the new pro-presidential majority. Yanukovych's deputies included senior members of the Party of Regions (Mykola Azarov), the Agrarian Party of Ukraine (Ivan Kyrylenko), Labor Ukraine (Dmytro Tabachnyk), and the Social Democratic Party (United) (Vitaliy Hayduk) (Meleshevich 2007, 71).[12] Our Ukraine, meanwhile, equivocated, not certain as to whether it should operate in opposition or strike a deal with Kuchma as he prepared to leave office in 2004 (Kuzio 2005, 32). Ultimately, however, the 2004 presidential election, and the corresponding Orange Revolution, would reset the political stage by bringing Yushchenko to power. Thus, in contrast to Russia's 2003 mixed-member elections where the ruling party, United Russia—and, by extension, Putin's Kremlin—emerged victorious, Ukraine's 2002 contests preserved the country's fragmented party system, one largely defined by elite-based and elite-biased parties (Turovsky 2011, 209).

The Nomination of District Deputies in Russia and Ukraine

As I discuss in more detail in subsequent chapters, various factors may influence which candidates parties decide to nominate for political office. A party may choose to prioritize internal cohesion by rewarding loyal politicians who toe the party line; it may choose to co-opt politicians previously affiliated with other parties; or it may strike a balance between the two. In other words, the politics of candidate selection introduces the possibility of co-optation, a tactic that is featured prominently in the literature on authoritarian politics. Stacher (2012, 43), for example, contends that co-optation may breed mutual dependence and regime cohesion:

> Authoritarian systems thrive on the cohesion and mutual dependence that co-optation produces. . . . Powerful elite figures try to make a president and other elites dependent on their usefulness. The president and ruling elites make agents . . . dependent upon them. With everyone trying to ensure the dependency of others, it produces and replicates an inherent logic of cohesion.

Yet parties in democratic regimes may also find value in co-opting politicians from rival parties, since such decisions influence the ability of their competitors to recruit candidates and mount viable electoral challenges.

Although Reuter and Remington (2009) present a convincing account of United Russia's ability to attract politicians and induce loyalty, their position rests heavily on how the Kremlin used the power at its disposal to skew the electoral playing field in the direction of the ruling party. Thus, while a marginalized opposition may be indicative of a dominant-party regime, the mechanisms used to achieve such marginalization can be the same ones characterizing the regime's authoritarian turn: a crackdown on independent media, restrictions on the freedom of association, voter intimidation, vote-buying, and the regime's ability to keep its opponents from competing for office (see, among others, Frye et al. 2014, 2019; Oversloot and Verheul 2006; Roberts 2012a; Robinson 2012). In other words, the ability of a ruling party to attract prospective candidates in authoritarian systems may say more about the regime's trajectory than the appeal of the party: winning loyalty from a broader cross-section of the political establishment should be easier when other options are under siege. In countries where coercion is less of an option and outcomes more uncertain, prospective candidates for legislative office will have more opportunities. They may form new parties, join historically smaller parties, or switch to the opposition (if they were not opposition members already). From this perspective, an investigation into the relationship between electoral system changes and party institutionalization should benefit from an examination of cases with diverging regime trajectories, as in Russia and Ukraine, since such contextual differences have the potential to influence the decision-making of prospective candidates.

Russia

In the initial round of voting of the 2003 Duma elections, Russia's ruling party, United Russia, won 103 SMD-plurality elections out of the 222 seats filled. In three of the 225 SMD elections (Districts 162, 181, and 207), the "against all" option won, which triggered another round of elections to fill the seats three months later.[13] At the time, winning 103 SMD seats was no small feat for a party in post-Soviet Russia. Prior to this, the largest share of SMD seats won by a party was the Communist Party of the Russian Federation's (KPRF) total of 58 in 1995. Thanks to United Russia's December 2003 success, many independents joined the United Russia bandwagon, and its seat share swelled to two-thirds, a constitutional majority (Clark 2005).[14] After United Russia, the next largest share of SMD seats in Russia's 2003 Duma elections went to self-nominated candidates or independents (67). In third place was the People's Party with 17, followed by the Communist Party (KPRF) with 12 and Rodina with 8 (see table 2.1). However, neither the People's Party nor Rodina competed independently in the 2007 Duma elections. Rather, they joined members of the Party of Entrepreneurial Development and the electoral bloc known as Party of Russia's Rebirth–Party of Life to form A Just Russia.

As a first step in the analysis of Russian and Ukrainian party nominations, I examine whether Russia's ruling party privileged district deputies who competed under its banner during the elections that preceded the move to a PR-only system over other district deputies. I begin by categorizing Russia's district deputies according to their official source of nomination during the 2003 elections. Since subsequent chapters examine whether the district deputies' electoral performances shape their prospects of a party nomination, and since victory in repeat elections is not the same as victory in the general elections, I exclude those deputies who filled the district seats where the "against all" option initially

TABLE 2.1. Distribution of Russia's 2003 SMD mandates

Political party / Electoral bloc	Number of district seats
United Russia	103
People's Party	17
Communist Party	12
Rodina	8
Yabloko	4
Union of Right Forces	3
Party of Russia's Rebirth–Party of Life	3
Agrarian Party	2
New Course–Automotive Russia	1
Entrepreneurial Development	1
Great Russia-Eurasian Union	1
Independents	67
Total	222

Source: Central Election Commission of the Russian Federation (2004, 192).

prevailed. In addition, four Russian district deputies died prior to the end of the 2003–2007 legislative session.[15] These cases are also removed from the analysis, reducing the total number of deputies under investigation to 218.[16] I also defer until chapter 3 the question of whether the decision to join the United Russia bandwagon influenced an incumbent deputy's nomination chances.

Although neither the KPRF nor A Just Russia compare to United Russia in terms of its status as the ruling party, both serve as useful points of comparison. Of all Russian parties, the KPRF represents the most organizationally developed party in Russia at the time. The KPRF is the successor to the communist regime's ruling party and won seats in every Duma since the collapse of the Soviet Union, and has demonstrated strong regional organization by having performed well in SMD contests and gubernatorial elections prior to their temporary elimination (see Reisinger and Moraski 2017; Slider 2001). If United Russia were to aspire to become a well-entrenched ruling party, then its investment in district deputies should resemble that of the KPRF.

However, A Just Russia was built on the remnants of parties that had competed previously, and in 2007 it was widely seen as a "quasi-opposition" party, or what March (2009) labels a "parastatal party"—one created with the support of the Kremlin and with the expectation that it would reciprocate. If United Russia nominated district deputies at a rate similar to A Just Russia, a party that more closely resembles a disposable party similar to those that characterized Russian politics in the 1990s, then the results would signal a failure to invest in party development.[17]

Figures 2.1–2.3 present data on how the 218 district deputies under investigation were distributed across the 2007 party lists of United Russia, KPRF, and A Just Russia. For figure 2.1, for example, the deputies are organized by the source of their 2003 nomination, with the corresponding bars comparing the number from each source landing on United Russia's 2007 party list ("yes") to the number not on United Russia's 2007 list ("no"). Figure 2.2 provides the numbers for placement on the Communist Party's 2007 list, while figure 2.3 presents those for A Just Russia.

Out of the 218 deputies under investigation, 119 made United Russia's list.[18] United Russia renominated 70 of its district deputies from 2003,

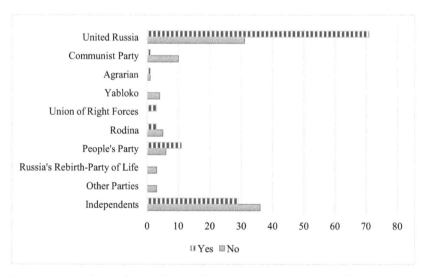

Figure 2.1. Russia's 2003 district deputies (by 2003 party nomination) and placement on United Russia's 2007 party list

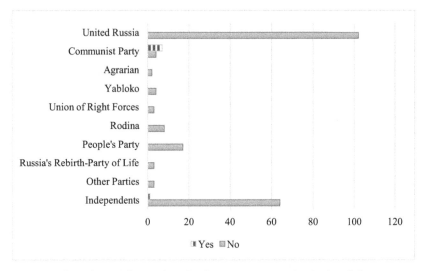

Figure 2.2. Russia's 2003 district deputies (by 2003 party nomination) and placement on the Communist Party's 2007 party list

or just under 70 percent of the 102 deputies who were still alive in 2007. This renomination rate surpasses that of the Communist Party's renomination rate of just under 64 percent (seven out of 11), which suggests an interest in party development by reinvesting, at a comparatively high level, in deputies with explicit geographic ties. By comparison, only five of the 24 district deputies (around 21 percent) to make A Just Russia's 2007 list were nominated by one of the party's predecessors in 2003.

Of the 119 district deputies making United Russia's 2007 list, 48 were politicians who had not committed to the ruling party during the 2003 elections.[19] In other words, while United Russia renominated the majority of district deputies who had affiliated with the party early, it also used list construction to co-opt a substantial number of deputies who had not committed to the party prior to the 2003 elections. Of previously uncommitted deputies, the largest share receiving positions in United Russia's 2007 list went to independents, who constituted almost a quarter of the spots that United Russia awarded to district deputies (29 out of the 119). The People's Party (a loose coalition of regionally based politicians) received the next largest share, with 11. To the extent that United

Russia sacrificed previously affiliated deputies for previously unaffiliated ones, its emphasis appears to have been on independent deputies or deputies from inchoate or less ideological parties rather than from more established parties such as the KPRF and Yabloko—two challengers that anchored opposite ends of Russia's ideological spectrum. These data reveal that while United Russia, as the ruling party, appears to have had an interest in co-opting deputies previously unaffiliated with it, some deputies were more prone to co-optation than others. Either United Russia saw deputies from these more established and more programmatic parties as less attractive candidates, or those individuals were less receptive to co-optation compared to independents and deputies from smaller parties. The data for the KPRF and A Just Russia not only differ significantly from those for United Russia; they also offer some insight into the ability of United Russia to attract district deputies as candidates by providing a sense of how other parties fared on this front.

Only eight district deputies landed on the KPRF's 2007 party list. One of these deputies competed as an independent; the remaining seven had been nominated by the party in 2003. It is notable that neither of the

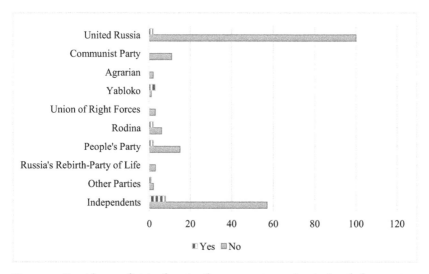

Figure 2.3. Russia's 2003 district deputies (by 2003 party nomination) and placement on A Just Russia's 2007 party list

district deputies nominated by the Agrarian Party, which was ideologically proximate to the KPRF, made the Communist Party's list in 2007. The paucity of previously unaffiliated district deputies on the KPRF's 2007 list, and the fact that United Russia's 2007 list included a district deputy previously nominated by the Agrarian Party, suggest that the KPRF was not in a position to compete with the ruling party for candidates—even those who may have been good ideological fits.

A Just Russia, meanwhile, nominated 18 district deputies in 2007. This number is notable because most of these deputies (13) did not compete under the banner of a party that later came to be part of A Just Russia. Many of the deputies who competed under those party banners instead secured a United Russia nomination in 2007, which again emphasizes the degree to which the swelling of United Russia's ranks likely reflected its ability to attract individuals with other options. In contrast to the Communist Party, however, A Just Russia did prove capable of attracting a reasonable number of previously independent district deputies (eight of them). A Just Russia also nominated three district deputies previously nominated by Yabloko. Since A Just Russia is widely considered to have been partly a Kremlin project, this outcome is noteworthy because it suggests that a majority of Yabloko's district deputies were open to co-optation. In other words, the failure of these deputies to make United Russia's 2007 list does not appear to be an indication of their disdain for a pro-Kremlin party as much as United Russia's lack of interest in nominating them as list candidates.

Ukraine

Ukraine's 2002 Rada elections took place in the context of President Leonid Kuchma using state authority for both political and private ends. Birch (2003, 526) notes, however, that, despite a growing gap between pro-presidential forces on one hand and opposition forces on another, the basic structure of Ukraine's party system changed little between independence and the 2002 Rada elections: The Communists and Socialists continued to dominate the left, while the right united for electoral purposes into the coalition Our Ukraine, led by the popular former prime minister Viktor Yushchenko. As I note above, faced with organized competition on the left and the right, several centrist—or, more accurately, ideologically amorphous—parties rallied

TABLE 2.2. Distribution of Ukraine's 2002 SMD mandates

Political party / Electoral bloc	Number of district seats
Our Ukraine	41
For a United Ukraine	66
Communist Party of Ukraine	6
Social Democratic Party (united)	5
Democratic Party-Democratic Union	4
Unity	3
Socialist Party	2
Ukrainian Naval Party	1
National Economic Growth	1
Independents	93
Total	222

Source: Official Website of Ukraine's Central Election Commission (www.cvk.gov.ua).

behind Kuchma, resulting in the pro-presidential coalition For a United Ukraine (Kuzio 2003, 25).

As in previous elections, the electoral performance of Ukrainian parties varied by electoral tier. The Communist Party and Socialist Party on the left and Our Ukraine and the Tymoshenko Bloc on the right won more than 57 percent of the 2002 PR vote. Of these parties, only Our Ukraine performed well in the SMD tier, coming in a distant second to FUU. Meanwhile, pro-presidential forces—For a United Ukraine and the Social Democratic Party (United)—received only 18 percent of the PR vote yet managed to win more district seats than their competitors (Kuzio 2003, 24–25).

Table 2.2 presents the distribution of Ukraine's SMD mandates across the organizations winning at least one district seat during the 2002 Verkhovna Rada elections. Since three of Ukraine's 2002 SMD contests were invalid,[20] table 2.2 presents only information on those deputies elected during the initial elections for the sake of consistency with the analysis of Russia. Comparing tables 2.1 and 2.2 reveals that, while district mandates in Russia were primarily divided between the ruling party and independents, in Ukraine most district mandates were split among independents and two parties: Our Ukraine (41) and For a United Ukraine (66).[21] As in Russian Duma elections prior to 2003 and previous legislative elections in Ukraine, independents as a group won the plurality of SMD seats (93) in the 2002 Rada elections.[22]

Based on the distribution of district seats in the 2002 Rada elections, Our Ukraine and For a United Ukraine serve as the most comparable cases to the Russian parties considered above. However, while Russia's ruling party emerged as a clear victor in 2003, the same cannot be said of FUU, which managed to win control of parliament only after picking off enough members of an opposition that had failed to unite once in office (D'Anieri 2007, 95). Indeed, For a United Ukraine disintegrated into seven factions three months after the 2002 elections (Kuzio 2003, 31).

As noted in the introduction, Ukraine's 2004 presidential election dramatically altered Ukraine's political trajectory. With election fraud and voter intimidation marring the second round of the contests, millions of Ukrainians took to the streets, holding 17 days of nationwide, nonviolent protests in harsh cold and sleet (Karatnycky 2005, 35). As evidence of fraud mounted,[23] Ukraine's Supreme Court annulled the results of the runoff, setting the stage for a third round, which Yushchenko would win (see, among others, Wilson 2005). At the time, these events were interpreted as providing Ukrainian democracy—and possibly its party system—a new lease on life. Way (2005b), in particular, submits that the Orange Revolution illustrated Kuchma's inability to preserve unity among his allies and that fragmentation at the top contributed to the eventual breakdown of Ukraine's authoritarian state institutions. Thus, in contrast to the 2002 Rada electoral campaigns (see Birch 2003, 527), opposition leaders "were neither intimidated nor denied access to the media" during Ukraine's first closed-list PR elections, leading international election observers to report that it largely met the standards of democratic elections (Hesli 2007, 509).

Besides improving the conduct of elections, the Orange Revolution also resulted in constitutional changes that transferred the power to nominate and dismiss the prime minister and several cabinet posts from the president to the parliament (D'Anieri 2007, 145; 2019, 132). This development is noteworthy because it raised the political profile of the Rada and increased the stakes of its elections.[24] In fact, given the switch to a PR-only electoral system, one might reasonably expect Ukraine's major parties to have focused on deepening their societal and organizational roots as they prepared to compete on a more level playing field for control over a newly empowered institution.

The ascension of Viktor Yushchenko to the presidency also changed the political landscape in Ukraine, as Our Ukraine went from a major opposition party to the party of the president. Its pro-presidential status did not make Our Ukraine a dominant ruling party, however. Indeed, the "Orange alliance" that helped Yushchenko win the 2004 presidential election emerged only when early polling indicated that Yulia Tymoshenko, a former deputy prime minister, would struggle to defeat Yushchenko at the ballot box. Although Tymoshenko had worked with Yushchenko in Kuchma's government, Tymoshenko became a member of the opposition, leading the "Ukraine without Kuchma" movement, at a time when Yushchenko stood by Kuchma (D'Anieri 2019, 141). Only after protracted negotiations between the two camps did Tymoshenko eventually agree to back Yushchenko for president in exchange for a promise that he would appoint her prime minister (Way 2016, Chapter 3, "Party Weakness . . ."). After the Orange Revolution, Our Ukraine emerged as one party within a larger ruling coalition, a coalition that depended on the Tymoshenko Bloc and the Socialists. Worse yet, the coalition suffered from in-fighting and eventually collapsed in October 2005 (D'Anieri 2007, 99). As a result, Our Ukraine's status going into Ukraine's first closed-list PR elections was drastically different from United Russia's. While both United Russia and Our Ukraine were pro-presidential parties, the constitutional reforms associated with the Orange Revolution actually weakened Ukraine's presidency and elevated the post of prime minister by giving the latter the power to appoint some ministers (D'Anieri 2019, 141–42). Even more problematic for Our Ukraine, the country's first post-Orange prime minister, who shared control over the executive with Yushchenko, was Tymoshenko. In less than nine months, the rivalry between Yushchenko's team and Tymoshenko's team deteriorated to such an extent that Yushchenko chose to dismiss Tymoshenko from office, a decision that moved the rivalry out of government and into the electoral arena as the sides competed with one another for centrist voters rather than uniting against the Party of Regions (D'Anieri 2019, 142).

While Our Ukraine and the Orange coalition collapsed, Viktor Yanukovych regained his footing. Thanks in part to the "most competitive, chaotic, and democratic" political period in Ukraine since the early 1990s, the Party of Regions experienced an unprecedented expansion (Way 2016, Chapter 3, "Party Weakness . . ."). Unlike the parties comprising the Orange coalition, which competed with one another for votes in western Ukraine, the Party of Regions consolidated its position in eastern Ukraine. By 2006, it had become a powerful opponent, one that appeared intent on learning from past mistakes with Yanukovych declaring that "it is better to be a strong party, than a weak bloc" (quoted in Way 2016, Chapter 3, "Party and State Strength"). Given these developments, one should expect the nomination of candidates by the Party of Regions in 2006 to have reflected its strong regional ties and emphasis on party unity.[25]

Before delving into the analysis, two issues merit discussion. First, although information on the district deputies' party memberships is available (Official Website of Ukraine's Central Election Commission, available at www.cvk.gov.ua),[26] in this chapter I focus only on the source of their 2002 nominations, which not only constitutes a reasonable indicator of the deputies' party ties but also is one more conducive to cross-national comparison. While the short electoral biographies for Russia's list deputies include party membership information, those for Russia's district deputies list only the source of the district nomination (i.e., a party or self-nominated) (Central Election Commission of the Russian Federation 2004).[27] Second, in addition to the three invalid district contests during the initial round of Ukraine's parliamentary elections, three of Ukraine's 2002 district deputies were unable to compete for office in 2006 and are, therefore, excluded from the analysis, lowering the total number of observations to 219.[28]

To explore the relationships between Ukraine's 2002 district deputies and placement on party lists in Ukraine's 2006 elections, figures 2.4–2.9 present the distribution of district deputies across the lists of the four parties that passed the legal threshold in 2006, plus two parties that did not win representation in the 2006 elections yet offer some additional analytical leverage. Figures 2.4 and 2.5 consider Ukraine's main pro-presidential party leading into the 2006 elections, Our Ukraine, and the Party of Regions, which was formerly part of For a United Ukraine in 2002 and FUU's main successor in 2006. In figure 2.4, for example, the

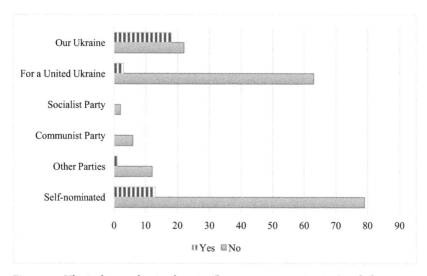

Figure 2.4. Ukraine's 2002 district deputies (by 2002 party nomination) and placement on the 2006 party list of Our Ukraine

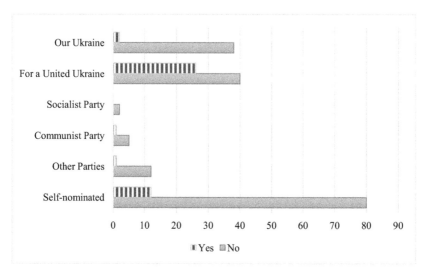

Figure 2.5. Ukraine's 2002 district deputies (by 2002 party nomination) and placement on the 2006 party list of the Party of Regions

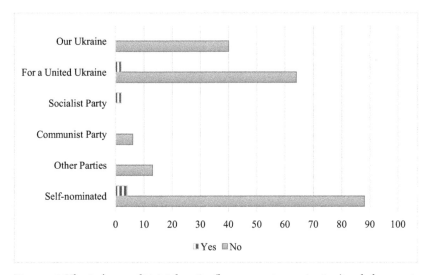

Figure 2.6. Ukraine's 2002 district deputies (by 2002 party nomination) and placement on the 2006 party list of the Socialist Party

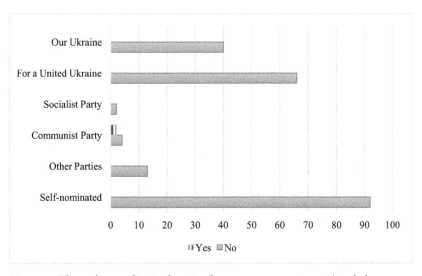

Figure 2.7. Ukraine's 2002 district deputies (by 2002 party nomination) and placement on the 2006 party list of the Communist Party

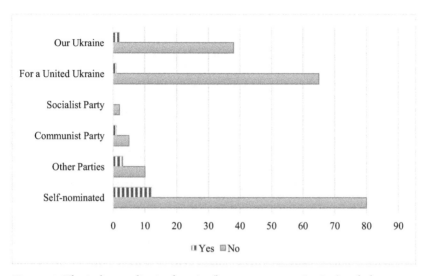

Figure 2.8. Ukraine's 2002 district deputies (by 2002 party nomination) and placement on the 2006 party list of the Tymoshenko Bloc

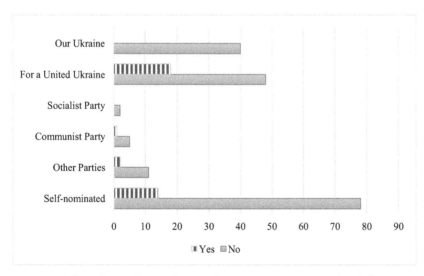

Figure 2.9. Ukraine's 2002 district deputies (by 2002 party nomination) and placement on the 2006 party list of the Lytvyn Bloc

deputies are organized by the different sources of nomination in 2002 with the corresponding bars comparing the number from each source landing on Our Ukraine's 2006 party list and the number not on Our Ukraine's 2006 list.

Since the Socialist Party and the Communist Party provide face-value assessments of how Ukraine's more ideology-oriented parties navigated the country's electoral system change, figures 2.6 and 2.7 present data for the Socialist Party, which won 33 seats in 2006, and the Communist Party, which failed to pass the 3 percent threshold in 2006. Figures 2.8 and 2.9, meanwhile, focus on two electoral blocs—the Tymoshenko Bloc and Lytvyn's People's Bloc—capable of competing successfully with Our Ukraine and the Party of Regions, respectively, for candidates.

Although the Tymoshenko Bloc competed and won seats in the 2002 elections, it did not win any district mandates. As alluded to above, although Our Ukraine and the Tymoshenko Bloc emerged from the Orange Revolution as victors and initially formed part of a ruling coalition, the two parties parted ways once burdened with the challenges of governing. Meanwhile, Lytvyn's People's Bloc was the successor to the Agrarian Party of Ukraine, the party that had joined with the Party of Regions, the People's Democratic Party, and other small parties to form For a United Ukraine in 2001. In fact, Lytvyn, who was the head of President Kuchma's administration at the time, held the top spot on the FUU list and became Rada speaker following the 2002 elections. Lytvyn broke with Yanukovych's camp in 2004, however, and helped defuse tensions during the Orange Revolution (Herron 2008, 553). These two blocs represent potential rivals to Our Ukraine and the Party of Regions, respectively. Explicitly examining the list placement of these parties therefore presents a fuller picture of list construction in a context not only where candidates are competing with one another for list placement but also where there is more competition among parties for candidates.

Figures 2.4–2.9 permit a number of interesting comparisons with regard to party nominations in 2002 and 2006. First, of the parties considered, the one with the highest renomination rate is the Socialist Party (see figure 2.6): Both district deputies nominated by the Socialist Party in 2002 received spots on the Socialist Party's list in 2006, for a renomination rate of 100 percent. In addition to these deputies, the Socialist Party nominated two district deputies previously nominated by For a United Ukraine and four previously self-nominated deputies. The placements of these deputies on the 2006 Socialist Party list ranged from three to 77.[29] These data suggest that the Socialist Party utilized the move to PR-only rules to preserve ties with its own district deputies and to co-opt other district deputies.

The finding that both United Russia and Ukraine's Socialist Party renominated a high percentage of its own district deputies while also co-opting previously unaffiliated deputies identifies a potentially common practice in weakly institutionalized party systems navigating the move to PR rules, one employed by the ruling party in an increasingly authoritarian regime as well as a smaller party in a nascent electoral democracy. If so, then the differences observed across parties within such states may not reflect differences between the parties, such as how ideological the parties are, as much as contextual differences, such as regime type or rule differences (including the size of the legal thresholds), that grant greater opportunities to some parties and fewer opportunities to others. In the case of this pairwise comparison, for example, while the strategy of Ukraine's Socialist Party may resemble that of United Russia, Ukraine's Socialist Party obviously does not compare to United Russia when it comes to the raw numbers of deputies renominated or co-opted. United Russia's advantage on both counts may be attributed to its status as Russia's ruling party rather than the strategy that it employed while navigating the move from a mixed-member electoral system to PR-only rules. Such a possibility matters to the study of electoral systems more broadly, because it reveals that parties in different regimes may be navigating similar electoral system changes in similar ways even if the final outcomes for the parties appear different. In other words, one cannot easily contend that United Russia's behavior when transitioning between electoral systems is unique to the authoritarian system that was in place, even if the party's success turns out to benefit from that system. It is possible that parties in democratic settings, if given the opportunity, would behave similarly in an effort to achieve the same result: a monopoly on legislative power.

When comparing Ukrainian parties to one another, it is striking how much list construction by the Socialist Party differs from that of the Communist Party (figure 2.7). In 2006, the Communist Party renominated only two of the six district deputies (or 33 percent) whom it had nominated in 2002, and neither won seats in the Rada. If one assumes that ideology drives party renominations, then this outcome is surprising, since one would expect ideology to matter at least as much to the Communist Party as to the Socialist Party. However, if one expects incumbent legislators, regardless of party affiliation, to be driven by an electoral motive (Mayhew 1974) when seeking nominations and to seek those nominations that increase their electoral prospects, then this result makes sense. In fact, of the six district deputies formerly nominated by the Communists, three received promising placements on the 2006 lists of other parties under investigation: one was nominated by the Party of Regions, one by the Tymoshenko Bloc, and one by Lytvyn's People's Bloc. Also, in contrast to the 2006 Socialist Party list, the 2006 Communist Party list did not include any district deputies not nominated by the Communist Party in 2002, an outcome that could reflect a desire to preserve party unity. However, given the Communist Party's poor performance in the 2006 elections and the ability of district deputies previously nominated by it to receive electable placements on other lists, one cannot rule out the possibility that the Communist Party, like the Socialist Party, had wanted to attract previously unaffiliated deputies but that, unlike the Socialist Party, it was not in a strong enough electoral position to do so.

While Our Ukraine and the Party of Regions had more district deputies to choose from, those parties exhibited relatively low renomination rates (figures 2.4 and 2.5). After nominating 40 of the deputies elected in district contests in 2002, Our Ukraine placed only 18 of these deputies on its 2006 list, a renomination rate of 45 percent. However, as noted above, Our Ukraine's status as the president's party is not equivalent to the ruling-party status that United Russia enjoyed with its constitutional majority in the Duma, especially since Our Ukraine had to contend with competition from another "Orange" victor—the Tymoshenko Bloc.[30] The Party of Regions, meanwhile, nominated 26 of the 66 district deputies (or 39 percent) who were officially candidates of For a United Ukraine in 2002. Thus, while Yanukovych's remarks during the 2006 legislative campaign suggest that he prioritized cohesion over co-optation, the party's renomination rate still proved to be substantially lower than United Russia's renomination rate of nearly 70 percent. It is worth reiterating, however, that although For a United Ukraine temporarily enjoyed a parliamentary majority in 2002, the coalition quickly fell apart, with the former head of the electoral coalition (and Rada speaker), Lytvyn, resurrecting the Agrarian Party of Ukraine as his People's Bloc for the 2006 elections. Thus, if one takes both the Party of Regions and Lytvyn's People's Bloc as successors to For a United Ukraine, then the renomination rate of deputies formerly nominated by For a United Ukraine improves to 67 percent (or 44 out of 66).[31] This finding suggests that what appears to be a relatively high renomination rate by United Russia may simply reflect its ability to stay united from one set of elections to the next, which again was likely helped by the nature of Russia's regime at the time. This cohesion, in turn, also likely allowed the regime to stay the course.

Finally, it is notable that both Our Ukraine and the Party of Regions, like United Russia, were more likely to nominate previously independent deputies to their lists when it came to deputies outside the party, with none of the three parties appearing to co-opt many deputies from other parties. Major parties across the two regimes appear to be not only balancing cohesion and co-optation—if at somewhat different rates—but also pursuing similar tactics, preferring independent deputies over those with party affiliations. At this point, however, such a finding should be viewed with skepticism, since this chapter does not investigate the range of characteristics that likely influenced the renomination or co-optation of incumbent legislators. For example, it does not examine whether the deputies' behavior within the outgoing legislature shaped party decisions. Moreover, the preceding discussion does not consider whether the deputies' legislative mandates (i.e., district or list) significantly influenced the likelihood of being nominated by one of the parties under investigation. Answering these kinds of questions requires closer examination of the parties and the deputies involved. Chapter 3 pursues such an approach by investigating the politics of United Russia's list construction in 2007, while chapter 4 examines the factors shaping party nominations of Our Ukraine and the Party of Regions in 2006.

Conclusion

In this chapter, I examine the extent to which parties in weakly institutionalized party systems nominated politicians with proven electoral records and legislative experience following the move to PR rules despite the possibility that these politicians might constitute risks to party discipline. Specifically, I consider whether the willingness of parties to take such risks reflects the electoral incentives influencing those in power when the new PR rules are implemented.

Since PR rules were adopted in Russia and Ukraine with a goal of removing the influence of more independent-minded district deputies, the analysis in this chapter focuses on the degree to which major parties in these states relied on this particular subset of incumbents when constructing party lists. Among the pool of politicians to include on a party list, district deputies are known quantities with proven electoral records representing constituents from a specific geographic territory. By examining party behavior toward incumbent district deputies, the analysis provides insight not only into whether Russian and Ukrainian parties sought to maintain some degree of local representation but also whether they strengthened existing elite bonds—by renominating politicians who had committed to the party when such commitments were optional—or built new ones, while also focusing on a group of prospective candidates who on average should have more influence in the candidate selection process than politicians seeking to win a national legislative seat for the first time.

The analysis reveals that Russia's ruling party was able to attract, and thus reinvest in, district deputies whom it had previously nominated at a much higher rate compared to Ukrainian parties. This outcome is not surprising given United Russia's preeminence, one that benefited from a postelection bandwagon effect in 2003 that gave the party a constitutional majority in the Duma. By contrast, no party in Ukraine could claim majority status, let alone dominant party status. In fact, the party of Ukraine's president, Our Ukraine, contested the 2006 elections as part of a larger electoral bloc. Meanwhile, although the main opposition party in 2006, the Party of Regions, had aspirations to consolidate its position and avoid the fate of the electoral bloc of which it was a part during the 2002 elections, the Party of Regions influence resided primarily in eastern Ukraine. In other words, its ability to co-opt district deputies from western Ukraine was limited.

Despite party-specific differences, however, all three of the major parties under investigation utilized list construction to co-opt at least some previously unaffiliated district deputies, and in all three cases there was a clear preference in favor of independents rather than other partisans. Yet the finding that even smaller parties, such as Ukraine's Socialist Party, could pursue a nomination strategy that utilized both co-optation and cohesion suggests that attempts to strike a balance between the two may be generalizable party behavior, at least in weakly institutionalized party systems—such as those that characterized many post-Soviet countries— and that this behavior may span regime type. To the extent that party nominations are expressions of power by political parties, the potential generalizability makes sense. Political organizations, from regimes to parties, have long been understood as seeking to navigate change by concentrating and expanding their influence: "[T]he great utility and the great appeal of the single-party system in modernizing countries is that it is an institution which, in large measure, promotes both concentration . . . and also expansion" (Huntington 1968, 146).

However, the presence of a shared desire to concentrate and expand power does not mean that regime type does not matter. It is likely that the ability of specific parties, especially pro-presidential parties, to succeed in their attempts to preserve party cohesion by renominating large numbers of district deputies and to co-opt a cadre of previously unaffiliated district deputies depends on the level of electoral competition in place in a country. As Huntington (1968, 147) notes, "More competitive two-party or multiparty systems may have considerable capacity for expansion and the assimilation of groups but less capability for the concentration of power." While there are plenty of reasons to expect that ruling parties in authoritarian states enjoy sizable advantages over their democratic counterparts, additional cross-national empirical work remains necessary, since party differences also clearly matter, even within a more competitive system.

3

Managing the Move to Proportional Representation in Russia

In chapter 1, I contend that periods of electoral system change are moments when parties and legislators are forced to adapt to different rules, creating novel opportunities to observe party priorities and tactics. In Russia and Ukraine, the adoption of closed-list proportional representation (PR) systems, at least theoretically, created opportunities to move toward greater party institutionalization. Regardless of the countries' regime trajectories, these new rules gave political parties a monopoly over who could run for legislative office. This change is notable because control over candidate selection is a function that conventionally defines political parties. Indeed, by many accounts, the election of large numbers of independent candidates in both countries not only reflected weak party institutionalization but also helped preserve it.

Chapter 2 presents an initial comparison of how the ruling party in Russia and two rival Ukrainian parties responded to the elimination of single-member-district (SMD) seats in the countries' legislatures with the adoption of solely closed-list PR systems. That initial analysis focuses on deputies who arguably were most affected by the electoral system change and who possessed traits that made them potentially attractive candidates: district deputies. As I note in the introduction, a general criticism of PR systems is that they prioritize inclusivity and horizontal accountability at the expense of the vertical relationships binding legislators to a specific subset of geographically identifiable constituents. While this criticism may fall short for PR systems with smaller district magnitudes (i.e., systems with many multimember districts that elect, say, five to twenty deputies each), PR systems that elect all representatives from a single national district—such as those under investigation—are subject to it. Examining the renomination rates of district deputies provides a sense of whether parties might seek to preserve some degree of vertical representation, even where elections are not free and fair, following the adoption of such a party-centered PR system.

This chapter delves deeper into the politics of candidate selection in Russia in an effort to better understand the interaction between PR rules and authoritarian politics. The topic is an important one as long as authoritarian regimes continue to utilize the institutional trappings of elections to establish domestic and international legitimacy. Given such practices, political science has witnessed a renewed interest in parties as vehicles of governance in illiberal states (Bogaards 2008; Greene 2010; Svolik 2012). While well-developed and cohesive ruling parties grant rulers more leverage for regulating societal discontent via elections and lower the risks of electoral defeat (Brownlee 2007), the relationship between electoral rule changes and party development in authoritarian regimes has received little attention. Yet, as this book contends, one key mechanism that facilitated the consolidation of Russia's ruling party was the adoption of the closed-list PR system that governed the country's 2007 and 2011 legislative elections. This chapter, as well as chapter 6, details how the ruling party, United Russia, utilized this electoral system, starting with an analysis of the relationship between United Russia and incumbent legislators during the transition to PR-only rules.

Electoral systems are conventionally seen as possessing the potential to shape party systems. Proportional methods relying on party lists are regarded as useful means for increasing party discipline within legislatures. From this perspective, the implementation of closed-list PR rules—regardless of whether a country is democratic or authoritarian—may facilitate greater party cohesion, as it allows party leaders to reward loyalty over opportunism. Yet, as chapter 2 illustrates, the elimination of district mandates does not automatically spell the end of district deputies' legislative careers: district deputies can become list candidates in the closed-list PR contests. However, party discipline may not be the only, or even the primary, motivation driving candidate nominations. For example, parties may recognize that politicians with proven electoral records and legislative experience can be valuable assets, even if they constitute potential risks to party discipline in the medium or long terms. In fact, party leaders may reasonably expect that the adoption of a PR-only system will substantially reduce the risks posed by previously unruly deputies, since such deputies can be sanctioned for violations of party discipline with worse, possibly unelectable positions on the party list down the road. This possibility likewise forces deputies to weigh the rewards of going their own way (either by forming a new party or by joining an opposition party) against losing the perks of office. With this tool now at their disposal, leaders of a ruling party may even be tempted to use closed-list PR rules to co-opt previously unaffiliated district deputies who add value to the party's electoral prospects or expand its geographic reach. In authoritarian regimes, where the electoral fortunes for ruling parties are brightest, those parties should be well positioned to pursue a strategy that utilizes some degree of co-optation. Indeed, a ruling party in an authoritarian regime may see co-opting district deputies during the first PR-only elections as an opportunity to preserve, or even deepen, its local presence and widen its electoral appeal while still keeping potential opponents at bay.

In this chapter, I examine how Russia's ruling party, United Russia, balanced the competing incentives of cohesion and co-optation as it navigated the shift to a closed-list PR system in 2007. Specifically, I investigate the extent to which the party prioritized the selection of candidates who were already affiliated with it, thereby maximizing the potential for cohesion, as well as the degree to which the party nominated previously unaffiliated but electorally proficient deputies, which is indicative of co-optation. These are topics that have largely been ignored in the study of authoritarian politics.

To analyze United Russia's nomination decisions during the country's first PR-only elections, I build on my previous work that focused on the list placements of district deputies (Moraski 2015). In a nutshell, while United Russia was more likely to nominate district deputies whom it officially nominated in the 2003 district contests, these deputies' list placements were not significantly better than those of district deputies who had competed under a different party label. However, district deputies previously nominated by United Russia did enjoy significantly better placement than previously independent deputies. My article did not, however, examine the party's interaction with the 225 deputies elected via party lists in 2003. As a result, it did not answer the question about whether United Russia valued previously elected district deputies differently from previously elected list deputies during the first PR-only elections. Neither did my previous article examine the party's relationship in 2007 with deputies who did not compete under its banner in 2003 but joined the party's faction once elected to office. This chapter fills in the gaps.

Legislative Mandates and Party Nominations in Russia

In a study of the origins and durability of single-party rule, Smith (2005) examines the degree to which fiscal and political constraints at a party's inception shape its development. According to Smith, authoritarian elites invest in party-building when well-organized parties are electorally necessary. Where rulers do not face an organized opposition and have ample access to resource rents that can be allocated to build electoral constituencies, the incentives to invest in a well-organized ruling party are few. Other observers, meanwhile, identify leadership succession as a critical factor shaping the development of party systems (Brownlee 2007; Reuter and Remington 2009; Weiner and La Palombara 1966). The creation of a durable ruling party can, among other things, manage elite conflict and limit much of the uncertainty that accompanies the succession process. If one views the ruling party's behavior toward district deputies after the adoption of PR through the lens of party-building, then a ruling party is more likely to find these deputies more attractive as candidates if it (1) faces a viable opposition, (2) lacks sufficient access to resource rents, or (3) expects to navigate leadership succession. As chapter 2 makes clear, the last characteristic describes Russian politics going into the 2007 Duma elections while the first two characteristics do not. Yet it is not evident from extant literature whether one condition alone—in this case, the succession process—is sufficient to promote much in the way of party-building.

As Reuter and Remington (2009) point out, the consolidation of a ruling party requires more rank-and-file elites to commit to it. Russia's ruling party established its position by emerging as the primary vehicle granting access to the corridors of power.[1] The Kremlin not only publicly endorsed United Russia; it also pursued institutional reforms that undermined the opposition's ability to successfully compete against it. These actions led politicians across Russia, including governors, to conclude that they stood a better chance of enjoying the spoils of office by affiliating with the ruling party than by maintaining separate political machines (see Reuter 2017, especially chapter 6). I return to the issue of gubernatorial affiliation with United Russia in chapter 6 and dedicate the remainder of this chapter to identifying the characteristics that increased the likelihood of incumbent deputies affiliating with the ruling party, as indicated by their placement on its party's list.

One expectation, discussed in chapter 2, is that Russia's regime trajectory influenced the evolution of its ruling party. When creeping authoritarianism is coupled with the move to closed-list PR, the path of least resistance for incumbent politicians seeking reelection is to join the ruling party. While joining, or even forming,[2] another party may allow politicians to secure higher list positions, the electoral benefits of this option are uncertain, since they depend on the number of seats that the party garners and since, in authoritarian elections, that amount will still likely be much lower than the number of seats awarded to the ruling party. Equally important, representation via another party (even another pro-presidential party) may yield fewer rewards—from influence over policy to career advancement—than what accompanies a position within the ruling party. Thus, while all politicians have agency and may choose an option besides joining the ruling party,[3] in an increasingly authoritarian regime it is unlikely that many politicians operating under the influence of the electoral motive would find these alternative options very attractive.

Of course, politicians are not driven solely by an electoral motive. Policy goals and personal values lead different politicians to associate with different parties. Moreover, one should expect the relationship between a party and a particular politician to deepen to the extent that the latter manages to win office by affiliating with the former. One might expect the party affiliations of incumbent deputies in the previous elections to influence those politicians' interactions with the ruling party during the first PR-only elections.

From this perspective, deputies who were officially nominated by United Russia in the 2003 elections should naturally be among those most likely to pursue positions on the ruling party's list during the first closed-list PR elections in 2007. Given their prior commitment to the party, these deputies are likely to have experienced little conflict between the electoral motive and other political interests (e.g., party loyalty, policy preferences).

In contrast, deputies nominated by parties that opposed United Russia in 2003 should be among those deputies who would be least likely to pursue spots on the ruling party's list. Although the electoral motive may have led those deputies to consider the advantages of affiliating with the ruling party given Russia's increasingly authoritarian regime (should the ruling party be interested), that motive is also likely to have been at odds with the deputies' other political interests. In other words, if winning a seat necessitates bending to the ruling party's will with little hope of pursuing one's preferred policies, then the politicians in this position may be less likely to seek the ruling party's endorsement than other politicians whose policy goals more closely align with those of the ruling party. In the aggregate, one should expect the conflicting motivations that opposition deputies encountered to have reduced their number on the ruling party's list, even if the ruling party wished to leverage the electoral motive to its advantage and co-opt these legislators.

Falling between these two poles are deputies who were not initially nominated by United Russia in 2003 but who did not necessarily oppose the party. The most obvious cases from Russia during this period are deputies who ran as independents or were nominated by a party other than United Russia but joined the United Russia faction within the Duma once the legislature convened.

District deputies elected in Russia's mixed-member electoral system regularly competed as independents during the district contests, only to join party factions after taking office. This behavior was not only electorally expedient (i.e., it allowed them to avoid risky affiliations with potentially unpopular parties); it also frustrated electoral accountability (Rose 2000; Smyth 2006). For United Russia's leadership, such behavior likely signaled political opportunism, and deputies exhibiting such behavior may have been less likely to be awarded spots—or were more likely to receive lower ranks—on United Russia's 2007 list compared to deputies who joined the party earlier.

Yet this outcome was not guaranteed. As I note in chapter 2, the move to PR offers a new mechanism for holding legislators within the party accountable, and part of the logic underpinning the construction and consolidation of a dominant party rests squarely on co-opting previously unaffiliated politicians, even if it means attracting political opportunists.

Another pool of potential candidates during the first closed-list PR elections consisted of deputies from Kremlin-friendly parties—or legislative factions—that regularly joined with United Russia to support the president's policies. For example, Remington's (2006) analysis of legislative voting in Russia's Third Duma (2000–2003) reveals that the Liberal Democratic Party's faction was an especially strong source of support for the president's legislative agenda. In fact, the LDPR's level of support fell somewhere between the level of support coming from Unity and Fatherland–All Russia (the two former rivals in 1999 that would merge to become United Russia). The two least supportive legislative factions during this period, meanwhile, were the Agrarians and the Communists (Remington 2006, table 3).

During the Duma's Fourth Convocation, five factions structured the Duma: United Russia, the Liberal Democratic Party, the Communist Party, A Just Russia–Rodina, and the People's Patriotic Union of Rodina. Of these factions, the LDPR represents one potential source of candidates, as the politicians who were affiliated with that party, much like those within United Russia, tended to support the president's agenda. While LDPR deputies might have been interested in running as United Russia candidates in 2007, it is not likely that United Russia's leadership would co-opt LDPR deputies, since the faction's members already supported the president. In fact, the presence of such "tamed" opposition parties works to United Russia's advantage to the extent that the Russian system relies on a veneer of competition. At the same time, it is likely that any deputies interested in joining United Russia would do so when the legislative factions were formed rather than wait until the 2007 election campaign. The data confirm this expectation: none of the deputies serving outside of United Russia's faction competed as a candidate on United Russia's 2007 list.[4]

United Russia's relationship with Rodina (or Motherland) in the 2003 elections is complicated by developments within this party and the legislative factions that resulted from it over the course of the Fourth Convocation. By most accounts, the Kremlin encouraged the emergence of Rodina, a coalition of small leftist and national parties, as a way to draw votes away from the Communist Party in the 2003 Duma elections (see, e.g., March 2012).[5] Two popular politicians, Dmitri Rogozin and Sergei Glaziev, led the coalition going into the 2003 Duma elections. However, after Rodina's legislative success (with more than 9 percent of the vote), Glaziev ran in the 2004 presidential election without the Kremlin's permission and was subsequently expelled from the party. Meanwhile,

Rodina's aggressively nationalist campaigning under the leadership of Rogozin led to that party being denied registration in several regional elections. Rogozin eventually resigned as party leader in 2006, as the Kremlin sponsored the formation of a new party, A Just Russia, which was itself the product of three previously established satellite parties, including the post-Rogozin Rodina (Gel'man 2015, 60).

With these developments in mind, the electoral prospects for politicians affiliated with the People's Patriotic Union of Rodina were likely to be dim due to tensions with the Kremlin. Meanwhile, the relationship between United Russia and those deputies affiliated with the A Just Russia–Rodina faction was more likely to resemble that of United Russia and the deputies comprising LDPR's faction: The deputies represent reasonably compatible candidates for the ruling party, but it is not likely that the United Russia systematically nominated deputies from this faction in 2007, since these deputies were already likely to be Kremlin-friendly and since their presence in a separate party contributed to Russia's democratic veneer.[6]

Another consideration complicating the relationship between prior party affiliation and a 2007 ruling party nomination was the degree to which the elimination of the Duma's district mandates itself reflected differences between district and list deputies. For example, in an analysis of legislative support for the president's agenda between 2000 and 2003, Remington (2006) finds that two Duma factions composed of district deputies—Russia's Regions and People's Deputy—were not particularly reliable sources of support on difficult issues, even though these factions supported much of the president's legislative agenda and did so at rates higher than independent district deputies or deputies affiliated with the Union of Right Forces. Thus, to the extent that the elimination of district mandates was designed to improve the manageability of parliament (White and Kryshtanovskaya 2011, 563) and to create "efficient" pro-presidential majorities (Remington 2006), one might expect incumbent district deputies to be less attractive candidates than list deputies given the history of independent behavior among the former.

However, there are at least two reasons to expect United Russia's 2007 list decisions to correlate more with the deputies' party affiliations than with their legislative mandates.[7] First, as Smyth (2006, 134) notes, during Russia's mixed-member elections, aspiring legislators could choose whether or not to affiliate with a party, but self-nominated candidates could compete only in the SMD elections. Those affiliated with a party, however, could decide whether to compete as a district-only candidate, as a list-only candidate, or as a district-and-list candidate. In practice, party insiders and other politicians with reputations embedded in a party would generally run as list-only or as district-and-list candidates (Smyth 2006, 152–53). From this perspective, truly independent candidates are not simply those who won district elections, but those who did so without a party affiliation.

Second, when focusing on United Russia's deputies, the party may not have treated its district deputies any differently in 2007 than its list deputies given that United Russia had already "exercised ironclad discipline" over the 300-plus deputies composing its faction after the 2003 elections (Reuter and Remington 2009, 507). As Remington (2006, 25) notes, United Russia's Duma faction initiated a series of rule changes that allowed it to assert strong control over the Duma immediately following the convocation of the Fourth Duma. Specifically, it increased the threshold requirement for deputy groups to register—from 35 to 55 deputies—and attain the same status as party factions. It eliminated the norm of proportionality in the distribution of leadership posts, thereby allowing United Russia to acquire all committee chairmanships and nearly all of the vice-chairmanships. In addition, United Russia's deputies comprised nearly all of the members comprising the Council of the Duma, the body that governs the chamber.

Analysis

To investigate the factors influencing United Russia's 2007 nominations of incumbent legislators, I begin with a multivariate logistic regression analysis to assess the likelihood of a deputy landing anywhere on the ruling party's list, then move to an analysis of list rank. As I note in chapter 2, I do not analyze deputies elected in by-elections, such as those elected to fill three district seats where the "against-all" option had prevailed among the voters. One of the variables of interest in the following analysis is electoral performance, which incorporates vote share for district deputies. However, the district vote share attained by a deputy in a by-election, which itself was a product of the "against-all" option garnering the most votes in the original round of voting (Central Election Commission of the Russian Federation, www.cikrf.ru), is not comparable to the vote share of deputies who won outright the first time around. Excluding these deputies reduces the number of observations to 447. In addition, seven deputies who were elected in the 2003 Duma elections died while in office and therefore were not available as candidates for the 2007 elections.[8] Their removal reduces the number of observations further, to 440. Of the 440 deputies under investigation, 188 (or about 43 percent) were nominated by United Russia in 2007 (Central Election Commission of the Russian Federation, www.cikrf.ru). Of these 188 legislators, 52 deputies were not nominated by United Russia in the 2003 elections, which suggests a reasonable amount of co-optation in the period between the two elections.

The logistic regression analysis includes independent variables designed to capture the effects of party affiliation, as theorized above. First, it examines whether United Russia renominated deputies who ran under its banner in 2003 at a significantly higher rate than deputies who were not previously affiliated with it. The dichotomous variable "United Russia nomination 2003" gives a score of one to deputies (district or list) who were nominated by United Russia in 2003 and scores of zero to everyone else (Central Election Commission of the Russian Federation 2004, 263–89).

To determine the willingness and ability of United Russia to co-opt incumbent deputies with other party affiliations in the manner that corresponds to the variation outlined above, I include four additional nomination dummies. The first three identify deputies who were affiliated with the parties, besides United Russia, that passed the 5 percent threshold governing the PR half of the electoral system in place at the time. Those parties are the Communist Party, the Liberal Democratic Party, and Rodina. Deputies nominated by one of these three parties in 2003 received a score of one, respectively, and zero otherwise. In addition, since about 15 percent of the seats in the elections went to deputies who ran in the district elections independently, I include another dichotomous variable where one indicates this (zero otherwise). The default category when these nomination variables are all included in the model, then, is nomination by a party that did not pass the 5 percent legal threshold.

Since consolidating a ruling party's position in a party system is built, at least partially, on co-optation, United Russia's leadership may have used the 2007 elections not only as an opportunity to reward politicians who joined the party early on (i.e., leading into the 2003 Duma elections) but also as a chance to reward those who were willing to break previous party ties and swell the ruling party's ranks following the elections. The latter group of deputies consists of candidates who did not compete under the party's banner in the 2003 elections but who joined United Russia's faction when the Duma convened. To identify postelection additions to United Russia's faction, I construct a dichotomous variable where deputies who were not nominated by United Russia in 2003 but then joined United Russia's legislative faction receive scores of one and all other deputies receive scores of zero.[9] This variable, however, introduces significant multicollinearity in the model estimating list placement when included alongside the nomination variables. Its effect on list placement, then, is examined separately (see table 3.3 below).

The logistic regression analysis of list placement includes several control variables that are intended to help better isolate the effects of party affiliation discussed above. First, to the extent that a ruling party values legislative experience, the model includes two variables that differentiate among the deputies along this dimension. One is a dichotomous variable where a score of one signifies a deputy who was an incumbent prior to the 2003 elections (zero otherwise) (Central Election Commission of the Russian Federation 2004, 259–62). The other distinguishes deputies who held leadership positions in the Duma during the Fourth Convocation from those who did not (Official Website of the State Duma, http://duma.gov.ru/). For this variable, a value of one indicates that a deputy held a position of chair or vice chair of a Duma committee, or higher (such as Duma speaker), between 2003 and 2007. To control for the potential impact of age on the deputies' nomination prospects, I subtract the year that the deputies were born (see Central Election Commission of the Russian Federation 2004, 263–89) from 2007 and use the resulting variable.

The logistic regression analysis also considers whether the likelihood of securing a position on United Russia's 2007 list varied systematically between district deputies and list deputies. To the extent that United Russia wished to use the new PR-only rules to co-opt district deputies and benefit from their more localized influence, district deputies should have been reasonably attractive candidates.[10] To evaluate whether the deputies' mandates (Central Election Commission of the Russian Federation 2004, 263–89) influenced the likelihood of the deputies landing spots on United Russia's 2007 party list, I use another dichotomous variable with a score of one indicating district deputies while party list deputies receive a score of zero.

Finally, previous works on candidate selection have uncovered a link between gender and list placement. While some scholars contend that certain parties may use list placement to increase female representation (Caul 1999; Reynolds 1999; Rule 1987), others interrogate how gender interacts with informal aspects of candidate selection (Bjarnegard and Kenny 2016). Although I am agnostic about the effects of gender in this case, I control for it using a dichotomous variable where a one indicates a male candidate and a zero signals a female candidate.

Table 3.1 presents two logistic regression equations. Both examine the impact of a deputy's nomination using the five nomination dummy variables—including a United Russia nomination—to determine the likelihood of independent deputies and those affiliated with the parties having passed the legal threshold of landing on United Russia's 2007 list relative to a deputy nominated by a party that did not pass the legal threshold in 2003, which I refer to as "small" or "minor" parties. The second equation differs from the first by broadening the definition of independent deputies and, as a result, employing an alternative measure (discussed below).

The results in table 3.1 highlight the importance of the legislators' party affiliation. Deputies nominated by United Russia in 2003 were over two times more likely to secure a position on United Russia's 2007 list than deputies affiliated with small parties, and this effect is significant at the .05 level for a two-tailed test. At the same time, deputies affiliated with one of the three parties besides United Russia to pass the 5 percent legal threshold in 2003 were significantly less likely to land on United Russia's 2007 list than deputies previously nominated by small parties. As a reminder, odds ratios range from zero to infinity with values below one indicative of negative relationships and those above one capturing positive relationships. Dividing one by the odds ratio makes the negative relationships comparable to positive odds ratios. Thus, the

TABLE 3.1. Party nomination and other correlates of placement on United Russia's 2007 party list

	Equation 1			Equation 2		
	Odds ratio (p value)	95% Confidence interval		Odds ratio (p value)	95% Confidence interval	
United Russia nomination, 2003	**2.460 (.042)**	1.035	5.847	**2.711 (.012)**	1.248	5.886
Self-nominated, 2003	0.822 (.673)	0.332	2.037	—		
Independent (self-nominated or no party tie), 2003	—			0.949 (.879)	0.481	1.871
Rodina nomination, 2003	**0.182 (.014)**	0.047	0.709	**0.204 (.012)**	0.060	0.702
Liberal Democrat nomination, 2003	**0.150 (.016)**	0.032	0.701	**0.164 (.021)**	0.035	0.764
Communist Party nomination, 2003	**0.036 (.002)**	0.004	0.309	**0.040 (.003)**	0.005	0.325
Male	0.942 (.874)	0.448	1.978	0.938 (.866)	0.446	1.971
Age	**0.974 (.044)**	0.949	0.999	**0.974 (.043)**	0.949	0.999
Duma or Committee Leader, 2004–2007	**2.030 (.002)**	1.292	3.188	**2.020 (.002)**	1.286	3.171
Incumbent, 2003	0.984 (.947)	0.612	1.581	0.100 (.999)	0.617	1.626
SMD deputy	**2.217 (.005)**	1.279	3.844	**2.197 (.006)**	1.248	3.869
Constant	1.407 (.699)	0.250	7.927	1.293 (.773)	0.226	7.384
Pseudo R^2	0.234			0.234		
Likelihood ratio χ^2 (significance)	140.83 (.000)			140.68 (.000)		
Number of cases	440			440		

Note: Numbers in bold indicate significance at the .05 level for a two-tailed test.

odds of a deputy nominated by a minor party in 2003 (the default category for the nomination dummies) landing on United Russia's 2007 list were more than five times those of a deputy nominated by Rodina (1/.182 = 5.5), almost seven times higher than those of a deputy nominated by the Liberal Democrats (1/.150 = 6.7), and almost 28 times those of a deputy nominated by the Communist Party (1/.036 = 27.8). The different magnitudes of these effects map closely onto the parties' histories, with the Communist Party enjoying the most organization and strongest reputation as an opposition party. It makes sense, then, that it would be the party least likely to lose deputies to the ruling party. By contrast, Rodina, which is widely recognized as a Kremlin creation, fares the worst. Still, on the whole, the results support the expectation that these parties would be unlikely sources of United Russia candidates during the first PR-only elections, which is a notable outcome given concerns about weak party development in Russia through much of its post-Soviet history prior to the period under investigation.

As expected, politicians who affiliated with United Russia early on were more likely to be nominated to its 2007 list when compared to politicians with other party ties, and among these politicians, deputies from parties that passed the legal threshold in 2003 were less likely to secure United Russia nominations than those from parties that did not pass the threshold. It is also notable that the variable signifying independents—here operationalized as self-nominated deputies—proves statistically insignificant. In other words, the prospects of these politicians being co-opted by the ruling party did not differ significantly from those deputies affiliating with a smaller party in 2003. However, equation 2 in table 3.1 (discussed below) revisits this finding since self-nominations are associated only with district deputies in this specification and since this equation also finds that district deputies from 2003 were twice as likely to make United Russia's 2007 list than deputies elected via a party list in 2003. Significant results for the mandate effect confirm a previous but untested assumption (Moraski 2015): United Russia used list construction to develop local representation in its ranks alongside the party centralization that is commonly associated with closed-list PR systems.

Table 3.1 also suggests that deputies serving in Duma leadership, such as committee chairs, were twice as likely to receive a position on United Russia's 2007 list as those who did not hold such positions, all else being equal. At the same time, United Russia appears to have privileged younger deputies, as the likelihood of list placement is negatively correlated with age. These findings suggest that, while the party leadership may have used the move to closed-list PR to develop a cadre of younger politicians, it also valued legislative experience.

As noted above, the results presented as the first equation in table 3.1 rely on a specific operationalization of "independent" deputy—that is, this variable identifies deputies who ran in district contests as self-nominated candidates. Although this indicator serves as a rigorous test of the mandate effect and emphasizes the robustness of that effect, it is possible to operationalize independents in Russia more broadly. In Russia, some list deputies identified themselves as party members in their candidate biographies, others listed positions within a specific party, and still others provided no information about their party affiliations (Central Election Commission of the Russian Federation 2004, 263–89). With this information in hand, I classified the last category of politicians as independents who were nominated to and elected via party lists in 2003. The second equation in table 3.1, then, replicates the previous analysis utilizing a dichotomous variable that relaxes the definition of "independent" to include deputies elected as self-nominated district candidates as well as list candidates who did not explicitly identify with a party in their corresponding candidate biographies.[11] This change does not radically alter the findings. The main difference is a stronger effect for deputies nominated by United Russia in 2003, with the odds of these deputies landing on United Russia's 2007 list increasing relative to those affiliated with small parties.

While the analysis so far has considered the likelihood of incumbent deputies receiving positions on United Russia's 2007 list, an equally important issue is how these different types of individuals fared when it comes to list rank.[12] In practice, list placement decisions represent a two-stage process. In the first stage, a party decides to nominate a candidate or not. The preceding analysis, then, compares different model specifications of this first stage in the process. In the second stage, the party ranks those politicians who were selected as candidates. Technically speaking, since the decisions are made by the same organization (here, United Russia), list rank decisions are subject to a nonrandom selection process (the first stage of receiving United Russia's backing), which may produce a selection bias that gives independent variables unwarranted significance when it comes to list rank (i.e., the second stage) (Berk 1983). To address this concern, the following analysis of list rank uses a Heckman selection model that estimates the decision to nominate a politician as a candidate with maximum likelihood, and list rank decisions are estimated using a corrected ordinary least squares (OLS) model (see Bushway et al. 2007; Drury et al. 2005; Heckman 1976).[13] For the first stage of the two-stage analysis, I use the first equation in table 3.1, which defines independent deputies more narrowly, thereby providing a more robust test of the mandate effect. The second stage, meanwhile, adds a few new variables while focusing on a smaller number of cases.[14]

As noted above, United Russia placed 188 deputies elected in the 2003 Duma elections on its party list in 2007.[15] All 188 of these deputies were either nominated by United Russia in 2003 (136) or joined United Russia's faction when the Duma convened (52). With this in mind, a key question is whether deputies who competed under United Russia's banner in 2003 received better list placements in the 2007 elections compared to those who joined the party's faction after the 2003 elections. To answer this question, one can use either the dichotomous variable for a 2003 United Russia nomination or a dichotomous variable capturing deputies nominated as independents or by other parties who then joined United Russia's faction (discussed below). I use the former. In other words, the dichotomous variable for a 2003 United Russia nomination in the second stage is used to differentiate deputies who affiliated with the party prior to its decisive 2003 electoral victory from those who joined it only after the elections. Missing from the second stage, then, are the other 2003 nomination variables used in the first stage—that is, those indicating whether deputies were self-nominated or nominated by Rodina, the Liberal Democratic Party, or the Communist Party.[16]

Another topic of interest is the list rank of district deputies relative to list deputies. As with list placement, the analysis of list rank uses the dichotomous variable for which a one signifies that a deputy is a district deputy. However, with the reduction in the number of cases in the second stage of the process, it is even more difficult to empirically separate any mandate effect from the question of who previously nominated the deputies, since 48 of the 52 deputies who joined United Russia's Duma faction after the 2003 elections were district deputies.

While the first and second stages of the model use several of the same independent variables, previous research reveals that the supply of proven politicians available as candidates for a United Russia regional sub-list significantly influences list rank for each individual candidate (Moraski 2015). For example, one peculiarity of the Russian system during the period under investigation was the placement of governors at the top of the ruling party's regional sub-lists. While chapter 6 examines the effects of this practice, it has implications for the current analysis. For one thing, in 2007, two of Russia's governors had been elected as district deputies in 2003 (Boos in Kaliningrad, and Denin in Bryansk) and one as a list deputy (Kanokov in Kabardino-Balkaria). To account for such cases in the list rank decisions, I use a dichotomous variable that gives any deputy elected in 2003, who was then governor in 2007,[17] a score of one (zero otherwise), since the new position likely improved their list ranks: governors often headed United Russia's regional sub-lists because they were expected to serve as "locomotives," tools that could drive votes in the ruling party's direction (Gel'man 2007).

Even if a Duma deputy under investigation did not become a governor by the time of the 2007 elections, the placement of governors on a deputy's regional sub-lists in 2007 likely reduced that deputy's list rank compared to deputies competing on sub-lists without a governor. To control for this possibility, I again use a binary variable where a one indicates the deputy in question was nominated to a regional sub-list that also had a governor on that sub-list and a zero indicates that no governor competed alongside the deputy. Similarly, the number of other incumbent deputies competing on the same regional sub-list should affect an individual deputy's list rank. Just as deputies nominated to a regional sub-list with a governor on the ticket will likely have worse ranks than those not competing with a governor for a top spot, the average deputy competing against other incumbent Duma deputies for a top position on a United Russia regional sub-list will likely be worse off than those not competing with their colleagues. To measure this difference, I include a count variable where the value indicates the number of other Duma deputies nominated by United Russia competing alongside the deputy on the same regional sub-list. The variable ranges from zero (indicating that no other deputy was nominated by United Russia to the regional sub-list) to ten (for deputies competing on the sub-list representing Moscow Oblast), with a median of 2.86.

Table 3.2 presents the results of the two-stage model in which the dependent variable in the second stage is each deputy's rank on one of United Russia's 2007 regional sub-lists in the first equation and the deputy's rank logged in the second and third equations. The rationale for logging list rank is that the transformation estimates the diminishing return of worse list placements. Specifically, the electoral prospects of a candidate on regional sub-lists are better when they are located at the

TABLE 3.2. Heckman Selection model for United Russia list placement, list rank, and logged list rank

Variables	Stage One
	List placement
United Russia nomination, 2003	0.565*
	(.271)
Independent (self-nominated or no party tie), 2003	−0.115
	(.286)
Rodina nomination, 2003	−0.965*
	(.388)
Liberal Democrat nomination, 2003	−1.042*
	(.431)
Communist Party nomination, 2003	−1.809*
	(.529)
Male	−0.017
	(.230)
Age	−0.016*
	(.008)
Duma or committee leader, 2004–2007	0.421*
	(.138)
Incumbent, 2003	−0.004
	(.145)
SMD deputy	0.495*
	(.168)
Constant	0.157
	(.534)
N=440	

TABLE 3.2. (cont.)

Variables	Stage Two		
	List rank	List rank, logged	List rank, logged
United Russia nomination, 2003	−2.077*	−0.189*	−1.563*
	(.809)	(.068)	(.539)
Male	−1.205+	−0.076	−1.288*
	(.658)	(.055)	(.620)
Age	0.019	8.41E-04	1.30E-02
	(.024)	(.002)	(.022)
Duma or committee leader, 2004–2007	−1.289*	−0.114*	−1.145*
	(.472)	(.040)	(.430)
Incumbent, 2003	−0.908*	−0.103*	−0.848*
	(.405)	(.034)	(.387)
SMD deputy	−0.662	−0.048	—
	(.624)	(.052)	
PR vote and district vote difference	—	—	−0.019
			(.015)
Governor, 2007	−2.550+	−0.526*	−2.730+
	(1.447)	(.123)	(1.439)
Governor on 2007 sublist	0.466	0.144*	0.582
	(.535)	(.045)	(.523)
Other Duma deputies on 2007 sublist	0.918*	0.067*	0.910*
	(.071)	(.006)	(.071)
Constant	6.488*	0.688*	5.462*
	(2.033)	(.170)	(1.618)
N=188			
Mills Lambda	−2.102+	−0.157	−1.367
	(1.200)	(.102)	(.857)
Heckman Model Chi-Square	226.23	229.45	228.81
Chi-Square probability	0.000	0.000	0.000

Note: Numbers in parentheses are standard errors. + indicates significance at the .10 level for a two-tailed test. indicates significance at the .05 level or higher for a two-tailed test.

top or near the top of a regional sub-list, while higher values are characterized by an increasingly diminishing likelihood of election. Logging the value of rank approximates this dynamic.

Since the results of the first stage of the analysis do not depend on how the dependent variable in the second stage of the analysis is measured, table 3.2 presents the results for the first stage only once. The results for list placement in the top panel of table 3.2 conform to those previously presented.[18] Specifically, comparing the first equation from table 3.1 to the first stage of the Heckman selection model reveals that the same independent variables prove significant and that they are significant in the same directions: deputies nominated by United Russia in 2003 were significantly more likely to be nominated by United Russia in 2007 than those nominated by parties not accounted for in the model, as were district deputies and incumbents who held leadership positions in the outgoing Duma. Meanwhile, deputies previously nominated by Rodina, the Liberal Democratic Party, or the Communists were significantly less likely to make United Russia's 2007 list than incumbent deputies from other, smaller parties. The fates of independents, however, demonstrate no significant difference from those of incumbents previously nominated by parties not accounted for in the model. Finally, older incumbents are less likely to have received a United Russia nomination in 2007, and prior incumbency (i.e., having been elected to the Duma in 1999) fails to matter.

The bottom panel of table 3.2 presents the second-stage results. As a reminder, in this case, a negative relationship works in the deputy's favor, since lower values for list rank indicate better placement. On most counts, the second-stage results resemble one another regardless of whether list rank is transformed (or not), with the primary exceptions involving the control variables for gubernatorial list placement. First, deputies whom United Russia nominated in 2003 received better list ranks (i.e., lower values) than those not previously nominated by the party. Deputies with more legislative experience—that is, those who were incumbents prior to the 2003 election—and those who held leadership positions within the Duma after the 2003 elections also enjoyed better list ranks in both equations. Moreover, as one would expect, a deputy's list rank is systematically worse as the number of other deputies nominated by United Russia on her regional sub-list increases.[19] In addition, although United Russia does not appear to have favored prior incumbents when selecting candidates among sitting legislators, it does appear to have allocated better list positions to prior incumbents who made the cut. Meanwhile, according to the first two equations, neither the age nor the mandate of the deputy significantly influence list rank. So, while United Russia was more likely to nominate younger deputies and those holding district mandates, these characteristics did not systematically translate into more electable list positions. The third equation in table 3.2 revisits the question of the mandate effect. I discuss that equation below.

Among the difference across the first two second-stage models, the result for gender suggests, at most, a marginal effect. For the equation when list rank is not transformed, male deputies are likely to receive better list positions, but the effect is significant at only the .10 level for a two-tailed test. Meanwhile, when the list rank is logged—and more electable list positions are given greater emphasis—the effect of gender disappears. In contrast, gubernatorial list placement has a much more significant effect when list rank is logged. Specifically, deputies who became governors enjoyed better ranks in the first equation, but the effect is significant only at the .10 level, while the presence of a governor on a regional sub-list does not significantly influence the deputies' ranks when all ranks on a regional sub-list are weighed equally. However, when list rank is logged, both variables capturing the gubernatorial list are significant at the .05 level for a two-tailed test. This outcome makes sense given the fact that most governors on regional sub-list held one of the top two list positions (see chapter 6).

It is possible that the null result for a mandate effect reflects a failure to differentiate among district deputies in a manner that identifies those whom the party valued more. Specifically, in a previous study of only district deputies, those with stronger electoral records (measured as district vote share) enjoyed better list placements (Moraski 2015). As I note in that 2015 article, especially high values may indicate more than a candidate's popularity with voters, such as the politician's ability to capitalize on electoral malfeasance and other administrative resources. To the extent that a ruling party in an electoral authoritarian state values decisive election results, regardless of how they are achieved, deputies winning under such conditions should emerge as attractive candidates. Adding list deputies to the analysis complicates matters, however, since a comparable indicator of these deputies' individual electoral influence or potential is not available.

One option is to develop a measure of electability for list deputies that is based on standardizing list placements, which I do in chapter 4 for the two Ukrainian parties under investigation. In Ukraine, however, parties propose a single national list, which facilitates the development of the measure used in chapter 4. In Russia, the reliance on regional sub-lists and the corresponding regional variation in what constitutes an electable list position with a party (reflecting population size and party performance; see chapter 6), even with the ruling party, impede this approach. So, instead, I measure deputies' electoral records by using United Russia's national PR vote share of 37.6 percent as the baseline and by assuming that all list deputies contributed to this total. District deputies, however, could have either overperformed or underperformed relative to the party's national total. A district deputy's electoral performance score, therefore, is the difference between his or her district vote share and the party's PR vote share. Of the 119 district deputies nominated by United Russia in 2007, the deputy with the lowest district vote share (17.5 percent) fell below United Russia's national total by 20.1 percent and thus receives a score of -20.1. The strongest performance was a district deputy who received 82.1 percent of the vote. That deputy receives a score of +44.5. All list deputies, meanwhile, receive scores of zero, which places them at the baseline. The third column in the lower panel of table 3.2 presents the two-stage analysis when this variable is used in lieu of the mandate variable. Like the mandate variable, however, this variable has no significant effect on list rank, although the substitution does influence the performance of three other variables in the model: when controlling for the electoral records of district deputies, gender matters, with male deputies now significantly more likely to receive better list placements. Meanwhile, the influence of both variables capturing the effects of gubernatorial list placement are appreciably weaker and resemble their effects in the first equation (in which list rank is not logged). While one should not read too much into these changes, they do seem to suggest that electoral performance may have indirect effects on list rank, interacting with other candidate characteristics that future research may wish to explore further. In this case, for example, especially high vote shares may have allowed Russian district deputies to compete more successfully with governors for the top spot on United Russia's regional sub-list.

Assessing the Effect of Changing Factions

As noted previously, a ruling party may seek to consolidate its position in a party system not only by rewarding politicians who joined the party early on but also by encouraging those politicians with previous affiliations to break ranks and join the ruling party. In fact, as I outline in chapter 4 in the context of Ukraine, a prior history of switching legislative factions may significantly influence party decisions about candidate selection. In Russia, the question of faction membership assumed the most salience when the Duma convened and a postelection bandwagon granted United Russia a supermajority of more than 300 deputies (see chapter 2). According to Reuter and Remington (2009, 507), after that point United Russia "exercised ironclad discipline" over its deputies.

To investigate the potential implications of postelection additions to United Russia's faction on United Russia's 2007 nominations, I employ a dichotomous variable where a score of one indicates deputies who were not nominated by United Russia in 2003 but then joined United Russia's legislative faction once in office. All other deputies receive scores of zero.[20] Table 3.3 replaces the dichotomous variable used in table 3.1 indicating a 2003 nomination by United Russia with this new variable, which identifies deputies who were not nominated by United Russia in 2003 but who joined United Russia's faction once the Duma convened.

With this new variable in place, the equations in table 3.3 examine the relationship between United Russia and those seemingly opportunistic deputies who affiliated with the party only after the elections. For example, if the party decided to co-opt these deputies at higher rates compared to other deputies, then these deputies should enjoy a higher likelihood of securing a position on United Russia's 2007 list compared to deputies from smaller parties who failed to join the bandwagon (the new default category). It is worth noting that deputies receiving a score of one on this variable means those deputies may have ran independently (as self-nominated candidates) or may have been nominated by any party other than United Russia, including those that passed the legal threshold: the Communist Party, the Liberal Democratic Party, and Rodina. As a result, the four dichotomous variables in the models in table 3.1, which previously indicated the sources of a deputy's nomination, now identify self-nominated deputies and deputies nominated by one of the three other parties represented in the Duma *who did not defect to the United Russia faction*. With these different combinations included in the model, the dummy variable for a United Russia nomination in 2003 is excluded due to multicollinearity.

TABLE 3.3. Faction membership and other correlates of placement on United Russia's 2007 party list

	Equation 1			Equation 2	
	Odds ratio (p value)	95% Confidence interval		Odds ratio (p value)	95% Confidence interval
Postelection addition to United Russia Faction, 2004	10.801 (.000)	3.972	29.371	4.886 (.000)	2.336	10.220
Self-nominated, 2003	0.072 (.000)	0.024	0.215	—		
Independent (self-nominated or no party tie), 2003	—			0.248 (.000)	0.126	0.488
Rodina nomination, 2003	0.030 (.000)	0.008	0.117	0.073 (.000)	0.023	0.233
Liberal Democrat nomination, 2003	0.032 (.000)	0.008	0.133	0.033 (.000)	0.009	0.128
Communist Party nomination, 2003	0.009 (.000)	0.001	0.074	0.016 (.000)	0.002	0.125
Male	0.871 (.716)	0.413	1.834	0.826 (.617)	0.391	1.748
Age	0.975 (.062)	0.950	1.001	0.974 (.052)	0.949	1.000
Duma or committee leader, 2004–2007	2.195 (.001)	1.381	3.489	2.265 (.000)	1.434	3.576
Incumbent, 2003	0.776 (.292)	0.485	1.243	0.727 (.186)	0.453	1.166
SMD deputy	1.376 (.227)	0.820	2.307	0.967 (.896)	0.580	1.611
Constant	3.697 (.098)	0.787	17.367	5.087 (.041)	1.068	24.227
Pseudo R^2	0.278			0.256		
Likelihood ratio χ^2 (significance)	166.97 (.000)			153.78 (.000)		
Number of cases	440			440		

Note: Numbers in bold indicate significance at the .05 level for a two-tailed test.

Equation 1 in table 3.3, which uses the narrower indicator of party independence from table 3.1, reveals that deputies who joined United Russia's faction were almost 11 times more likely to land on United Russia's 2007 list than those nominated by smaller parties who did not join the faction. Meanwhile, deputies who were self-nominated or were nominated by one of the three parties besides United Russia to pass the threshold *but did not* join United Russia's faction were significantly less likely to make United Russia's 2007 list than those deputies nominated by smaller parties who did not join United Russia's faction (again, the default category).

Equation 1 in table 3.3 reaffirms the finding that United Russia favored deputies who held leadership positions in the Duma as candidates in 2007, while the effects for younger deputies fall short of conventional significance levels in this model. More notable, the mandate effect observed in table 3.1 dissipates. A likely explanation for this outcome is that the deputies not nominated by United Russia and more likely to join United Russia's faction in the Duma were district deputies. Indeed, of the 87 deputies not nominated by United Russia in 2003 who subsequently joined United Russia's Duma faction, 76 were district deputies.[21] Overall, then, the results from table 3.1 and the first equation in table 3.3 demonstrate a tendency of United Russia to use the move the PR rules to co-opt politicians who did not commit to the party earlier, which includes an emphasis on district deputies.

Equation 2 in table 3.3 repeats the analysis using the alternative measure of independent deputies that includes list deputies without an explicit party affiliation (aside from the source of their nomination) alongside self-nominated district deputies. The effects of postelection membership in United Russia's faction and nonpartisanship are smaller using this specification. Meanwhile, self-nominated deputies and those nominated by parties other than United Russia who joined United Russia's faction are now almost five times more likely to land on United Russia's 2007 list than those nominated by smaller parties who did not join the faction. While the odds of independents (broadly defined) landing on United Russia's 2007 list are also not great, at 4:1 ($1/.248 = 4.0$) they are better than those estimated for self-nominated deputies—almost 14:1 ($1/.072=13.9$)—in the first equation of table 3.3. These changes reflect the fact that defining independents broadly includes deputies who not only competed on United Russia's 2003 list but also appear to have been rewarded for this early commitment even if they did not explicitly define themselves as party members at the time. Under this specification, holding a leadership position within the Duma continues to improve a deputy's chances of being nominated by United Russia in 2007, while the effect of age once again falls short of convention, meeting significance at only the .10 level for a two-tailed test.

As I note above, using the dichotomous variable for faction membership significantly alters how to interpret the dichotomous nomination variables that are included in the models in table 3.3 relative to the models

TABLE 3.4. Effects of nomination and faction membership combinations on United Russia's 2007 party list

	Equation 1			Equation 2		
	Odds ratio (p value)	95% Confidence interval		Odds ratio (p value)	95% Confidence interval	
United Russia nominee in 2003 and faction member	7.169 (.000)	4.488	11.452	—		
Postelection addition to United Russia Faction	—			1.603 (.078)	0.949	2.707
Male	0.984 (.965)	0.477	2.031	0.875 (.692)	0.453	1.693
Age	0.972 (.023)	0.949	0.996	0.979 (.055)	0.959	1.000
Duma or committee leader, 2004–2007	1.697 (.018)	1.096	2.628	1.805 (.004)	1.211	2.689
Incumbent, 2003	0.998 (.994)	0.640	1.557	0.871 (.180)	0.581	1.306
SMD deputy	4.034 (.000)	2.535	6.420	2.433 (.000)	1.590	3.725
Constant	0.445 (.272)	0.105	1.886	1.153 (.828)	0.320	4.160
Pseudo R^2	0.20			0.069		
Likelihood ratio χ^2 (significance)	118.57 (.000)			41.53 (.000)		
Number of cases	440			440		

Note: Numbers in bold indicate significance at the .05 level for a two-tailed test.

in table 3.1 by changing the default category. Moreover, since the variable for a 2003 United Russia nomination is excluded from the models in table 3.3 due to multicollinearity, the results cannot speak to the question regarding the list chances of deputies who committed to the party prior to the elections relative to more opportunistic deputies who joined the party's faction after the elections. To address this question, table 3.4 presents two simplified estimations of list placement. The first equation compares the likelihood of list placement for deputies nominated by United Russia in 2003 and serving in United Russia's legislative faction relative to all other deputies by employing a single dichotomous variable that gives deputies possessing both attributes a score of one and all other deputies a score of zero. The variables for gender, age, prior incumbency, leadership positions in the Duma, and legislative mandate are included again as controls. The second equation replaces the variable capturing those deputies who committed to United Russia early and served in its faction with the variable that captures only postelection additions to United Russia (i.e., the dichotomous variable used above, where a one indicates deputies who were not nominated by United Russia but who joined United Russia's faction in the Duma). Comparing the two sets of results suggests that, while members of United Russia's faction were more likely to be nominated by United Russia in 2007 as compared to other deputies, the odds are significantly better for those deputies who also competed under the party's banner in 2003 than for those who did not but then joined the faction after the elections. These results, then, suggest that United Russia prioritized the nomination of deputies who committed to the party prior to the 2003 elections over deputies who joined the party's faction after the election results were in.

Conclusion

While the effects of proportional representation are conventionally investigated in democratic regimes, this chapter uses Russia's implementation of a closed-list PR system as an opportunity to examine the development of a ruling party (United Russia) operating under an increasingly authoritarian regime. The adoption of a closed-list PR system followed four legislative elections that were governed by a mixed-member electoral system: those held in Russia in 1993, 1995, 1999, and 2003. Unlike the mixed-member system—which gave independents a strong presence in the national legislature—the PR-only rules allowed Russia's parties to control access to the Duma. The monopoly given to parties had combined with the increasingly authoritarian nature of the regime to grant United Russia the opportunity to consolidate its position in the national legislature. How this actually unfolded, however, has gone largely unexamined. Yet, as noted in chapter 2, a similar consolidation of power had escaped previous pro-presidential parties in Russia, and United Russia's success on this front likely reflected preparations for the 2008 presidential election that would transfer the office from Putin to his handpicked successor. With this in mind, United Russia's 2007 nominations of deputies elected in 2003 provide a rare opportunity to scrutinize whether concerns about cohesion and co-optation shaped the ruling party's development. Specifically, this chapter analyzes whether the party's relationship with incumbent Duma deputies, as a pool of potential candidates with greater leverage vis-à-vis the party than many other politicians, varied systematically on the basis of the deputies' previous party affiliations, legislative positions, legislative mandates, ages, genders, and faction memberships.

Comparing United Russia's 2007 nominations of Duma deputies elected in 2003 confirms several expectations while providing new insights. When investigating the factors influencing the likelihood of a United Russia nomination, I find that the party was, in fact, significantly more likely to nominate deputies in 2007 whom it had nominated in 2003 as opposed to those affiliated with other parties in 2003, regardless of whether or not those parties passed the 5 percent legal threshold. However, the analysis also reveals that the chances of self-nominated district deputies making United Russia's list did not differ significantly from deputies previously nominated by small parties that failed to pass the legal threshold. In other words, United Russia appears to have been willing and able to co-opt seemingly independent deputies as well as deputies from minor parties with little prospects of passing the 7 percent threshold governing the 2007 Duma elections. It can be surmised that United Russia pursued a strategy in 2007 of co-opting politicians without ties to other parties as well as politicians from electorally weak parties while preserving its relationship with deputies who had already committed to the party before the elections. One caveat to these findings entails deputies elected in 2003 who then joined United Russia's faction following the elections. While those who competed under United Russia's banner in 2003 had better United Russia list prospects in 2007 than postelection faction members, the latter were better off than other deputies elected in 2003.

The analyses also reveal that United Russia was more likely to nominate district deputies—that is, deputies who had been directly elected by geographically defined sets of constituents—than list deputies who owed their election more to the appeal of a party. Even when controlling for prior party affiliations, United Russia seems to have preferred deputies with proven electoral records, as evidenced by their ability to win district contests. This outcome suggests that United Russia used list construction during Russia's first PR-only elections to capitalize on the existing local ties of incumbent legislators alongside the opportunities for party centralization commonly associated with the implementation of closed-list PR rules.

Perhaps even more interesting is the evidence of greater party *system* institutionalization in Russia. While United Russia was significantly more likely to nominate its own 2003 nominees than self-nominated politicians or those nominated by minor parties, it was also significantly less likely to nominate deputies previously nominated by Russia's largest "opposition" parties: the Communists, the Liberal Democratic Party, and Rodina.[22] Yet the results do not simply capture a reasonable degree of organizational distinctiveness between Russia's ruling party and what observers of Russian politics call the "systemic" opposition. Rather, the variation uncovered also maps nicely onto one might expect given the parties' political histories and ideological origins. The likelihood of a deputy from the Communist Party—the main opposition party in the 1990s—receiving a United Russia nomination was significantly lower than that of a deputy from the Liberal Democratic Party—an opposition party that has consistently competed in Russia's post-Soviet elections but that often proved more deferential to the Kremlin. Meanwhile, the odds of a deputy from Rodina (commonly depicted as a Kremlin project) making United Russia's list were the best among the three but still appreciably worse than deputies previously nominated by minor parties.

Changing the focus from party nominations in general to the prospects of election via a United Russia nomination adds another set of findings and insights. First, deputies nominated by United Russia in 2003 were not only more likely to make the party's 2007 list; these deputies were also more likely to receive electable list placements compared to the other incumbent deputies United Russia nominated in 2007 (all of whom had joined the party's faction after the 2003 elections). While United Russia also appears to have privileged younger deputies when selecting candidates, age does not appear to have been a factor driving list rank. Rather, legislative experience—indicated by prior incumbency and, depending on the model, holding leadership positions within the Duma—appears to have been more important. However, neither gender nor legislative mandate exhibits an independent influence on list rank, although there is some evidence to suggest that the stronger electoral showings of some district deputies may have indirectly influenced their list ranks.

Finally, the analyses of list rank identify the placement of governors on the ruling party's regional sub-lists as an intriguing practice in Russian legislative elections that merits further investigation. Since these politicians already enjoyed powerful posts, the decision to head a regional sub-list is not likely to have been driven by electoral motivations. Chapter 6 examines this practice. Chapter 4 analyzes the relationships between two of Ukraine's main parties at the time of that country's first legislative elections governed by closed-list PR and the incumbent legislative deputies there. Since the Ukrainian elections occurred in the aftermath of the 2004 Orange Revolution, the analysis in chapter 4 provides a reference point for understanding how parties in more competitive electoral contexts navigate major electoral system changes. Chapter 4 also lays the foundation for a direct comparison of Russian and Ukrainian party behavior (chapter 5), which seeks to systematically analyze party behavior across regime types. Taken together, the chapters offer theoretical and empirical baselines to scholars interested in understanding how individual parties in weakly institutionalized party systems utilize changes in their electoral systems.

4

Contending for Power under Proportional
Representation in Ukraine

Chapter 3 uses a case study of the Russian 2007 Duma elections to examine how ruling parties in authoritarian regimes may utilize the adoption of a closed-list proportional representation (PR) electoral system to strengthen their positions. Specifically, I contend that parties have to decide how much they value retaining loyal politicians (cohesion) and how much they are interested in recruiting new politicians, such as previously unaffiliated politicians with proven electoral records and legislative experience (co-optation).

Ukraine's 2006 Rada elections represent a particularly useful point of comparison to the Russian case. In contrast to Russia, Ukraine's first PR-only contests occurred in a fiercely competitive political climate following Ukraine's 2004 Orange Revolution. As discussed in chapter 2, Viktor Yushchenko, the former prime minister–turned–presidential contender, would eventually defeat President Leonid Kuchma's preferred successor, Viktor Yanukovych, thanks in part to large public protests against the electoral fraud that marred the second round of the 2004 presidential election. The events not only led Ukraine's Supreme Court to rule in favor of repeating the vote; they also set the stage for constitutional changes that gave the legislature, rather than the president, control over the prime minister and several cabinet posts. During the months to come, opponents to Kuchma's regime failed to unite around Yushchenko, while Yanukovych's Party of Regions strove to consolidate its position as a dominant force in eastern Ukraine. In this context, the outcome of Ukraine's 2006 elections proved far more uncertain than that of Russia's 2007 elections, with no single party enjoying a decisive advantage when recruiting prospective candidates. As a result, while some party leaders may have wished to pursue a strategy of co-optation as a way to keep potentially influential politicians from forming new parties or affiliating with rival parties, not all parties were in a strong position to do so. Moreover, to the extent that such a strategy places party discipline in jeopardy should these politicians win seats, the leaders of some parties in the position to co-opt previously unaffiliated deputies may have decided to emphasize cohesion over co-optation. From this perspective, one should expect a strategy of cohesion to prevail among parties in more competitive environments as parties will be either less willing to risk party discipline or less able to attract "free agents," such as those created by the elimination of district mandates in the cases under investigation.

This chapter focuses on the candidate nominations of the two Ukrainian parties with the largest contingent of district deputies leading into the 2006 Rada elections: Our Ukraine and the Party of Regions. It begins by addressing a limitation in chapter 2's initial comparative analysis: the potential for the district deputies' 2002 party memberships to influence 2006 list placement in Ukraine. It then moves to a multivariate analysis of party list construction similar to that presented in chapter 3 for Russia. The multivariate analysis builds on previous work that examines the placements of only district deputies on party lists (Moraski 2017). The benefit of that analysis was the ability to explore whether geographic differences across Ukraine—a key aspect of Ukrainian electoral politics—influenced party decisions. The 2017 analysis found that deputies who represented regions widely viewed as strongholds for the Party of Regions in 2002 were more likely to secure positions on that party's 2006 list. This chapter casts a wider net: it examines list placement during the first closed-list PR elections for all legislative deputies previously elected—that is, district deputies and party list deputies alike. By doing so, the current analysis explicitly considers whether two of Ukraine's major parties treated legislators with district mandates differently from those with list mandates. It turns out that they did, although at different stages in the process. This approach not only closely parallels the one pursued in chapter 3 but also adds two case studies of party behavior that can be compared to the behavior of United Russia, which I address more directly in chapter 5.

Revisiting the Nomination Strategies of Ukraine's Main Parties

As I note in chapter 2, neither Our Ukraine nor the Party of Regions possessed as much leverage over Ukraine's legislature, the Verkhovna

Rada, as United Russia did over the State Duma. In fact, the governing party following the 2002 Rada elections, For a United Ukraine, disintegrated after a few months in office. Given these developments, it is reasonable to expect that the leadership of the Party of Regions would be attuned to the question of internal party discipline when selecting prospective candidates for its list in the first PR-only elections, leading it to treat party members differently than those deputies whom were only nominated by For a United Ukraine in 2002. Accordingly, I begin this chapter by revisiting the comparative analysis of the nominations by Ukrainian parties presented in chapter 2.

As in chapter 2, I examine list construction in Ukraine's 2006 elections by comparing the nomination decisions of Our Ukraine and the Party of Regions to one another as well as to the Socialist Party and the Communist Party, which represent organizations with distinct ideological positions that could serve to preserve party allegiance. In addition, I examine the 2006 lists of the Tymoshenko Bloc and Lytvyn's People's Bloc; the former was positioned to draw votes and candidates away from Our Ukraine, while the latter was positioned to draw votes and candidates away from the Party of Regions.

While chapter 2 privileges comparability across Russia and Ukraine by focusing on the rates by which the main parties in the countries renominated district deputies whom they had nominated in the preceding elections, this chapter more carefully considers the nuances of the Ukrainian case. As chapter 2 illuminates, renomination rates by Our Ukraine and the Party of Regions were not only substantially lower than those of United Russia; the renomination rate of the Party of Regions was also appreciably lower than that of Our Ukraine. Chapter 2 points out that this outcome likely reflects the fact that the Party of Regions had to compete with another successor to For a United Ukraine—Lytvyn's People's Bloc (also known simply as the Lytvyn Bloc)—for candidates. However, a second possible explanation for this result is that the Party of Regions may have privileged party membership when selecting district candidates for its 2006 PR list to a greater extent than Our Ukraine given the disintegration of For a United Ukraine after the 2002 Rada elections. Thus, I revisit the analysis from chapter 2 by focusing on the party memberships of district deputies, then move on to the analysis of all deputies, both list and district.[1]

The electoral rules in place during Ukraine's 2002 Rada elections allowed independents (i.e., candidates with no party membership) as well as self-nominated candidates (i.e., candidates without a party nomination). While one could reasonably interpret those competing under a party banner as signaling greater commitment to that party than self-nominated candidates, it is unclear how party-nominated deputies compare to party members in general, let alone those who chose to forgo a party nomination in favor of self-nomination. Indeed, the relative importance of these signals may depend on the organization in question, and for reasons already discussed, one could expect the Party of Regions to be less comfortable than Our Ukraine with renominating previously elected deputies who were not party members. Figures 4.1–4.6 present the rates by which the six Ukrainian parties in question renominated district deputies who were party members in 2002.[2]

As figures 4.1–4.6 illustrate, the impact of this more stringent test of party loyalty varies by party. For the Socialist Party and the Communist Party, the outcomes in figures 4.3 and 4.4 appear largely unchanged when compared to figures 2.6 and 2.7, which employ the 2002 party nominations: The Communist Party struggled to retain its district deputies, and

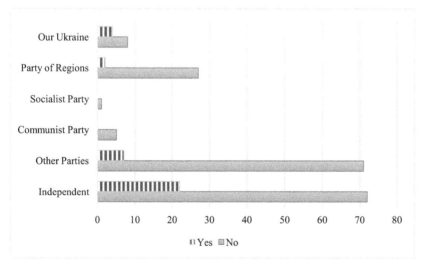

Figure 4.1. Ukraine's 2002 district deputies by 2002 party membership and placement on the 2006 party list of Our Ukraine

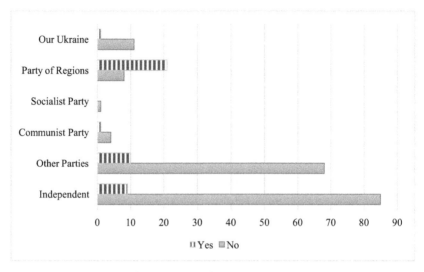

Figure 4.2. Ukraine's 2002 district deputies by 2002 party membership and placement on the 2006 party list of the Party of Regions

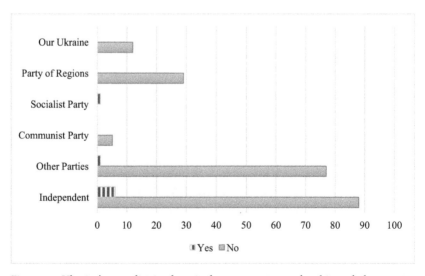

Figure 4.3. Ukraine's 2002 district deputies by 2002 party membership and placement on the 2006 party list of the Socialist Party

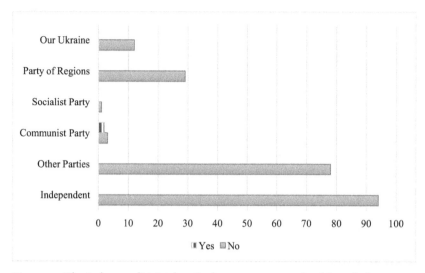

Figure 4.4. Ukraine's 2002 district deputies by 2002 party membership and placement on the 2006 party list of the Communist Party

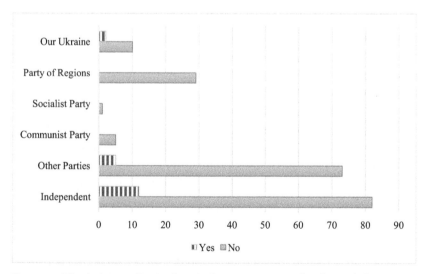

Figure 4.5. Ukraine's 2002 district deputies by 2002 party membership and placement on the 2006 party list of the Tymoshenko Bloc

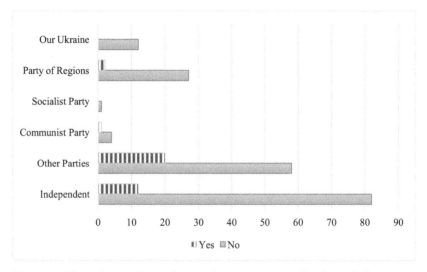

Figure 4.6. Ukraine's 2002 district deputies by 2002 party membership and placement on the 2006 party list of the Lytvyn Bloc

the Socialist Party renominated its own. Figure 4.3 also confirms the Socialist Party's willingness to support deputies who had competed as independents in 2002 and even a member of another party. Moving to Our Ukraine and the Party of Regions (figures 4.1 and 4.2), the new emphasis on party membership shows that Our Ukraine's renomination rate was actually lower for 2002 party members (33 percent) than it was for those who simply had been nominated by the party in 2002 (45 percent). In fact, district deputies without party affiliations in 2002 outnumbered any other group on Our Ukraine's 2006 list, holding 22 of the 35 spots allocated to 2002 district deputies. As expected, the Party of Regions demonstrates a high rate of renomination of district deputies who were party members in 2002. The rate of 72 percent is substantially higher than its renomination rate of 39 percent for deputies who had been nominated by the party in 2002 (see chapter 2). The only party to exceed the level of reinvestment in party members by the Party of Regions is the Socialist Party, with a renomination rate of 100 percent. However, since the Socialist Party elected just one party member as a district deputy in 2002, the only other option was 0 percent. A better point of comparison may therefore be the Communist Party. For this party, five party members were elected as district deputies in 2002, but only two, or 40 percent, were nominated by the party in 2006. Our Ukraine, meanwhile, elected 12 party members as district deputies in 2002, but only 33 percent of those individuals made Our Ukraine's 2006 list. Overall, then, the data suggest that leaders of the Party of Regions privileged 2002 party membership in its 2006 list construction to a greater extent than Our Ukraine or the Communist Party.

Figures 4.5 and 4.6 also support the contention that the Tymoshenko Bloc and Lytvyn's People's Bloc had emerged as alternatives that could draw district deputies, even party members, away from Our Ukraine and the Party of Regions, respectively. The 2006 list of the Tymoshenko Bloc included two individuals who were members of Our Ukraine in 2002 alongside 12 independents, plus five deputies who were members of other parties in 2002 (figure 4.5). Likewise, the 2006 list of the Lytvyn Bloc included two individuals who were members of the Party of Regions in 2002 alongside 12 independents, one Communist Party member, and 21 deputies who were members of other parties in 2002. Finally, it is worth noting that no Our Ukraine party members from 2002 landed on the 2006 list of the Lytvyn Bloc, and no Party of Regions members from 2002 became candidates on the 2006 list of the Tymoshenko Bloc.

List Construction and Ukraine's 2006 Legislative Election

Ukraine's Orange Revolution not only prevented the outgoing president's handpicked successor, Viktor Yanukovych, from taking office; it also meant that control over the executive branch switched hands between the decision to change the electoral system and the elections in which the new system was first used. This change recalibrated electoral politics in ways that likely influenced the electoral tactics of the blocs and parties competing in 2006. Specifically, one could expect the victory of Our Ukraine's presidential candidate, Viktor Yushchenko, and the organization's new pro-presidential status to have worked in its favor as Our Ukraine prepared for the 2006 elections. To the extent that formerly independent district deputies and deputies affiliated with small parties uncertain of their electoral fortunes under the new PR rules were looking to change parties, Our Ukraine should have been an attractive option. In contrast, although the Party of Regions existed as an organization independent of its presidential candidate,[3] the defeat of Yanukovych meant that it was relegated to the political opposition.[4] Since the Party of Regions no longer had ties to the national executive or played a role in distributing appointments within it, one could expect the party's ability to co-opt previously unaffiliated legislators to be lower than that of Our Ukraine.

Although events during and following the Orange Revolution give cause to question the position of the Party of Regions leading into the 2006 elections, these developments did not necessarily guarantee Our Ukraine a monopoly on incumbent deputies seeking spots on a party list during the first PR-only contests. For one thing, the compromise to re-run the second round of the 2004 presidential election granted Ukraine's parliament, the Verkhovna Rada, the power to nominate and dismiss the prime minister and most deputy ministers. This reallocation of power raised the stakes of the 2006 elections. Accordingly, parties across the spectrum in Ukraine may have been more motivated to pursue nomination strategies that would strengthen their organizations and enhance their electoral prospects.

Other factors that likely undermined Our Ukraine's ability to capitalize on the new PR-only rules include shortcomings within the coalition that came to power after the Orange Revolution. For example, Kuzio (2006) submits that President Yushchenko failed to use the powers at his disposal to press charges against senior members of the Kuchma regime, leaving members of the Party of Regions in a position to regroup. Yushchenko also failed to push through a radical government program during his first year in office. As a result, the legislative contingent of Our Ukraine had no signature policy achievement to highlight. Finally, the removal of the Tymoshenko government in September 2005, just seven months before the elections, and a January 2006 gas deal with Russia stoked existing divisions in the Orange coalition (Kuzio 2006). As a result, political observers, politicians, and voters had plenty of reasons to expect the first PR-only elections in Ukraine to be fiercely contested.

To shed light on the politics of list construction during Ukraine's first closed-list PR elections, the multivariate analyses begin with logistic regression models of placement anywhere on the 2006 lists of Our Ukraine and the Party of Regions before moving on to the analyses of list rank. The logistic regression analyses include five dichotomous variables drawn from the exploratory analyses presented earlier in this chapter and in chapter 2. If Our Ukraine and the Party of Regions pursued strategies that reinvested in deputies who had committed to them prior to the electoral system change, then deputies whom they nominated (as For a United Ukraine in the case of the latter) or those who were party members in 2002 should have had better list prospects in 2006 than other deputies, all else being equal.

The first two variables in each equation compare the likelihood of a deputy nominated by another party landing on the list in question relative to a deputy whom that party or coalition nominated in 2002. For example, since both parties' 2006 lists include deputies nominated by the other in 2002, the logistic regression analyses capture this by including a dummy variable for a 2002 nomination by their rival. In addition, the models include dichotomous variables where a one indicates that a deputy was nominated by another party or was self-nominated (for district deputies) in 2002 (Other Nomination 2002)—that is, not by For a United Ukraine or by Our Ukraine. Given the models' construction, significance for any of the nomination variables indicates that the specific 2002 nomination (e.g., For a United Ukraine or another party in the first equation) influenced a deputy's chances of landing on the list under investigation. To the extent that Our Ukraine (or the Party of Regions) privileged deputies who committed to it by accepting its nomination in 2002, the dummy variables included in the equation should be negatively correlated with placement. The next three variables in each equation pursue the same logic but replace the nominating party with the deputies' party memberships. In addition, a dichotomous variable is used to indicate those deputies who were independents. For this variable, those deputies without a party membership at the time of the 2002 elections receive a score of one (and zero otherwise).[5]

In addition to the 2002 nominations and party memberships, the logistic regression models include a number of controls. First, as in chapter 3, the equations include a dichotomous variable where a one indicates male as well as the deputies' age (calculated by subtracting the deputy's birth year from 2006). Another characteristic that may correlate with list placement is legislative experience. I employ one dichotomous variable where a one identifies deputies who were incumbents prior to the 2002 elections (zero otherwise) and another to distinguish deputies who held leadership positions in the Rada from those who did not. For this variable, a value of one indicates that a deputy held a position of chair or vice chair of a Rada committee, or higher (such as Rada speaker), between 2002 and 2006.[6]

The willingness of deputies to move among parliamentary factions during a legislative session represents one critical factor that undermined party development in Ukraine. Several postcommunist states have experienced high levels of electoral volatility, largely as an artifact of elite behavior (Tavits 2005; 2008; Zielinski et al. 2005, 365). Ukrainian politics has been no exception (Thames 2007a; 2007b; Whitmore 2004). The analysis, therefore, includes the number of factions to which each deputy belonged prior to the beginning of the 2006 campaign season.[7] The more faction memberships a deputy possessed, the less that deputy appears committed to any one party and the less attractive that deputy should be as a candidate to party leaders constructing lists with concerns about future party discipline in mind. In addition, since several deputies lacked any affiliation with a faction at the start of the election campaign, which might be interpreted as a signal of their availability (or "free agency"), I include a dichotomous variable where such deputies receive a score of one and others who are members of a faction at the start of the election campaign receive a score of zero.

Finally, the analyses consider whether Our Ukraine and the Party of Regions treated district deputies differently as compared to list deputies.[8] While district deputies are the ones whose legislative mandates disappeared with the elimination of the single-member-district (SMD) contests, parties could have decided that district deputies were more attractive candidates than those deputies who had been elected previously via the party list. In fact, a widely cited advantage of SMD electoral systems is their ability to bind the electoral prospects of politicians to the preferences of a specific geographic constituency. To win such elections, politicians are expected to be more attuned to local needs and interests, and they are more likely to respond to local demands while in office. As a result, parties interested in preserving some degree of local influence despite the move to a closed-list PR system may see district deputies as attractive candidates.

To the extent that the Party of Regions was, in fact, a party of regional interests, it makes sense that it might be drawn to district deputies as candidates for its 2006 party list. However, since the party also likely privileged loyalty given the aftermath of the 2002 elections, and since district deputies are on the whole more likely to put local demands above those from the party leadership, it is possible that district deputies did not enjoy any particular advantage over their list counterparts. Similarly, while the decision to invest in local representation by placing district deputies on its 2006 party list would be indicative of Our Ukraine developing (or at least preserving) some degree of party organization, this outcome could be achieved by balancing the nomination of district and list candidates as opposed to privileging the former over the latter. To assess whether the deputies' mandates, elected via a single-member district or via a party list, influence the likelihood of the deputies landing spots on the 2006 party lists of Our Ukraine or the Party of Regions, the first equation in table 4.1 includes a dichotomous variable in which deputies formerly elected via single-member-district contests receive a score of one and party list deputies receive a score of zero.[9]

Table 4.1 presents two logistic regression equations: one for Our Ukraine (equation 1), and one for the Party of Regions (equation 2). Each model yields a statistically significant likelihood ratio χ^2. Equation 1 identifies seven factors that significantly influenced the odds of a deputy landing on Our Ukraine's 2006 list, if one uses significance at the .05 level for a two-tailed test as the cutoff.[10] When interpreting the odds ratios, remember that they range from zero to infinity, with values below one indicative of negative relationships and those above one capturing positive relationships. Dividing one by the odds ratio makes the negative relationships comparable to positive ones. Thus, the odds of a deputy nominated by Our Ukraine in 2002 securing a position on Our Ukraine's 2006 list (the default category for the nomination dummies) were 10 times those of a deputy nominated by For a United Ukraine ($1/.099 = 10.1$) and almost 17 times those of a deputy nominated by another party or self-nominated ($1/.059 = 16.9$). By contrast, independent deputies were more than eight times more likely to land on the party's list than Our Ukraine party members (again the default category, this time for the party membership variables), while members of parties other than Our Ukraine or the Party of Regions were more than four times more likely to land on Our Ukraine's list than deputies who were Our Ukraine members in 2002. These results suggest that Our Ukraine

TABLE 4.1. The effect of mandates and other correlates on the 2006 party lists of Our Ukraine and the Party of Regions

	Our Ukraine			Party of Regions		
	Equation 1			Equation 2		
	Odds ratio (p value)	95% Confidence interval		Odds ratio (p value)	95% Confidence interval	
For a United Ukraine nomination, 2002	**0.099 (.000)**	0.030	0.330	—		
Our Ukraine nomination, 2002	—			**0.171 (.002)**	0.055	0.534
Other nomination, 2002	**0.059 (.000)**	0.027	0.129	**0.284 (.004)**	0.122	0.662
Party of Regions member, 2002	1.575 (.633)	01.245	10.142	—		
Our Ukraine member, 2002	—			0.315 (.314)	0.033	2.994
Independent, 2002	**8.117 (.000)**	2.834	23.243	**0.312 (.007)**	0.133	0.730
Other party member, 2002	**4.705 (.019)**	1.286	17.222	**0.081 (.001)**	0.020	0.337
Male	0.496 (.319)	0.125	1.969	0.973 (.969)	0.243	3.894
Age	1.014 (.378)	0.983	1.045	0.994 (.747)	0.961	1.029
Incumbent, 2002	**0.495 (.041)**	0.252	0.973	0.795 (.550)	0.379	1.686
Rada or committee leader, 2002–2006	1.386 (.358)	0.692	2.776	1.048 (.905)	0.486	2.260
Number of factions prior to July 7, 2005	**0.772 (.032)**	0.610	0.976	**0.729 (.011)**	0.572	0.930
No faction memberships on July 7, 2005	0.151 (.099)	0.016	1.431	—		
SMD deputy	**3.085 (.020)**	1.173	8.118	1.038 (.943)	0.368	2.930
Constant	0.278 (.243)	0.032	2.386	3.233 (.354)	0.270	38.727
Pseudo R^2	0.27			0.22		
Likelihood ratio χ^2 (significance)	109.66 (.000)			72.90 (.000)		
Number of cases	444			431		

Note: Numbers in bold indicate significance at the .05 level for a two-tailed test.

systematically renominated incumbents whom it had nominated for office in 2002 at a higher rate than incumbents from other parties. While this is not surprising given Our Ukraine's status as an electoral bloc, Our Ukraine also appears to have nominated independents and members of other parties at a significantly higher rate than deputies who had been Our Ukraine party members in 2002. While initially surprising, this result likely reflects the relative scarcity of Our Ukraine members (12) elected as part of its legislative delegation in 2002, which also indicates the degree to which it was undeveloped as an organization at the time.

These results contrast significantly from those reported in chapter 3 for United Russia. In Russia, deputies nominated by the ruling party in 2003 were no more likely to land on that party's 2007 list than deputies nominated by other parties. However, any cross-party comparisons should proceed with caution, since the construction of the models differ, at least in part due to the kinds of data available.[11] In chapter 5, I tackle the challenge of comparison directly by constructing independent variables and models that better facilitate direct cross-national assessments.

Table 4.1 also reveals that the odds of deputies making Our Ukraine's 2006 list significantly decreased as the number of factions they belonged to in the Rada prior to the start of the campaign for the 2006 elections increased. This outcome suggests that, even though the move to PR-only rules was partially intended to overcome party-switching by elected politicians, Our Ukraine was still concerned about the issue when selecting among incumbent deputies. If one relaxes the level of significance to .10 for a two-tailed test, then deputies who were not affiliated with a faction at the start of the election campaign were also less likely to be nominated by Our Ukraine in 2006. Our Ukraine also appears less likely to nominate legislative holdovers, as deputies who were incumbents in the Rada prior to the 2002 elections were less likely to land on Our Ukraine's 2006 list.

One particularly important result is the significance for a mandate effect: district deputies were significantly more likely than party list deputies to make Our Ukraine's 2006 list. It is notable that this effect emerges even while controlling for independent deputies. However, while independents were more likely to be district deputies, this relationship was not universal. Independents could be nominated on party lists as well as by parties in district contests in 2002. In fact, the data reveal that 41 of the 225 list deputies elected in 2002 were independents, compared to 94 of the 219 district deputies under investigation.[12] The results therefore suggest that Our Ukraine's 2006 list did, in fact, privilege district deputies over list deputies when constructing its 2006 list.

Equation 2 in table 4.1, which presents the results for the Party of Regions, tells a different story. First, much like Our Ukraine, the Party of Regions was significantly more likely to renominate deputies nominated by For a United Ukraine in 2002 relative to those previously nominated by Our Ukraine or those who were self-nominated or nominated by another party. However, unlike Our Ukraine, independents and deputies who were not members of the Party of Regions were significantly less likely to receive, or perhaps pursue, a Party of Regions nomination in 2006. Surprisingly, the exception to this pattern is if a deputy was an Our Ukraine party member in 2002. Taken together with the results from equation 1, these findings round out the parallel dynamics of the two parties' list construction: With Our Ukraine more likely to nominate individuals who were not party members in 2002 relative to existing Our Ukraine party members in 2002, the Party of Regions likely struggled to attract non–party members.

Several additional results are worth discussing. First, the dichotomous variable for no faction membership at the start of the 2006 election campaign predicts failure perfectly for 13 observations in equation 2. As a result, these observations are dropped from the analysis, which in turn reduces the number of observations to 431. Despite this change, the Party of Regions, like Our Ukraine, stayed away from deputies with a history of changing factions, as deputies who belonged to more factions were significantly less likely to receive a spot on the 2006 list of the Party of Regions. However, deputy mandate does not have a significant effect for the Party of Regions like it does for Our Ukraine. District deputies were no more likely to land on its 2006 list than list deputies. For neither party does age appear to have a significant effect on the likelihood of a deputy making a list. This outcome across both equations differs from the finding for United Russia, where the party appears to have used the new PR-only rules to favor younger deputies.

While table 4.1 yields interesting findings, one missing consideration is the degree to which party list construction in Ukraine's 2006 elections reflected the deputies' electoral performances in 2002. For a study limited to only district deputies, comparing electoral performance across the potential candidates is straightforward. Each district deputy's electoral potential can be measured using vote percentage. In SMD-plurality elections with multiple candidates, deputies who win with higher vote shares should be more attractive compared to those with lower vote shares but the same margin of victory.[13] As chapter 3 notes, especially high values do not necessarily signal only a candidate's popularity with voters; they may also capture electoral malfeasance and the administrative resources at a prospective deputy's disposal. To the extent that political parties value election outcomes more than the means by which they are achieved, deputies winning under such conditions should remain attractive candidates. Adding list deputies to the analysis complicates matters, however.

One option for assessing the impact of the 2002 electoral outcomes on 2006 list construction would be to repeat the analysis in table 4.1 with a measure like the one I use for Russian deputies in chapter 3. In that chapter, I measure the deputies' electoral records by using the ruling party's PR vote share as the baseline and by assuming that all list deputies contributed to this total. All list deputies receive scores of zero (which places them at the baseline), and district deputies' vote shares are used to indicate whether they overperformed or underperformed relative to the party's national total. To the extent that the goal is to measure regionally concentrated levels of support, this measure is reasonable. A problem with this approach, however, is that all PR deputies are treated equally. While no clear alternative exists to produce some degree of uniformity across the regional sub-lists in the Russian case, a reliance on a single national list by parties in Ukraine permits an opportunity to rank the deputies according to their relative electability in the 2002 elections. I pursue this option. In closed-list PR systems, the electability of list candidates depends on their list rank. Since parties performed differently in the PR portion of Ukraine's 2002 elections, the relative value of rank on a party list for a specific deputy also varies by party. While all candidates ranked first on a party list passing the legal threshold were elected with certainty, those at lower ranks did not enjoy the same likelihood of election. For example, the 27th candidate on Our Ukraine's list was located solidly in the upper half of the 99 candidates elected from its list, but the candidate ranked 27th on the Socialist Party's 2002 list was the lowest-ranked candidate to win election.[14] With this variation in mind, I standardized the list ranks across the different parties as a way to create a common measure of the list deputies' electability. The first step in the process rescaled the ranks so that higher ranks corresponded to better electoral prospects. To do this, I added one to the maximum value of list rank for each party (e.g., 27+1 for the Socialist Party) and then subtracted each deputy's rank from this number. Adding one to the maximum before subtracting the list rank ensures that deputies at the top of each list receive the highest standardized score and avoids using zeros for those at the low end. To standardize the rescaled ranks, I then divided each deputy's rescaled rank by the difference between the maximum rescaled value and the minimum rescaled value.[15]

While standardizing the list ranks of the different deputies across different parties yields a measure of list deputies' electability, the measure is not comparable to the district deputies' vote share. At the same time, although including both measures alongside one another in the analysis would allow one to assess whether the electability of the different deputies influenced their list prospects, this approach does not permit the opportunity to explicitly test for a mandate effect. The preferred option would be to include a single electability measure across all deputies and the dichotomous variable differentiating district deputies from list deputies. To accomplish this, I use the district deputies' vote shares and standardize them in a manner similar to the standardization of list rank: each deputy's vote share was divided by the difference between the maximum and minimum vote shares of elected district deputies.

Table 4.2 presents the results of the logit analysis that includes the standardized electability measure alongside the dichotomous variable where a one indicates that the deputy in question is a district deputy. The results for the first equation in this table resemble the results in the first equation of table 4.1. Once again, the chances of a deputy landing on the 2006 list of Our Ukraine appears significantly higher for independents and deputies who were members of parties other than Our Ukraine or the Party of Regions in 2002. The odds were also significantly lower if a deputy had previously been nominated by For a United Ukraine or a party other than Our Ukraine or For a United Ukraine, as well as for deputies who held more faction memberships. Two notable changes include the increased significance for deputies who did not belong to a faction at the start of the 2006 election campaign. The negative effect is now significant at the .05 level for a two-tailed test. In contrast, the effect for incumbency prior to 2002 is not significant using this model specification. While the standardized electability score has a negative impact on the odds of a deputy receiving an Our Ukraine nomination in 2006, the effect is significant at only .10 level for a two-tailed test. The mandate effect, meanwhile, remains significant at the .05 level with the odds of a district deputy making Our Ukraine's 2006 list three times higher than the odds of list deputies.

Turning to the Party of Regions, the second equation in table 4.2 also largely duplicates the results in table 4.1. All variables differentiating membership of a party other than the Party of Regions yield significantly negative effects, with the exception of Our Ukraine party members. Likewise, deputies with sources of nomination besides For a United Ukraine in 2002 were also less likely to make the list of the Party of Regions in 2006. In addition, the likelihood of landing on the 2006 list of the Party of Regions decreased as the number of factions that a deputy belonged to prior to the start of the 2006 campaign season increased. As before, no mandate effect emerges: district deputies do not appear any more likely to have been nominated by the Party of Regions in 2006 when compared to list deputies. At the same time, the variable for electability fails to significantly affect the likelihood of placement on the 2006 list of the Party of Regions.

One shortcoming of the logistic regression models is that they cannot determine whether the observed effects in a party's list construction result from pull or push—that is, whether deputies are drawn to specific parties or repelled by them. However, examining the parties side by side does provide an opportunity to consider the parties' priorities and abilities. As the analyses suggest, the party membership variables appear to have consistently influenced the list construction of Our Ukraine and the Party of Regions, operating in different directions: Independents and other party members were not only more likely to be nominated by Our Ukraine in 2006; such deputies were also less likely to be nominated by the Party of Regions. This outcome supports the expectation that the party's status as the president's party likely helped it co-opt previously unaffiliated, but electorally proven, candidates. The finding implies that independents and other party members saw Our Ukraine

TABLE 4.2. The effect of deputy electability, mandate, and other correlates on the 2006 party lists of Our Ukraine and the Party of Regions

	Our Ukraine		Party of Regions	
	Equation 1		Equation 2	
	Odds ratio (p value)	95% Confidence interval	Odds ratio (p value)	95% Confidence interval
For a United Ukraine nomination, 2002	**0.096 (.000)**	0.029 0.322	—	
Our Ukraine nomination, 2002	—		**0.174 (.003)**	0.056 0.541
Other nomination, 2002	**0.053 (.000)**	0.023 0.119	**0.307 (.007)**	0.130 0.722
Party of Regions member, 2002	1.566 (.635)	0.246 9.967	—	
Our Ukraine member, 2002	—		0.297 (.292)	0.031 2.843
Independent, 2002	**8.047 (.000)**	2.818 22.975	**0.294 (.005)**	0.124 0.697
Other party member, 2002	**4.229 (.030)**	1.146 15.599	**0.078 (.000)**	0.019 0.325
Male	0.562 (.430)	0.134 2.354	0.925 (.913)	0.229 3.734
Age	1.016 (.327)	0.985 1.048	0.994 (.714)	0.960 1.028
Incumbent, 2002	0.594 (.149)	0.293 1.204	0.729 (.426)	0.336 1.585
Rada or committee leader, 2002–06	1.442 (.307)	0.714 2.909	1.040 (.921)	0.480 2.251
Number of factions prior to July 7, 2005	**0.787 (.049)**	0.619 0.999	**0.736 (.013)**	0.578 0.937
No Faction Memberships on July 7, 2005	**0.096 (.047)**	0.009 0.969	—	
Standardized 2002 electability score	0.313 (.076)	0.087 1.129	1.962 (.374)	0.444 8.668
SMD deputy	**2.962 (.029)**	1.116 7.864	1.017 (.975)	0.360 2.871
Constant	0.406 (.426)	0.044 3.730	2.528 (.478)	0.195 32.707
Pseudo R^2	0.28		0.23	
Likelihood ratio χ^2 (significance)	112.92 (.000)		73.68 (.000)	
Number of cases	444		431	

Note: Numbers in bold indicate significance at the .05 level for a two-tailed test.

as an attractive option in 2006 and that Our Ukraine's leadership saw independents as attractive candidates. In contrast, independents, as well as those with other party memberships, were significantly less likely to secure a position anywhere on the 2006 list of the Party of Regions. While the results cannot speak definitively as to whether the relationships are an artifact of independents and members of other parties in

2002 eschewing the Party of Regions in favor of Our Ukraine, the evidence does fit this pattern. The results also reveal how the factors shaping the lists of Our Ukraine and the Party of Regions in 2006 were not simply mirror images. The nomination variables not only influenced list construction for the two parties; those effects worked in the same direction: self-nominated deputies and those previously nominated by parties other than Our Ukraine or For a United Ukraine were significantly less likely to receive an Our Ukraine or a Party of Regions nomination in 2006, all else being equal.

As in chapter 3, I examine how the factors shaping list rank differ from those influencing list placement (i.e., receiving a spot anywhere on a party list) using a Heckman selection model. The preceding logit analyses of list placement guide the construction of the model's first stage. Specifically, the first stage in the models for both Our Ukraine and the Party of Regions are the models used in table 4.2—that is, those with measures that capture both the deputies' mandates and relative electability. Once again, a key difference between the two stages is the reduction in the number of cases under investigation, as the second stage excludes deputies who are censored out in the first stage. Also as in chapter 3, the independent variables for nominating party and party membership are simplified in the second stage relative to the first. As in the preceding logit analyses, the first stage compares the list prospects for deputies with various party (or nonparty) nominations and party memberships to default categories that capture the nomination by and membership in the party under investigation (i.e., either Our Ukraine or the Party of Regions). In the second stage of the Heckman selection model, I use dichotomous variables to explicitly capture the previously omitted category. For example, in the first equation in table 4.3, the second stage of the model uses a dummy variable for a 2002 Our Ukraine nomination to identify whether deputies previously nominated by Our Ukraine were ranked higher on that party's 2006 list than deputies not nominated by Our Ukraine in 2002. Similarly, the second stage of that model employs a dichotomous variable indicating members of Our Ukraine in 2002 to determine whether such deputies were rewarded, relative to other deputies who were not members in 2002, when it came to their placements on Our Ukraine's 2006 list. The process is repeated for the Party of Regions in table 4.3's second equation. Table 4.3 therefore reports two sets

TABLE 4.3. Heckman selection models for Our Ukraine and the Party of Regions

Variables	Stage One OU list placement	Stage One PoR list placement
For a United Ukraine nomination, 2002	−1.271*	—
	(.316)	
Our Ukraine nomination, 2002	—	−0.812*
		(0.294)
Other nomination, 2002	−1.673*	−0.618*
	(.221)	(.235)
Party of Regions member, 2002	0.168	—
	(.458)	
Our Ukraine member, 2002	—	−0.736
		(0.568)
Independent, 2002	1.105*	−0.679*
	(.282)	(.238)
Other Party member, 2002	0.806*	−1.291*
	(.365)	(.351)
Male	−0.381	0.023
	(.385)	(.389)
Age	0.009	−0.006
	(.009)	(.009)
Rada or committee leader, 2002–6	0.249	0.034
	(.193)	(.209)
Incumbent, 2002	−0.324	−0.191
	(.198)	(.210)
Number of factions prior to July 7, 2005	−0.107+	−0.131*
	(.063)	(.062)
No faction memberships on July 7, 2005	−1.082+	—
	(.579)	
SMD deputy	0.602*	0.032
	(.272)	(.275)
Standardized electability, 2002	−0.674+	0.529
	(.367)	(.391)
Constant	−0.487	0.278
	(.622)	(.698)
N=444		

Table 4.3. (cont.)

Variables	Stage Two OU list rank	Stage Two PoR list rank
Our Ukraine nomination, 2002	33.367	—
	(24.077)	
Our Ukraine member, 2002	1.568	—
	(20.565)	
For a United Ukraine nomination, 2002	—	0.494
		(19.420)
Party of Regions member, 2002	—	−50.719*
		(14.726)
Male	−5.481	8.838
	(19.398)	(21.916)
Age	0.750+	0.783
	(0.443)	(.535)
Rada or committee leader, 2002–2006	−27.539*	−11.609
	(9.947)	(11.669)
Incumbent, 2002	−21.749+	−7.773
	(11.693)	(13.594)
Number of factions prior to July 7, 2005	0.004	11.198*
	(3.811)	(4.613)
No faction memberships on July 7, 2005	−17.389	—
	(45.479)	
SMD deputy	6.961	−25.030+
	(11.095)	(13.874)
Standardized electability, 2002	−77.536*	−81.731*
	(20.279)	(25.856)
Constant	45.120	121.040*
	(43.058)	(53.580)
N	74	54
Mills Lambda	17.169	−27.108
	(19.625)	(20.609)
Heckman Model Chi-Square	50.97	43.24
Chi-Square Probability	0.000	0.000

Note: Numbers in parentheses are standard errors. + indicates significance at the .10 level for a two-tailed test. * indicates significance at the .05 level or better for a two-tailed test.

of results. As a reminder, while positive correlations in the first stage indicate a better chance of receiving a spot on a particular party's list,[16] negative correlations in the second stage are associated with better list positions, since higher ranks are captured by lower values.

As table 4.3 illustrates, both Heckman models yield statistically significant chi-square values. Looking at the equation for Our Ukraine, the first stage results confirm that the chances of a deputy landing on the 2006 list of Our Ukraine appears significantly higher for independents and deputies who were members of parties other than Our Ukraine or the Party of Regions in 2002 as well as district deputies. Meanwhile, the likelihood of an Our Ukraine nomination was significantly lower if a deputy had been nominated previously by For a United Ukraine or a party other than Our Ukraine or For a United Ukraine. Of the remaining variables, the model suggests that Our Ukraine was also less likely to nominate deputies who held more faction memberships during the previous Rada session, were not affiliated with a faction at the start of the election campaign, or demonstrated higher standardized electability scores, although these effects are significant only at the .10 level for two-tailed tests.

While electability in the 2002 elections had, if anything, a negative effect on Our Ukraine list placement according to the first stage of the model, the second stage reveals that higher standardized electability significantly improved a selected candidate's rank on Our Ukraine's 2006 list. The only other variable to have an impact at the .05 level (for a two-tailed test) is whether a chosen candidate held a leadership position within the outgoing Rada. Deputies who were incumbents going into 2002 also received better placements on Our Ukraine's 2006 list, but this effect is significant at only the .10 level. These findings suggest that Our Ukraine used better placements on its 2006 party list to attract more experienced legislators. However, one should not equate experience with age, since older deputies, all else being equal, tended to be ranked lower on Our Ukraine's 2006 list, but again the effect attains significance at only the .10 level.[17]

Turning to the Heckman selection model for the Party of Regions, the first stage again reveals that the Party of Regions, in contrast to Our Ukraine, was significantly less likely to nominate deputies who were independents or members of a party other than the Party of Regions or Our Ukraine in 2002. Similarly, in 2006, the Party of Regions was less likely to nominate deputies who had not been nominated by For a United Ukraine in 2002. Meanwhile, as the number of factions that deputies belonged to prior to the start of the 2006 campaign season increased, the likelihood of landing on the 2006 list of the Party of Regions decreased. As before, no other variables prove significant. For example, there is no mandate effect, and electability fails to matter.

In contrast, the story is different when it comes to list rank. First, prior membership in the Party of Regions continues to be highly valued, as party members enjoyed significantly better ranks than other deputies, all else being equal. This apparent emphasis on loyalty and its effect on list rank for the Party of Regions is echoed in the result for the effect of the number of factions that deputies joined in the outgoing Rada: of the deputies who were nominated by the Party of Regions in 2006, those who changed factions more often received significantly worse ranks.

Aside from these results, the second stage of the model for the Party of Regions suggests that the party, much like Our Ukraine, gave better ranks in 2006 to deputies with higher standardized electability scores in 2002. In other words, district deputies who won election with higher vote shares and list deputies who were ranked higher in the previous elections received better list placements in 2006 regardless of the party, whether Our Ukraine or the Party of Regions. In addition, the second stage of the second equation in table 4.3 reveals that the Party of Regions tended to favor district deputies, all else being equal, with these candidates also receiving better positions on its 2006 list. While this mandate effect may be limited since it is significant at only the .10 level, a similar mandate effect does not emerge in the analysis of list rank for Our Ukraine. Instead, for that party, the mandate effect comes in the selection stage: district deputies have a higher likelihood of being nominated by Our Ukraine than their list counterparts.[18]

Conclusion

This chapter uses party nominations in Ukraine's first PR-only elections to investigate how different parties balance the challenges of winning elections, improving party organization, and preserving party discipline under new electoral rules. Specifically, the analyses explore the issues that Our Ukraine and the Party of Regions likely took into consideration when determining the degree and nature of legislative continuity that emerged during Ukraine's transition to a closed-list PR system. Since political parties play decisive roles in determining which legislators are most likely to stay in office, the chapter focuses on that process in order to highlight the complexities that accompany electoral system change. These complexities matter because they can undermine the ability of electoral system changes to solve the perceived pathologies in legislative politics—from seemingly unaccountable representatives to weak party discipline—that scholars and other political observers identify.

In contrast to the initial comparison of the renomination rates of district deputies by the parties presented in chapter 2 and the first part of this chapter, the systematic multivariate analyses of list placement find support for the expectation that Ukraine's pro-presidential party, Our Ukraine, was better positioned than the Party of Regions to co-opt previously independent deputies. In addition, by casting a wider net, the multivariate analyses reveal that, while Our Ukraine was more likely to nominate district deputies than list deputies, the Party of Regions did not systematically discriminate between mandates when nominating incumbent legislators. Nevertheless, there is some evidence that the Party of Regions may have rewarded district deputies with better list ranks, something that Our Ukraine did not do. These findings lend support to the expectation that parties may use the move to PR rules to develop greater party organization by relying on incumbent deputies less beholden to other parties as well as with existing ties to specific geographically defined constituencies, even if the mechanism—candidate selection or candidate ranking—varies by organization.

In addition, while electoral system scholars may expect closed-list PR rules to facilitate party discipline among elected legislators by granting party leaders control over the deputies' electoral prospects, the analyses reveal that both Ukrainian parties—despite different levels of co-optation—proceeded with an eye toward party unity following the elections. Both Our Ukraine and the Party of Regions practiced caution when nominating incumbent legislators and were more likely to nominate deputies who had changed legislative factions less frequently in the preceding Rada. To the extent that both parties pursued this practice, the results highlight a level of risk aversion among parties competing in weakly institutionalized party systems that may be expected to advance the cause of party discipline once the newly elected legislators take office. It is particularly notable that deputies who changed factions more frequently in the previous Rada also received less electable list placements on the 2006 list of the Party of Regions. While this outcome may reflect Viktor Yanukovych's expressed desire to build a "strong party" rather than rely on a "weak bloc" (see chapter 2), the discovery that a similar relationship does not emerge for Our Ukraine makes the question of party discipline in Our Ukraine following the 2006 elections a topic of special interest, one that I return to in chapter 7.

As noted, differences in the kinds of data available for candidates in Russian and Ukrainian legislative elections limit the ability to make direct comparisons between the nomination decisions by United Russia, which were examined in chapter 3, and those made by Our Ukraine and the Party of Regions, which were the subject of this chapter. While some speculation is possible given the country- and party-specific findings thus far uncovered, I instead pursue a more direct comparison of the parties' behavior using the analyses from this chapter and chapter 3 as a guide. Chapter 5 presents those results.

5

Cohesion and Co-optation in Russia and Ukraine

In chapters 3 and 4, I analyze party nominations in the first solely pro-portional representation (PR) elections in Russia and Ukraine while limiting comparisons across the two countries in an effort to focus on explanations that more closely conform to the specific developments in each case. Yet, as chapter 1 emphasizes, an overarching goal of this work is to use the insights drawn from Russia and Ukraine to develop an understanding of how political parties across regime types inter-act with incumbent deputies while navigating major electoral system changes. Chapter 2 takes an initial step in this direction: it conducts a cross-national comparison of the rates by which parties nominate district deputies following the adoption of PR-only electoral systems. Since the actions of one party, including a pro-presidential party, can influence and be influenced by those of other parties, the analysis in chapter 2 casts a wider net than those in chapters 3 and 4. It examines the nomination strategies of multiple parties within Russia and Ukraine to determine whether they differ from one another in terms of their levels of co-optation and cohesion. Thus, while chapters 3 and 4 look more carefully at the individual characteristics of incumbent legisla-tors as prospective candidates for the ruling party in Russia and two major parties in Ukraine, chapter 2 includes more parties but limits the individual characteristics under consideration to prior party affiliations while focusing exclusively on district deputies (i.e., those deputies who technically lost their legislative mandates). Chapter 2's analysis reveals that two quite different parties—Russia's ruling party, United Russia, and Ukraine's Socialist Party—nominated district deputies in a man-ner indicative of balancing co-optation and cohesion, though on vastly different scales. In addition, I note that one might reasonably expect any but perhaps the most ideological of parties to nominate politicians who were already affiliated with the party as well as other politicians who could add value to the party, either in terms of electoral impact or legislative experience. If the desire to balance cohesion and co-optation spans parties, then differences in their observed levels may largely reflect differences in the opportunities and constraints that the parties face.

As chapter 2 notes, regime type emerges as one potential determinant of the opportunities and constraints that parties encounter when recruiting prospective legislative candidates. In regimes governed by competitive, multiparty elections, more parties are in a position to offer prospective candidates a route to legislative office and the possibility of shaping legislation. In regimes where elections are not competitive, few—perhaps only one party—can reasonably promise candidates a high probability of election and legislative influence. From this perspective, while all parties may wish to balance co-optation and cohesion when navigating major electoral system changes, one should expect ruling parties in authoritarian regimes (or authoritarian regimes in the making) to execute this approach more successfully than ruling parties in more competitive, if not fully democratic, regimes.

Another potentially influential factor shaping a party's opportunities and constraints when adapting to electoral system change is its level of organization and institutionalization. While chapter 2 highlights the low level of party institutionalization in Russia and Ukraine throughout the 1990s and early 2000s, one critical difference between the two countries' party systems prior to the implementation of closed-list PR rules was United Russia's ability to win a majority of legislative seats in the preceding elections. In fact, United Russia's 2003 performance was an unprecedented victory in post-Soviet Russian politics, one that would prove even more decisive after dozens of deputies, who had not competed under United Russia's banner during the 2003 elections, joined its faction at the start of the legislative session. In Ukraine, however, the main pro-presidential party during the mixed-member elections preceding the move to closed-list PR was, in fact, an electoral alliance. For a United Ukraine was primarily assembled to defend the Kuchma regime (Diuk and Gongadze 2002, 162; Wilson 2002, 92). Thus, to the extent that For a United Ukraine resembled a Russian pro-presidential party, it resembled Unity in 1999, not United Russia in 2003. As I discuss in chapter 2, after Russia's 1999 Duma elections, United Russia resulted from a postelection merger between Unity and its main rival, Fatherland–All Russia. In the years that followed, United Russia proved to be a driving force in the Duma

(Kunicova and Remington 2008; Reuter and Remington 2009) as well as a party that won the support of key regional actors (Reuter 2010; 2017). It also touted 1.66 million members leading into Russia's first closed-list PR elections (Sakwa 2011, 23). For a United Ukraine, by contrast, disintegrated into seven factions three months after the 2002 elections (Kuzio 2003, 31), with the Party of Regions and Lytvyn's People's Bloc emerging as separate successor organizations during the 2006 elections.

While, hypothetically, the Orange Revolution that accompanied the second round of Ukraine's 2004 presidential election may have created the opportunity for a new pro-presidential party in Ukraine to consolidate power, in practice the "Orange victors" also proved to be divided. The ruling alliance of Yushchenko's Our Ukraine, the Tymoshenko Bloc (of Yulia Tymoshenko), and the Socialist Party proved fragile, and the coalition collapsed within a year (D'Anieri 2007, 99). In 2006, Our Ukraine competed with its former partners for candidates and votes.

Combining these party-specific differences with differences in regime type provides ample reason to expect that United Russia would be in a better position to renominate its own deputies as well as to attract other, previously unaffiliated politicians than either Our Ukraine or the Party of Regions. Although the initial analysis presented at the end of chapter 2 supports this expectation, it does not examine the parties' interactions with deputies elected via party lists in the previous elections; neither does it investigate the range of deputy-specific characteristics that might systematically influence the nomination prospects of incumbent legislators. Yet, as chapters 3 and 4 illustrate, these characteristics can matter.

The goal of this chapter is to compare how a broader range of legislator characteristics influenced the likelihood of a United Russia nomination to their effects on a nomination with Our Ukraine or the Party of Regions. As a result, the structure of this chapter diverges from those of chapters 3 and 4. Although similar—but not identical—variables and explanatory models are used in those earlier chapters, the findings are presented as specific to the parties and deputies, while cross-country comparisons are limited. This chapter compares the phenomenon of list construction in the aftermath of electoral system changes across the two countries. It does so by pooling specific subsets of the deputies across the countries, by testing for country- and party-specific effects on the likelihood of list placement, and by discussing similarities and differences across the results to identify relationships that are common across, or specific to, the parties and countries.

By definition, the process of comparison requires some loss in specificity. While quantitative analysis, even within a single country at one moment in time, may be criticized for using thin measures to capture thick concepts, cross-national quantitative analyses push the envelope even further (Coppedge 1999). Such risks, however, are unavoidable if a scholar wishes to move beyond country- and time-specific narratives in an effort to tackle larger disciplinary questions in political science (Fleron 2016). The next section discusses the modifications to the data used in chapters 3 and 4 that enable the cross-national comparisons before presenting the analyses and summarizing the findings. Following this discussion, I turn to the question of list rank, contending that some cross-national comparison remains possible despite substantial differences in how party lists are constructed across the two countries. Specifically, I contend that context-specific models designed to identify observable patterns in list placement can also be used to assess the degree to which candidate selection across parties may reflect largely unobservable mechanisms such as bribery.

Cross-National and Cross-Party Comparisons

In chapters 3 and 4, I note that information for district candidates are reported differently across the two countries and that this difference might signal different practices that could also influence list placement. In Ukraine, the party affiliations and sources of nomination for district deputies were explicitly identified in 2002. The candidates' short biographies indicate whether candidates have a particular party affiliation or are nonpartisan; they also note whether candidates are nominated by a party or are self-nominated deputies. In turn, the analyses in chapter 4 examine the potentially differential effects of partisanship and the source of a candidate's nomination. However, in Russia's 2003 Duma elections, district candidates are identified by the Central Election Commission (CEC) as party-nominated or self-nominated. While some district deputies reported positions within a party in 2003, they did not explicitly report party memberships, regardless of whether they were party-nominated or self-nominated. For example, several incumbent deputies who held committee positions, such as chairs or vice chairs, within the previous Duma competed without identifying a party membership. The practice emerges for self-nominated candidates as well as those nominated by specific parties, including United Russia (Central Election Commission 2004, 274–75). From this perspective, categorizing Russia's district deputies as nonpartisan on the basis of what the deputies chose to report and not to report is riskier terrain than it is for list deputies where the practice of reporting one's party membership was common. As a result, the pooled analysis of Russian and Ukrainian district deputies operationalizes independence as self-nominated rather than as nonpartisan, since only the former information about candidates in district contests is available in both Russia and Ukraine, and since self-nominated deputies in Russia may not have been independent deputies from the perspective that they lacked party affiliation. Indeed, some self-nominated Russian legislators may have consciously sought to avoid any potentially detrimental baggage that would come from associating with a particular party during election campaigns only to affiliate with a party in the Duma by joining that party's legislative faction after the elections. Other politicians, meanwhile, formed their own party factions, essentially creating legislative organizations in the absence of corresponding electoral organizations.

With these cross-national differences in mind, any analysis of list construction that combines parties from Russia and Ukraine is limited by the data that are available for district deputies. So, while partisanship versus nonpartisanship receives particular attention in the chapter focusing only on Ukrainian parties, analyses that include Russian parties limits one to the data that are comparable—that is, the source of nominations (e.g., self-nominated or not). This adjustment in turn limits the conclusions that one can draw from a cross-national analysis of district deputies. However, it is noteworthy that the electoral system changes in Russia and Ukraine, from mixed-member systems to closed-list PR, as well as the data available, still permit an opportunity to assess the effects of partisanship relative to nonpartisanship on party list construction across the two countries: this opportunity comes from pooling all of the list deputies into a single analysis.

Like district deputies, list deputies in Ukraine are listed as party members or not party members, with the source of party nomination corresponding to the deputies' party lists. In Russia, the partisanship of list deputies is not as starkly presented as it is in Ukraine, but most Russian list candidates explicitly identified themselves as party members (e.g., "chlen LDPR") or as holding a position with a party, while others provided no particular party information.[1] By treating the latter politicians as nonpartisan, I can pool data on all list deputies across the two countries to investigate the impact of nonpartisanship on list placement for the three parties under investigation: United Russia from Russia, and Our Ukraine and the Party of Regions from Ukraine. As this discussion suggests, reasonable comparisons across the parties then require separate analyses for the list placement of district deputies and the list placement of list deputies.

To identify commonalities in list construction across the two countries during their first PR-only elections, I begin by pooling the list deputies from both countries together and include a dichotomous variable to differentiate list deputies from Ukraine (who score a one on this variable) and those from Russia (who score a zero). This variable allows one to determine whether the likelihood of Russian list deputies making United Russia's 2007 party list was higher (or lower) than the likelihood of Ukrainian list deputies making the 2006 lists of Our Ukraine or the Party of Regions.

Since Russian party list construction differed from Ukrainian list construction by utilizing regional sub-lists rather than a single national list, which in turn impedes the construction of a reasonably comparable dependent variable for list rank, I examine only the likelihood of securing a position on one of the parties' lists. The dependent variable is dichotomous, with a one indicating nomination by one of the parties under investigation—United Russia, Our Ukraine, or the Party of Regions—at the time of the first PR-only elections. In each set of analyses—that is, for list deputies and district deputies—list placement during the closed-list PR elections is identified using three different party-based combinations: (1) nomination via either United Russia's 2007 list or Our Ukraine's 2006 list; (2) nomination via either United Russia's 2007 list or the 2006 list of the Party of Regions; and (3) nomination via any of the three parties' lists. The explanatory variables used in the following logistic regression analyses depend on whether the deputies under investigation are Russian and Ukrainian list deputies or Russian and Ukrainian district deputies.

Besides testing for the country- and party-specific effects, the explanatory models for the list deputies examine whether the likelihood of list placement varies systematically on the basis of the deputies' prior source of nomination—specifically, whether the parties under investigation nominated the deputy in question during the previous elections. In other words, the model comparing list placement for United Russia and Our Ukraine during Russia's and Ukraine's first PR-only elections includes a dichotomous variable where deputies receive scores of one if they were nominated by United Russia in 2003 or Our Ukraine in 2002 (and zero otherwise). For the model comparing list placement for United Russia and the Party of Regions, the dichotomous variable provides a score of one for deputies nominated by United Russia in 2003 or For a United Ukraine in 2002. In the model that pools all of the parties together, deputies receive values of one for the corresponding dummy if they were nominated by any of the three in the elections governed by the mixed-member electoral system preceding the first closed-list PR contests.

Since data on party membership exist in Russia and Ukraine for list deputies, the models also include dichotomous membership variables that are constructed in a manner similar to the nomination variables, with a score of one indicating deputies who were members of the parties under investigation at the time of the elections that preceded the first PR-only elections (and zero otherwise). In addition, the models include the dummy variable "nonpartisan," for which a score of one indicates that the deputy in question was not a member of a party in the elections prior to the first closed-list PR ballot, while a zero indicates that the deputy was a member of a party. Including this variable alongside the variable that indicates membership in one of the parties under investigation in the model means that the default category for each model (i.e., zeros on both counts) captures deputies who were party members but not members of one of the parties under investigation. Thus, to the extent that either the party membership variable or the variable for nonpartisanship matters, the impact of the variable is relative to this default category.

As in previous chapters, the models include a series of control variables. These variables are gender (one for male and zero for female), age (higher values indicate older deputies), positions in the outgoing legislature (with deputies holding leadership positions in the legislature

TABLE 5.1.A Correlates influencing the likelihood of list deputies making the party lists of Our Ukraine and the Party of Regions in 2006 and United Russia in 2007

	Equation 1		
	Odds ratio (p value)	95% Confidence interval	
Nomination: UR or OU	**25.390 (.000)**	11.001	58.597
Nomination: UR or FUU	—		
Nomination: UR, OU, or FUU	—		
Membership: UR or OU	0.945 (.920)	0.318	2.815
Membership: UR or PoR	—		
Membership: UR, OU, or FUU	—		
Nonpartisan	1.126 (.779)	0.492	2.577
Male	0.446 (.071)	0.185	1.073
Age	0.990 (.486)	0.963	1.018
Legislative or committee Leader	**2.010 (.017)**	1.135	3.560
Incumbent	0.635 (.134)	0.350	1.150
Ukrainian	0.871 (.762)	0.357	2.125
Constant	**0.141 (.032)**	0.023	0.846
Pseudo R^2	0.316		
Likelihood ratio χ^2 (significance)	156.28 (.000)		
Number of cases	447		

Note: Numbers in bold indicate significance at the .05 level for a two-tailed test. UR = United Russia; OU = Our Ukraine; FUU = For a United Ukraine; PoR = Party of Russia.

as a whole or on legislative committees scoring values of one and zero otherwise), and prior incumbency (with deputies who were already incumbents prior to the elections that preceded the 2002 elections in Ukraine or the 2003 elections in Russia receiving scores of one and zero otherwise).[2]

Table 5.1 presents three logistic regression equations. The first pairs United Russia and Our Ukraine, while the second pairs United Russia with the Party of Regions. Accordingly, these two models test for common practices across parties from the different countries. Put another way, in both equations significance for any of the independent variables, except the country dummy, identifies common factors that influence

TABLE 5.1.B Correlates influencing the likelihood of list deputies making the party lists of Our Ukraine and the Party of Regions in 2006 and United Russia in 2007

	Equation 2	
	Odds ratio (p value)	95% Confidence interval
Nomination: UR or OU	—	
Nomination: UR or FUU	**5.425 (.001)**	2.029 14.505
Nomination: UR, OU, or FUU	—	
Membership: UR or OU	—	
Membership: UR or PoR	**6.090 (.004)**	1.790 20.718
Membership: UR, OU or FUU	—	
Nonpartisan	2.761 (.055)	0.977 7.798
Male	0.844 (.721)	0.333 2.137
Age	0.970 (.071)	0.939 1.003
Legislative or committee Leader	1.362 (.324)	0.737 2.518
Incumbent	0.693 (.283)	0.355 1.354
Ukrainian	0.567 (.194)	0.240 1.335
Constant	0.225 (.141)	0.031 1.638
Pseudo R^2	0.347	
Likelihood ratio χ^2 (significance)	146.63 (.000)	
Number of cases	447	

Note: Numbers in bold indicate significance at the .05 level for a two-tailed test. UR = United Russia; OU = Our Ukraine; FUU = For a United Ukraine; PoR = Party of Russia.

the likelihood of list placement across the two parties being compared. Significance for the variable "Ukrainian," meanwhile, indicates that the likelihood of list deputies landing on the Ukrainian party's list differs significantly from list deputies in Russia securing positions on United Russia's party list, all else being equal. The third equation pools all three parties together to identify effects that are common across all three parties. In this third model, significance for the country dummy moves any party-specific result in the direction of a country-specific finding.

As table 5.1 illustrates, despite the reduced specificity that comes with the data constraints discussed above, the models for the nomination of list deputies still explain a quarter to a third of the variance, and all

TABLE 5.1.C Correlates influencing the likelihood of list deputies making the party lists of Our Ukraine and the Party of Regions in 2006 and United Russia in 2007

| | Equation 3 | | |
	Odds ratio (p value)	95% Confidence interval	
Nomination: UR or OU	—		
Nomination: UR or FUU	—		
Nomination: UR, OU, or FUU	**18.521 (.000)**	7.954	43.131
Membership: UR or OU	—		
Membership: UR or PoR	—		
Membership: UR, OU, or FUU	1.652 (.300)	0.639	4.268
Nonpartisan	1.441 (.345)	0.675	3.075
Male	0.659 (.324)	0.288	1.509
Age	0.989 (.398)	0.963	1.015
Legislative or committee leader	**1.726 (.046)**	1.010	2.948
Incumbent	0.659 (.142)	0.378	1.150
Ukrainian	1.035 (.933)	0.465	2.301
Constant	**0.097 (.009)**	0.017	0.553
Pseudo R^2	0.284		
Likelihood ratio χ^2 (significance)	147.57 (.000)		
Number of cases	447		

Note: Numbers in bold indicate significance at the .05 level for a two-tailed test. UR = United Russia; OU = Our Ukraine; FUU = For a United Ukraine; PoR = Party of Russia.

produce significant likelihood ratio χ^2s. In addition, the results reveal that, regardless of how the parties are grouped, list deputies were significantly more likely to make party lists in the first PR-only elections if they were nominated by those parties (or its antecedent in the case of the Party of Regions) in the prior elections. The main difference on this count is the impact of the effect, which varies greatly. When comparing United Russia and Our Ukraine, previously nominated list deputies are 25 times more likely to land on these parties' lists in the closed-list PR elections compared to list deputies who were not nominated by these parties. This finding suggests that these two parties, which were affiliated with the executive branch in Russia and Ukraine, respectively, significantly reinvested in those politicians who committed to them earlier on. While this behavior also holds for the Party of Regions, as equation 2 demonstrates, the magnitude of the effect drops to five times the likelihood when only United Russia and the Party of Regions are analyzed. Part of the reduced effect is likely the increased impact of party membership in that equation (discussed below). On the whole, these results reveal that all parties—pro-presidential and opposition parties, parties in increasingly authoritarian regimes, as well as parties in regimes where elections are hotly contested—are likely to utilize list construction following the move from a mixed electoral system to closed-list PR to buttress preexisting relationships with their incumbent legislative deputies.

While the effect of prior nomination is consistently significant across the equations, the observed effect of party membership is not. In the first equation, membership in Our Ukraine in 2002 or United Russia in 2003 has no significant effect on the likelihood of a deputy receiving a position on the parties' lists in 2006 or 2007, respectively. However, what does matter (besides the source of prior nomination) is whether a list deputy held a leadership position in the outgoing legislature. These deputies were twice as likely as other deputies to receive a position on the 2006 list of Our Ukraine or the 2007 list of United Russia. However, when United Russia is paired with the Party of Regions, positions in the outgoing legislature do not matter, while party membership does. For this pairing, the odds of receiving a spot on the 2006 list of the Party of Regions or on the 2007 list of United Russia are almost six times that for list deputies who were members of these parties in the previous elections relative to list deputies who were members of other parties (i.e., the default category), all else being equal. In addition, the odds of a nonpartisan list deputy in the previous elections securing a position on the 2006 list of the Party of Regions or the 2007 list of United Russia are almost three times those of list deputies who were members of other parties, although this effect falls short of significance at the .05 level for a two-tailed test. These results suggest that United Russia navigated the move to closed-list PR in one way that was similar to Our Ukraine— nominating experienced legislators at a higher rate—and in another way that was similar to the Party of Regions—nominating party members at a higher rate. Such practices should be understood as party-specific as opposed to reflecting practices that parties in one regime type might pursue that parties in another regime type would not.[3] Indeed, the lack of a significant effect for Our Ukraine likely reflects a party-specific fact at the time: only one list deputy elected by Our Ukraine was an Our Ukraine party member. For a United Ukraine, meanwhile, six of the elected list deputies identified as Party of Regions members in 2002. In contrast, 102 of the list deputies under investigation and elected by United Russia in 2003 identified themselves as affiliated with that party.

As suggested above, analyzing how the main parties in Russia and Ukraine compared to one another when nominating district deputies to party lists requires that one rotate the analytical lens. While the analysis of list deputies includes party membership, the analysis of district deputies is limited to information on their sources of nomination in the previous elections. However, since the focus is now on deputies who did not have to be nominated by a party, the indicator of independence becomes a dummy variable where a one indicates that the deputy was self-nominated and a zero indicates that a party nominated the deputy. Including this variable in the analysis alongside the variable indicating whether deputies were nominated by the parties under investigation makes the default category (i.e., scores of zeros for both of these dichotomous variables) district deputies who were nominated by a party other than United Russia or Our Ukraine in the first equation, by a party other than United Russia or For a United Ukraine in the second equation, or by a party other than United Russia, Our Ukraine, or For a United Ukraine in the third equation. Thus, to the extent that a nomination variable is significant, that significance indicates an effect relative to an "other party" nomination.

In addition to the same control variables used in the analysis of list deputies, the analysis of district deputies includes a variable that captures the potential impact of these politicians' electoral performance in the district elections on party list decisions. As in chapters 3 and 4, I include the district deputies' vote shares in the elections preceding the first PR-only elections to determine whether those with more decisive victories were more likely to be nominated by the parties under investigation.

Table 5.2 presents three logistic regression equations with the first two, once again comparing United Russia's list construction to the list construction of Our Ukraine and the Party of Regions, respectively, and

TABLE 5.2.A Correlates influencing the likelihood of district deputies making the party lists of Our Ukraine and the Party of Regions in 2006 and United Russia in 2007

	Equation 1		
	Odds ratio (p value)	95% Confidence interval	
Nomination: UR or OU	**6.060 (.000)**	3.277	11.206
Nomination: UR or FUU	—		
Nomination: UR, OU, or FUU	—		
Self-nominated	1.778 (.069)	0.957	3.306
District vote share	0.997 (.709)	0.982	1.013
Male	1.899 (.197)	0.717	5.032
Age	0.993 (.577)	0.967	1.019
Legislative or committee leader	**1.645 (.042)**	1.017	2.660
Incumbent	0.971 (.908)	0.594	1.589
Ukrainian	**0.216 (.000)**	0.130	0.357
Constant	0.332 (.258)	0.049	2.241
Pseudo R^2	0.219		
Likelihood ratio χ^2 (significance)	124.02 (.000)		
Number of cases	437		

Note: Numbers in bold indicate significance at the .05 level for a two-tailed test. UR = United Russia; OU = Our Ukraine; FUU = For a United Ukraine.

the third comparing the construction of all three party lists simultaneously. Although the overall performance of the three models varies appreciably, with the pseudo-R^2s ranging from .09 to .21, the effects for the explanatory variables are relatively consistent.

According to table 5.2, district deputies nominated by the parties (or, again, in the case of the Party of Regions, its antecedent) in the prior elections were significantly more likely to land on the parties' lists during the first PR-only elections than deputies nominated by other parties. For the equation examining the lists of United Russia and Our Ukraine together, the likelihood is six times that of deputies nominated by other parties. For the equation comparing United Russia and the Party of Regions, the effect drops but is still over five times as likely. In contrast, the parties do not appear to have systematically privileged self-nominated

TABLE 5.2.B Correlates influencing the likelihood of district deputies making the party lists of Our Ukraine and the Party of Regions in 2006 and United Russia in 2007

	Equation 2		
	Odds ratio (p value)	95% Confidence interval	
Nomination: UR or OU	—		
Nomination: UR or FUU	**5.136 (.000)**	2.746	9.604
Nomination: UR, OU, or FUU	—		
Self-nominated	1.558 (.175)	0.821	2.957
District vote share	1.004 (.590)	0.989	1.020
Male	1.158 (.749)	0.472	2.842
Age	0.993 (.553)	0.969	1.017
Legislative or committee leader	**1.666 (.032)**	1.045	2.656
Incumbent	1.037 (.886)	0.630	1.709
Ukrainian	**0.239 (.000)**	0.148	0.384
Constant	0.419 (.337)	0.071	2.477
Pseudo R^2	0.187		
Likelihood ratio χ^2 (significance)	107.68 (.000)		
Number of cases	437		

Note: Numbers in bold indicate significance at the .05 level for a two-tailed test. UR = United Russia; OU = Our Ukraine; FUU = For a United Ukraine.

deputies relative to deputies previously nominated by other parties. Only for the equation comparing United Russia and Our Ukraine is the difference substantively significant, suggesting that the self-nominated deputies were almost twice as likely to be nominated by these parties as those nominated by other parties; however, the effect is significant at only the .10 level for a two-tailed test. Taken in conjunction with the results from table 5.1, the results in table 5.2 reveal that parties will likely reinvest in previously nominated deputies when navigating the move from mixed electoral rules to closed-list PR and that this behavior not only spans parties and regime types but also holds regardless of the deputies' prior mandate.

Similarly, when it comes to the nomination of district deputies, all three equations suggest that the parties under investigation valued

TABLE 5.2.C Correlates influencing the likelihood of district deputies making the party lists of Our Ukraine and the Party of Regions in 2006 and United Russia in 2007

	Equation 3	
	Odds ratio (p value)	95% Confidence interval
Nomination: UR or OU	—	
Nomination: UR or FUU	—	
Nomination: UR, OU, or FUU	**3.708 (.000)**	1.960	7.014
Self-nominated	1.481 (.239)	0.770	2.849
District vote share	1.001 (.891)	0.987	1.015
Male	1.293 (.556)	0.550	3.044
Age	0.998 (.843)	0.976	1.020
Legislative or committee leader	**1.575 (.040)**	1.021	2.428
Incumbent	0.866 (.531)	0.555	1.358
Ukrainian	**0.429 (.000)**	0.277	0.664
Constant	0.417 (.295)	0.076	2.596
Pseudo R^2	0.087	
Likelihood ratio χ^2 (significance)	52.30 (.000)	
Number of cases	437	

Note: Numbers in bold indicate significance at the .05 level for a two-tailed test. UR = United Russia; OU = Our Ukraine; FUU = For a United Ukraine.

legislative leadership experience, as deputies who held leadership positions in the outgoing legislatures were more than one and a half times more likely to receive a spot on a party list. The main difference across deputy mandates appears to be the behavior of the Party of Regions. While legislative leadership does not appear to have had a significant effect on that party's nomination of list deputies, this characteristic does appear to matter for its nomination of district deputies.

Perhaps the most important finding from table 5.2 is the discovery of a country effect that proves significant across all three equations. Specifically, the likelihood of list placement was significantly lower for Ukrainian district deputies than it was for Russian district deputies. When all three parties are analyzed collectively (equation 3), Russian district deputies were more than two times as likely (1/.429 = 2.3), all else being equal, to land on United Russia's list than Ukrainian district deputies were to land on the lists of Our Ukraine or the Party of Regions. Indeed, when the parties are analyzed as pairs, the differential prospects of the district deputies are even greater (1/.216 = 4.6 and 1/.239 = 4.2, respectively). Since chapter 4 finds that the Party of Regions was significantly more likely to nominate district deputies than list deputies, while Our Ukraine tended to nominate them at similar rates, the current finding suggests that the difference in practice between parties in Ukraine is not as great as the difference that emerges among the parties from the different countries. Of course, the use of regional sub-lists in Russian legislative elections alone indicates a commitment to ensuring some degree of regional representation in the Duma, despite the elimination district mandates. However, the construction of regional sub-lists predates the move to closed-list PR, and there is no reason to assume that Russian parties, including the ruling party, would rely on district deputies to populate the sub-lists.

Testing for Hidden Effects on List Rank

As the discussion thus far suggests, evaluating whether a particular party in one country is more willing or able to nominate certain types of politicians than a party in another country is a complicated and imperfect process. Nevertheless, the preceding analysis does provide an approach that scholars who are interested in questions related to candidate selection may replicate in future cross-national research, which may in turn help move investigations of candidate selection beyond the study of "a single party in a particular country at a specific time" (Hazan and Rahat 2006a, 110). In fact, if parties from the different countries under investigation all nominate their candidates using national party lists, one can imagine deploying a similar approach to examine how country- and party-specific considerations influence list rank. Unfortunately, a key difference in how party lists are structured prevents such an approach for Russia and Ukraine. While Russian candidates are primarily elected via regional sub-lists,[4] with their party's performance in a region determining how many candidates are elected from the sub-list, candidates in Ukraine are ranked on a national party list, with their party's national vote share determining how many seats the party wins and, accordingly, whether deputies with worse ranks on the national list receive mandates. This difference makes the rank of a typical candidate on a Russian party sub-list essentially incomparable to the rank of a candidate on a Ukrainian party list. Given this limitation, I take a different approach, one that investigates list rank in Russia and Ukraine by analyzing the potential impact of unobserved behavior on these decisions.

One important shortcoming for statistical work in the social sciences is the danger of excluding a potentially important explanation from the analysis. While omitted variable bias may occur unwittingly (i.e., because the researcher had not realized that a certain variable might matter), it also may occur due to a lack of data. For example, one may be aware that certain behavior occurs but is not able to observe such behavior, let alone measure it systematically. A solution is to find a way to control for the potential effect of the omitted variable, even if the control is less than ideal. In the case of candidate selection, for example, I contend in chapter 1 (see note 14) that limiting the analysis to incumbent deputies should reduce the influence of informal mechanisms such as bribery associated with the "costs of entry." Moreover, should the costs of entry increase, these politicians are well positioned, and should be sufficiently motivated, to continue to "pay to play." In this section, I build on the analyses of list rank in Russia and Ukraine from chapters 3 and 4 to assess the validity of this assertion, contending that the direction and size of the discrepancy between these politicians' predicted list ranks versus actual list ranks offer an opportunity to compare the degree to which the parties' decisions stemmed from the observable considerations modeled in those chapters rather than other, potentially hidden mechanisms.

While the Heckman selection models in chapter 3 and chapter 4 differ from one another so as to take into consideration the specific contexts, both attempt to estimate the candidates' electoral prospects using characteristics that are largely observable to scholars. I do not doubt that other factors may shape party decisions; rather, I present the models with an interest in developing some insight that may be helpful to others interested in systematically understanding what Gallagher and Marsh (1988) call the "secret garden of politics."

One way to explore the potential influence of missing factors that may allow politicians to ascertain better list ranks is to determine how many deputies selected to the lists hold positions that are significantly higher, in terms of electability, than the models would predict. To do this, I calculated the predicted value from each party's Heckman selection model for every legislator securing a position on the party's respective list.[5] I then subtracted the actual value (say, 10) for each candidate's rank from the predicted value (say, 25). The resulting score (15) measures the difference between the predicted and actual values, with higher scores indicating a rank that is better than predicted. To determine what qualifies as "significantly overranked," I used the standard deviation for the list rank variable and identified all cases for which the difference between the predicted and actual values was equal to or greater than the value of two standard deviations. I consider these candidates to be "overachievers." For the sake of comparison, I also used the two standard deviations metric to identify "underachievers"—that is, candidates ranked significantly lower than the respective models would predict. The results are informative.

Among the 188 United Russia candidates, only three were overachievers (i.e., they received list ranks that were two standard deviations better than predicted). In contrast, none of United Russia's candidates qualify as underachievers. Looking more closely at United Russia's three overachievers, the ability of two of them—one list deputy and one district deputy—to secure a top spot in 2007 on one of United Russia's regional sub-lists likely reflects the prominence of their positions at the time, something that was not fully captured in the statistical analysis. One candidate, Aleksander Zhukov, was a deputy prime minister who, upon election in 2007, declined his mandate ("Zhukov, Aleksandr" n.d.). The other was a top party leader: former minister and chairman of the State Duma, Boris Gryzlov. In other words, both individuals still possessed observable characteristics that a party—democratic or not—should value and that most politicians could use to their advantage when seeking a party nomination.[6] The third candidate with a list rank significantly higher than predicted, Vladimir Vasil'ev, appears to have lacked such influence. While Vasil'ev had served in Moscow's local government prior to winning a district contest in 2003, online biographies say little else about his political life aside from noting that he was deputy chairman of a Duma committee ("Vasil'ev Vladimir Alekseevich" n.d.), which is a characteristic that is already included in the analysis. While one might be tempted to speculate about the informal mechanisms that may have worked in this candidate's favor, the presence of one such overachieving candidate is not particularly strong evidence that a failure to explicitly control for an explanation, such as bribery, systematically biased the results reported in chapter 3.

Moving to the Ukrainian parties, none of the 74 deputies making Our Ukraine's 2006 list qualify as overachievers. Our Ukraine does, however, have two candidates who appear appreciably underranked: Anatolii Korchin'skii and Vadim Litvin. In 2002, these candidates were elected as list deputies from separate parties, both of which opposed Yushchenko and Our Ukraine: the Social Democratic Party (United) and the Communist Party, respectively. One plausible explanation for their unexpectedly low placements may be that, while Our Ukraine co-opted candidates from a range of other parties going into the 2006 elections, it might have ranked candidates from parties that were particularly hostile to Our Ukraine lower than those from other, less adversarial parties.

The results for the 54 candidates nominated by the Party of Regions, meanwhile, resemble those for United Russia, with three overachievers and, again, no underachievers. All three of these candidates were elected in 2002 as deputies representing a single-member district. Of the three, one candidate, Vasilii Gorbal', resembles the more politically networked overachievers in Russia, thanks to his close ties with both For a United Ukraine and the Party of Regions in Ukraine's capital, in addition to having actively worked on Viktor Yanukovych's 2004 presidential campaign ("Gorbal' Vasilii Mikhailovich" n.d.). Another, Viktor Turmanov, not only competed as a self-nominated candidate from Donetsk but also appears to have capitalized on the prominent position he held in the union representing workers in Ukraine's coal industry ("Turmanov, Viktor Ivanovich" n.d.). As with United Russia, two of the overachievers associated with the Party of Regions possessed observable characteristics that could readily explain their higher-than-predicted list ranks. Although these politicians may have enjoyed these positions thanks to the informal connections that often pervade professional life in the former Soviet Union, they still constitute explanations that make allegations of bribery, in particular, difficult to sustain. The third overachiever associated with the Party of Regions, Dmitrii Svyatash, not only lacked the organizational ties that his colleagues may have leveraged for political gain; both his professional background—as one of the largest players in Ukraine's domestic automobile market—and rumored links to political figures with questionable reputations ("Svyatash Dmitrii" n.d.) are more likely to be sources of suspicion. But again, this is only a single case.

Overall, the preceding comparison of predicted and actual list ranks should help reduce concerns that unobservable mechanisms such as bribery systematically influenced the decisions of the parties under investigation about where to rank incumbent deputies on their lists of candidates. And although the work says little about the costs that aspiring legislators may have to pay to gain entry initially, it does at least offer an approach that future scholars may replicate in their efforts to identify candidates for whom unobservable, and perhaps illicit, behavior may be determinative.

Conclusion

A primary goal of this chapter has been to systematically compare the nominations of incumbent legislators by Russia's ruling party with those made by the pro-presidential party and a primary opposition party in Ukraine during the two countries' first PR-only elections. Since the two countries employed closed-list PR for the first time in regimes with significantly different levels of electoral competition, few would be surprised to learn that Russian and Ukrainian parties might have behaved differently from one another. However, since all parties, regardless of regime type, are interested in winning elections and establishing majority control over the legislature, one might also reasonably expect some commonalities across the parties to emerge. The only way to know which kinds of behavior reflect the fact that parties are operating in democratic rather than authoritarian regimes (or vice versa) is to explicitly compare how parties in both types of regimes respond to similar changes. The study of the electoral system changes in Russia and Ukraine provides such an opportunity.

The preceding analyses reveal that parties will likely navigate the move to closed-list PR by reinvesting in a core of seemingly loyal and experienced deputies. As observed above, incumbent deputies, both district and list, were consistently more likely to be nominated by one of the parties during the first closed-list PR elections if the deputies were previously nominated by the party in question. This finding holds regardless of whether the parties are pro-presidential or opposition and regardless of whether the parties are in an increasingly authoritarian regime or in a regime where elections were hotly contested. Likewise, it appears that all parties—regardless of regime type and status (i.e., pro-presidential or not)—value the legislative experience of incumbent deputies; again; this holds for deputies with either district or list mandates. Although the effect of this variable fails to attain significance in one model (the model comparing the nomination of list deputies by United Russia and the Party of Regions), the null finding in this case likely reflects the significant effect of prior party membership among list deputies, which itself can be expected to have determined the allocation of key positions in the outgoing legislature.

The analyses also yield insight into the degree to which parties may view party affiliation differently. At least for the cases under investigation, which again operate in weakly institutionalized party systems, previous party affiliation among list deputies (i.e., the only deputies for whom party membership data are consistently available) in the form of a prior party nomination is not the same thing as party membership. As that particular analysis highlights, prior party membership mattered to United Russia and the Party of Regions but not to Our Ukraine. Since Our Ukraine and United Russia constitute the two pro-presidential parties, and the Party of Regions and United Russia competed in different regimes, this finding cannot be explained as resulting from pro-presidential status or as a regime-type effect. With this in mind, the importance of party membership to nomination decisions during periods of electoral system change should be understood as a party-specific concern and as one that can span regime types and party status.

Finally, the cross-party statistical analysis of district deputies reveals an important difference across the two countries: in all three equations presented in table 5.2, Ukrainian district deputies were significantly less likely to be nominated by one of the two Ukrainian parties under investigation than Russian district deputies were to be nominated by United Russia. This finding emphasizes the value of the cross-national analysis because it reveals that the difference between the Ukrainian parties on this count, identified in chapter 4, is less than the difference between parties operating in different countries. Future cross-national research may wish to examine the degree to which such an outcome constitutes a regime effect, a party-system effect, or an institutional effect. Given the differences between Russia and Ukraine, the finding could reflect Russia's authoritarian trajectory, United Russia's stronger position in its developing party system, or Russia's federal structure and reliance on regional sub-lists.

6

Proportional Rules and Majoritarian Outcomes in Russia

While the Kremlin's ability to capitalize on the move to proportional representation (PR)-only rules is only part of the story explaining the renewal of authoritarian politics in Russia,[1] the Russian experience serves as an important example of how electoral rules and party decisions interact in electoral authoritarian regimes where legitimacy rests squarely on convincing electoral victories. Unlike the voluminous literature on the manipulation of electoral rules for political gain in democratic settings, particularly studies on gerrymandering and malapportionment (e.g., Erikson 1972, Niemi et al. 1990, Samuels and Snyder 2001), scholars have only begun to unpack the interaction between electoral systems and party systems under electoral authoritarianism (e.g., Golosov 2006; 2016). This chapter considers how nominally proportional electoral rules may contribute to ruling-party majorities in authoritarian settings by using Russia as a case study. Specifically, I examine an intriguing dynamic that emerged from the analysis in chapter 3 of United Russia's list construction: the nomination of governors to the ruling party's regional sub-lists. This chapter demonstrates that, while conventional wisdom expects the placement of governors on regional sub-lists to drive votes in the ruling party's direction, this effect holds in the empirical analysis only when one controls for a previously unconsidered effect that comes from excluding certain governors from the party's list. In addition, this chapter reveals how the institutional effects that allow PR rules to be effective in authoritarian contexts may prove temporary: in Russia, the effects of gubernatorial list placement dissipate in 2011. This outcome does not mean that Russia's PR system was not influential in 2011, however. Regions that enjoyed greater representation within the ruling party in the first elections governed by PR-only rules (2007) relative to the previous elections were more likely to deliver votes for that party in the last Russian elections governed by a PR-only system (2011). In sum, since United Russia's overwhelming electoral victory in the 2007 Duma elections served as a formative step in the development of Russia's authoritarian regime, I consider the role that Russia's closed-list PR system played in this outcome as well as why United Russia's performance in 2011 (the second Duma elections to be governed by closed-list PR rules) fell short of 2007 levels. The chapter sets the context for the book's conclusion and its discussion of the return of Russia's mixed-member system in 2016.

Russia's Regional Locomotives

While United Russia is commonly thought of as "Putin's party" (e.g., Ivanov 2008; Roberts 2012a), it has evolved since the merger of Unity and Fatherland–All Russia in December 2001. The new ruling party began asserting itself by appropriating the majority of the committee chairmanships in the Duma. Then, in the December 2003 Duma elections, United Russia won more than 49 percent of the vote and established a legislative majority (see chapter 2). Perhaps just as important, it amassed a membership of 1.66 million (Sakwa 2011, 23) and co-opted a majority of Russia's governors (Reuter 2010; 2017) going into the 2007 Duma elections. As Roberts (2012a, 3) notes, the placement of Russian governors on United Russia's party list in the 2007 elections highlighted the degree to which the party had become "the primary mechanism for elite circulation and career advancement within the political system."

Despite these changes, however, United Russia has not strayed far from its origins as the party of Vladimir Putin. In 2007, for example, President Putin aligned himself with United Russia in a way that President Boris Yeltsin never did with any party: Putin personally led United Russia's 2007 party list. As expected, this move helped maximize United Russia's vote tally in 2007, and United Russia became the first ruling party in Russia to emerge victorious in two consecutive legislative elections (2003 and 2007). While this development may have indicated that the Kremlin had finally established a "lasting party of power" (Moraski 2006; 2007), doubts lingered about whether United Russia, at least at the time, qualified as a dominant party. As Hale (2014, 279) explains, Putin's decision did not simply help the party's electoral prospects; it also meant that United Russia's delegation to the Duma would consist of deputies who would owe their seats to Putin. In other words, the outcome reinforces Sakwa's (2011, 12) position: "Although parties are the main actors in [Russian] parliamentary elections, they are at best accessories to the processes taking place within the regime," and "[t]his applies to UR [United Russia] as much as to other parties, hence its role as a 'dominant party' is limited." Hutcheson (2013, 911) takes a similar stance:

> UR's hegemony can be overstated. Its role in securing leadership succession and distributing resources in strategic economic areas—key functions of a dominant party—is limited. Its executive-led formation means that leading figures' membership of the party is a formality rather than the basis of their power, and recent rotation of regional governors has diminished its patronage network to some extent. UR also remains a coalition of different elite groups—evinced by its internal discussion clubs spanning the political left to right and its subdivision in the Duma into four sub-factions. Most significantly, the continued presence of the [Communist Party of the Russian Federation] in the party system also challenges UR's hegemonic nature. The CPRF remains a vocal critic of Medvedev's and Putin's social and economic policies while colluding on or tacitly accepting certain party and electoral reforms.

While United Russia may not be the primary source of political power in Russia, it does appear to be the dominant party in Russia's party system,[2] making it an object of interest for scholars of elections generally and electoral systems specifically. At the same time, United Russia's position at the pinnacle of legislative power, especially during the four-year interregnum between the Putin presidencies, and perceived role in political recruitment and career advancement justify taking a closer look at how Russia's PR electoral system not only contributed to the party's success but also interacted with Russia's governors.

Coattail effects constitute a prime example of how influential actors at different levels of government shape election results (Born 1984; Campbell and Sumners 1990; Ferejohn and Calvert 1984; Gaines and Crombez 2004; Gelineau and Remmer 2006; Rodden and Wibbels 2011). Scholars have shown that coattail effects not only work down the party ticket; they can flow up a ticket as well. According to Broockman (2009, 421), the coattail logic rests on the contention that voters utilize the better-defined and more cognitively accessible attitudes that they possess about certain political candidates to evaluate others whom they know less about. A theory of reverse coattails, then, rests on the assertion that subnational elites can function as political cues for voters in national elections, especially in federal systems.

Ames (1994), for example, submits that a critical yet underappreciated aspect of the 1989 Brazilian presidential election was the effort that every candidate put into winning endorsements from other politicians at various levels of government (i.e., legislative deputies, governors, and mayors). According to Ames, Brazil's presidential candidates pursued the backing of local officials and local party organizations because Brazilian municipalities depended heavily on transfer payments, which were generally allocated on the basis of discretionary and political criteria. As a result, any sensible local leader would be delivering votes for someone. At the same time, Brazil's strong local machines possessed tools—from patronage to media influence—that were capable of shaping voter choice (Ames 1994, 96). Samuels (2000), meanwhile, contends that Brazil's governors not only are often better known than presidential candidates but also possess more developed and broader clientelistic networks than other local politicians. Thus, Brazilian presidential candidates regularly turn to these provincial leaders for support and to appear less foreign to voters. Taken together, these studies illustrate how reverse coattails may operate outside of established democracies, identifying causal mechanisms that may have little in common with the sincerity of voter preferences (see also Magar 2012). Thus, while reverse coattails are commonly understood as operating in democratic states, there are reasons to expect them to matter in authoritarian regimes that rely on elections for their rule.

In Russia, the term "locomotives" refers to high-profile politicians who serve on the ruling party's list as a way to drive votes in that party's direction (Nisnevich 2014, 72). Governors in particular tend to decline the legislative mandates, which then allows the seats to go to the next candidate on the party's list.[3] However, since Russia's incumbent presidents topped the ruling party's list in both elections under investigation (Putin in 2007 and Medvedev in 2011), both conventional and reverse coattails were possible. While an incumbent president's presence on United Russia's list represents a constant across all the regions during the elections in question, his ability to operate as a locomotive may vary across the regions. With this in mind, the following analysis includes the president's vote share in the executive election preceding the legislative ones to control for this variation.

One obvious difference between the Russian system and others, such as Brazil's, is Russia's lack of competitiveness. From 2007 on, Russian governors are widely believed to have had little choice but to deliver votes for the Kremlin's preferred candidate or party in national elections. Yet this has not always been the case. Even before the collapse of the Soviet Union, Russian president Boris Yeltsin sought to mobilize provincial support in his struggle with Mikhail Gorbachev by encouraging the regions within the Russian union republic to "[t]ake as much independence as you can hold on to" (quoted in Kahn 2002, 95). As Russia's transition from authoritarian rule progressed, the regional executives' control over patronage and ability to influence electoral outcomes undermined the development of the national party system, with governors developing their own political machines that often served as alternatives to national party organizations (Hale 2006).[4] Even Russia's most developed political party, the Communist Party of the Russian Federation, enjoyed little leverage over governors who competed under its party banner (Kahn 2001). Thus, by the late 1990s, many of Russia's governors were seen as powerful and largely independent political players. In fact, with the fate of the Russian presidency after Yeltsin uncertain, some of Russia's most powerful regional executives united to form the bloc All Russia with the goal of winning seats in the 1999 Duma elections. Then, in August 1999, All Russia joined with Fatherland, the party of Moscow mayor Yuri Luzhkov, to form the center-left Fatherland–All Russia party. In response, the Kremlin created Unity, a center-right party that also had direct ties to regional politicians: among its founding members were 13 governors (Brudny 2001, 159). Only after Putin's decisive victory in the 2000 presidential election did Unity and Fatherland–All Russia merge to become United Russia.

As discussed in chapter 2, Putin's Kremlin recognized that it needed the help of the country's governors to win elections and therefore invested heavily in extending United Russia's reach. While regional elites who chose to cooperate with the ruling party were likely to receive greater influence over policy and rents (Reuter and Remington 2009, 507), Reuter (2010) finds that governors were not uniformly co-opted.

Governors with more political resources at their disposal (i.e., those in better positions to deliver votes) were more reluctant to join the party than their less influential counterparts. However, the replacement of gubernatorial elections with a system of presidentially appointed governors greatly reduced the room that even Russia's most powerful governors had to maneuver. Under the new system, which went into effect in 2005, governors who were able to deliver votes for the Kremlin's preferred candidate or party during national elections stayed in office longer than those either unwilling or unable to deliver such votes (Reisinger and Moraski 2013; Reuter and Robertson 2012; Sharafutdinova 2010). In other words, during the appointment period, Russia's president controlled the governors' fates, and by most accounts the deciding factor was the regional delivery of votes in the Kremlin's desired direction. The following analysis controls for variables commonly associated with vote delivery across Russia's regions, including regional regime type.

While the number of locomotives increased dramatically with the partisan and institutional co-optation of Russia's governors, another factor that likely explains the dramatic increase in locomotives between 2003 and 2007 is the change in the Duma's electoral system. With the move to a fully closed-list PR system, list construction in Russia assumed greater importance in 2007 than it did in 2003, when party lists populated half as many seats. In the 2003 Duma elections, the first following the merger of Unity and Fatherland–All Russia, 29 out of Russia's 89 governors acted as locomotives, rounding up votes for the "party of power" (to use the nomenclature of many observers of Russian politics). In 2007, the first Duma elections to follow the elimination of gubernatorial elections, the number grew to 65 governors (Gel'man 2007, 6).

Thanks to United Russia's strong affiliation with the Kremlin, it is reasonable to assume that governors not on United Russia's list during the appointment era may have perceived their exclusion as indicating that they were vulnerable to replacement. Indeed, Gel'man (2007, 6) contends that gubernatorial decisions to join United Russia and gubernatorial placement on the party's list were strongly correlated: "By the spring of 2007, 70 of 85 governors announced that they were participating in the party of power. Sixty-five of these joined the regional lists of United Russia in the Duma elections." Gel'man (2007, 6) also notes that these decisions fit a particular electoral and partisan pattern, one that signaled the end of select governors' time in office: "The few governors who did not join United Russia typically were elected to their posts before 2004 with the support of the Communists and have little chance of being reappointed."

Since previous work has already examined when and why governors joined United Russia (Reuter and Remington 2009; Reuter 2010; 2017), which in turn are strongly correlated with landing on its 2007 list, this chapter considers whether gubernatorial list placement influenced electoral support for United Russia across regions.[5] While list placement decisions were made behind closed doors,[6] I contend that the signals (whether intended or unintended) sent by those decisions mattered.

The party may have deemed governors unattractive list candidates for a host of reasons: an absence of genuine support (elite or public) in the region, appearing too independent, personal scandal, poor economic performance in their region, or the presence of other, more attractive options. To the extent that excluded governors were unpopular, the decision to leave them off United Russia's 2007 list could be seen as an attempt to maintain some distance between these governors and the party. While this tactic would allow the party to avoid the costs of such an affiliation, there is little reason to expect that United Russia would perform better in these regions than it would in regions where the governors made its list. In other words, keeping unpopular governors off United Russia's list would—at best, it seems—allow United Russia's performance in such regions to match its performance in other regions where governors were on the list. Where popular governors were excluded from United Russia's list for reasons such as an affiliation with the Communist Party, one might expect these governors to respond by driving votes in a direction other than toward United Russia. In fact, this behavior would create the kind of cross-regional variation that would support the conventional locomotive hypothesis.

It is also plausible, however, that some governors felt compelled to drive votes in United Russia's direction despite having been left off of its list. I call this possibility the "gubernatorial vulnerability hypothesis." To the extent that subordinate politicians in authoritarian regimes are risk-averse, those who perceive a potential threat to their positions of privilege could respond by demonstrating their fealty and value. In other words, given United Russia's expressed position as the party of

President Putin, as well as the system of presidentially appointed governors in place, governors left off United Russia's list may have marshalled the resources at their disposal to produce electoral results in favor of United Russia as a way to compensate for whatever shortcomings may have kept them off its list. Similarly, should governors have turned down list candidacy, the provision of votes for United Russia could have served as an immediate and meaningful signal of their loyalty—despite previous affiliations—and value to the regime.

While a ruling party should desire a strong performance throughout the country, Russia's governors during the appointment era were not all equally capable of delivering favorable or highly favorable vote totals. As Hale (2014, 112–14) notes, Russian politicians who landed in the governors' seats in the 1990s had the opportunity to amass the political and economic resources necessary for building powerful political machines. On average, longer-serving governors can be expected to have competed in and won more elections; in addition, all else being equal, they are likely to have developed stronger regional networks that could become cogs in the national authoritarian machine. Put differently, governors with proven electoral track records—having governed during previous national elections and having won election themselves—are better positioned to compensate for list exclusion by delivering higher regional vote shares for United Russia.

Focusing on gubernatorial tenure has the additional benefit of separating gubernatorial influence from other traits that make regions positively or negatively predisposed to proregime vote totals. Theoretically, a region could be represented among the list of locomotives in 2003 and 2007 even though the governor in office in 2007 is different from the governor who held the position in 2003. This scenario may occur because the party finds the region particularly attractive for, say, possessing an especially high proportion of national voters. Controlling for gubernatorial tenure differentiates regions where the practice of locomotives continued despite a change in governor (i.e., one with a short tenure) from regions where it continued without a change in the regional chief executive (one with a long tenure).

The idea that previously elected governors can prove their electoral salt better than governors without such electoral experience also has potentially important implications for the continued effectiveness of the locomotive strategy. By the December 2011 legislative elections, the appointment process was fully institutionalized following the 2008 transfer of the presidency—and with it the power of appointment—to President Putin's handpicked successor, Dmitri Medvedev. Since one aim of the appointment process was to penetrate the regions and reintegrate them into a more tightly knit executive hierarchy, several appointed governors came from the federal government or were other outsiders (Blakkisrud 2011). This turnover in the gubernatorial corps likely undermined the electoral benefits of locomotives, since the locomotive strategy hinges on governors who are well known and entrenched in the regions that they govern (Samuels 2000). Moreover, having not competed in direct elections or governed during Russia's more competitive national elections, newly appointed governors likely lacked the kinds of electoral machines of those whom they replaced. Thus, while the regions' experiences with the locomotive practice continued to vary in 2011, governors left off the list—having little to no personal electoral experience or lacking the necessary regional network—should have been less able to compensate for list exclusion by driving more votes toward United Russia than their counterparts were in 2007.

To untangle the electoral consequences of gubernatorial list placement in Russia across its regions, I use multivariate regression analysis.[7] The dependent variables are United Russia's regional vote shares in the 2007 and 2011 Duma elections. In 2007, United Russia's mean regional vote share was 66 percent and ranged from a minimum value of 49.7 percent (Nenets) to a maximum of 99.5 percent (Chechnya), with a standard deviation of 11.1. While numbers at the high end suggest greater amounts of falsification, the ability and willingness of regional actors to produce such results are at the heart of the research question. In 2011, United Russia's mean regional vote share was lower, at 49 percent. The range was also wider with a minimum of 29 percent (Yaroslavl) and a maximum of 99.5 percent (Chechnya), yielding a standard deviation of 16.8.[8]

The data for the dependent variables come from Russia's Central Election Commission (Official Website of the Central Election Commission of the Russian Federation, www.cikrf.ru). Although one might question whether the CEC itself is complicit in data manipulation, thus undermining the data's validity, existing studies attribute electoral violations to actors working at lower levels of aggregation (i.e., regional and local politicians and local electoral commissions) (Bacon 2012; Myagkov et al. 2009). Moreover, any effort by the CEC to pad United Russia's vote shares across the board or boost its vote share randomly across regions should actually work against identifying the hypothesized regional patterns. While a systematic attempt to manipulate vote shares in accordance with gubernatorial list placement would raise issues for the analysis, I know of no compelling theory for why this might have occurred.

To test the conventional locomotive hypothesis in a way that can be easily converted into a test of the gubernatorial vulnerability hypothesis, the first step in the analysis uses a dummy variable where a one indicates that a region's governor was left off United Russia's list and a zero indicates that a governor was on its list. A significantly negative coefficient will support conventional wisdom. While a lack of significance may suggest that governors left off the ruling party's list (as well as those on the list) succeeded in delivering votes in the Kremlin's favor, the analysis tests the gubernatorial vulnerability hypothesis more directly by employing an interaction term. The term multiplies the dichotomous variable for regions where the governor was left off United Russia's 2007 list and the tenure of the governor in office at the time of the elections, which ranges from two months to 203 months.[9] A positive and significant effect for the interaction term indicates that United Russia systematically benefited from leaving long-serving governors off its list—that is, its share of the vote is higher in these regions. To receive an unbiased coefficient for the interaction term, the model controls for the interaction term's components (Brambor et al. 2006).

In addition to the main explanatory variables, the multivariate regression analyses control for regional support for the incumbent president in the most recent Russian presidential election—that is, national executive coattails—and variations in regional regime type. The latter may affect an incumbent governor's ability to convert the regional system in place into one that can reliably deliver votes in the Kremlin's desired direction. Data on the former come from the CEC for the 2004 and 2008 Russian presidential elections. To measure variations in regional regime type, which varies appreciably at the subnational level in Russia (Moraski and Reisinger 2007), I use an index of regional democracy for the 2002–2006 period in the analysis of the 2007 Duma elections and another for the

2006–2010 period in the analysis of 2011. These indices are compiled by Petrov and Titkov (2013, 25–28). For each region, they sum expert ratings (on a scale of one to five) across 10 political characteristics, ranging from openness of political life and quality of elections to media independence and corruption. A higher value on the index indicates a more democratic polity. For the 2002–2006 period, data on Chechnya are missing, which reduces the number of cases in the corresponding analysis.

Besides these variables, the analysis includes measures that estimate regional demographic and economic conditions. Previous research has found that the greatest amount of variation in regional support for the Kremlin's preferred party or candidate during the Putin era can be explained using the percentage of non-Russians in the regions (Reisinger and Moraski 2010). This result may be attributed to the liberty that the governors of Russia's larger ethnic regions (republics) enjoyed from the federal government when it came to developing political machines within their borders (Stepan 2000).[10] According to Hale (2007, 231), the geographic concentration of ethnicity provided governors the capacity not only to monitor but also to reward voting with "preferential treatment in education, state employment, territorially concentrated investment, and status."[11] Golosov (2011, 401) notes that, while the political trajectories of Russia's smaller ethnic regions (autonomous okrugs) more closely resembled other nonrepublics during the 1990s, they also possess characteristics—such as small populations, dense ethnic networks, and distant locations—that could undermine competitive politics. I use 2002 and 2010 Russian census data to measure the percentage of non-Russians in the regions.[12]

Aside from ethnic composition, scholars regularly emphasize the potential susceptibility of rural voters to machine politics. In the United States, Monroe (1977) contends that the ability of local politicians to distribute government jobs in the rural counties of Illinois explain why these counties enjoyed higher voter turnout. In Putin's Russia, Myagkov et al. (2009, 90) find suspiciously high levels of turnout to be significantly more common in rural districts. At the same time, education levels and economic conditions are commonly identified as determinants of voting behavior in consolidated democracies as well as many postcommunist states, including at the subnational level in Russia (Konitzer 2005; Tucker 2006). Given these considerations, the analysis controls for the percentage of rural voters at the time of the elections, percentage of the population with higher education, change in real income over the four years between elections, as well as change in regional unemployment measured as a percentage of the economically active population.[13]

In an ordinary least squares analysis testing the core hypotheses, five outliers emerged. Two were on the high end with studentized residuals above 2, and three were on the low end with studentized residuals below -2. List placement for the outliers varied at both ends of the spectrum. Among the high outliers, one (Merkushkin in Mordovia) was on United Russia's list, while the other (Batdyev in Karachayevo-Cherkessia) was not. On the low end, two (Yevdokimov in Murmansk and Mamsurov in North Ossetia) were on United Russia's list, while one (Potapenko in Nenets) was not. Given the presence of these outliers, table 6.1 presents the results of a robust regression analysis, which corrects for their impact by down-weighting them when calculating coefficients (Andersen 2008).

Equation 1 presents the model estimating the conventional locomotive hypothesis. Given the inclusion of what is essentially a lag for previous pro-Kremlin voting in the regions (i.e., the share of the regional vote for Putin in 2004), the equation's R^2 of .74 is not surprising.[14] As expected, regions that supported Putin in 2004 yielded significantly higher vote shares for United Russia in 2007. The effect proves significant at the .001 level for a two-tailed test. Looking at the coefficient, almost a half of a percentage point jump in support for United Russia in 2007 can be expected with each 1 percent increase in the regional vote share for Putin in 2004, all else being equal. In addition, United Russia enjoyed significantly higher vote shares in 2007 in regions with more ethnically non-Russian residents and where incomes rose between 2003 and 2007. Both variables are significant at the .01 level for two-tailed tests. A 1 percent increase in the number of non-Russians in a region is associated with more than a 0.1 percent increase in United Russia's vote share in 2007. Meanwhile, a 1 percent rise in real income levels in a region between 2003 and 2007 yields more than a 0.25 percent increase in United Russia's regional vote share, again all else being equal. The latter result suggests that the regime's economic performance continued to influence election results in 2007 despite its authoritarian turn during this period. The former confirms previous findings that regions with more ethnically non-Russian residents

TABLE 6.1. Correlates of regional support for United Russia in 2007

	Equation 1	Equation 2
Off 2007 List	−1.56	−9.53*
	(1.53)	(2.67)
Tenure, 2007	−4.76E-03	−0.01
	(0.01)	(0.01)
Off 2007 List X Tenure, 2007	—	0.09*
		(0.03)
Vote for Putin, 2004	0.48*	0.52*
	(0.11)	(0.10)
Regional Democracy Index, 2002–2006	−0.45*	−0.44*
	(0.13)	(0.12)
Percent non-Russian, 2002	0.12*	0.12*
	(0.04)	(0.04)
Percent with higher education, 2002	−0.19	−0.20
	(0.20)	(0.19)
Change in real income (2007–2003)	0.20*	0.27*
	(0.09)	(0.09)
Change in regional unemployment (2007–2003)	−0.25	−0.40
	(0.35)	(0.33)
Percent rural, 2007	−2.36E-4	−0.05
	(0.07)	(0.07)
Constant	44.31*	39.69*
	(8.61)	(8.22)
R^2	0.74	0.77
N	82	82

Note: Coefficients are unstandardized while the numbers in parentheses are standard errors.
* indicates significance at the .05 level or better. All tests are two-tailed.

have been cornerstones in the provision of pro-Kremlin vote totals. By contrast, regions rated as more democratic during the 2002–2006 period witnessed more competitive Duma elections in 2007, evidenced by the negative coefficient meeting significance at the .001 level for a two-tailed test. A one-point increase in the democracy index is associated with 0.45 percent decline in United Russia's regional vote share, all else being equal.

The key findings from equation 1 are the null results for list placement and months in office. As conventional wisdom would expect, regions where governors were left off United Russia's 2007 list are associated with less support for United Russia than regions where the governors have been described as locomotives. However, this effect is not significant in an equation that does not control for the behavior of long-serving governors left off the list. Likewise, while the relationship between gubernatorial tenure and United Russia's regional vote shares is negative, it is not significant, and each additional month in office has a negligible effect.

Equation 2 tests the conventional locomotive hypothesis alongside the gubernatorial vulnerability hypothesis. The model in equation 2 also explains around three-fourths of the variance in United Russia's regional vote share. Temporarily setting aside the question of gubernatorial list placement, the results resembles those from equation 1: Presidential coattails correlate highly with United Russia's 2007 vote share, while United Russia performed worse in regions that were more democratic during the 2002–2006 period. Moreover, regions with more ethnically non-Russian residents and where incomes rose between 2003 and 2007 yielded significantly higher vote shares for United Russia. The main differences are the results supporting the conventional locomotive and the gubernatorial vulnerability hypotheses. In line with the conventional locomotive hypothesis, the presence of a locomotive (i.e., where the value of the variable—off the 2007 list—is zero) yields a 9.5 percent increase in United Russia's vote share, all else being equal, according to equation 2. Meanwhile, the positively significant interaction term supports the gubernatorial vulnerability hypothesis. While a one-month difference in tenure for governors on the list equates to only a .09 percent increase in United Russia's vote share, an entirely plausible difference of 100 months would result in a 9 percent increase.[15] As in equation 1, tenure alone is insignificant, suggesting that the length of time that a governor held office on its own failed to influence United Russia's 2007 regional vote shares.

Figure 6.1 graphs the marginal effect of list exclusion on tenure using 10-month increments. Doing so better illustrates the relationship between tenure and list exclusion that underpins the gubernatorial vulnerability hypothesis. It demonstrates that the difference between list placement and list exclusion is significant when both the upper and lower bounds of the confidence interval are below or above

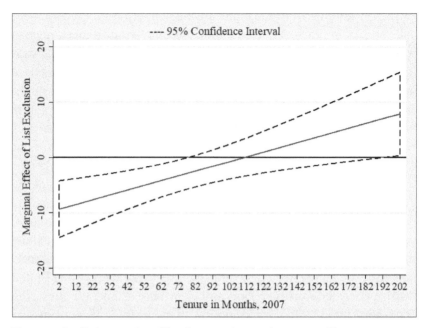

Figure 6.1. Predictive margins of list placement in 2007, by tenure, with 95 percent confidence intervals

the zero line (Brambor et al. 2006, 76), that is, below the 75-month mark and above the 200-month mark. In other words, regional vote shares for United Russia were significantly lower where governors with tenures below 75 months were left off of United Russia's 2007 list, as the locomotive hypotheses predicts. Above 75 months (and below 200 months), the effects of list placement and list exclusion are not significantly different from one another, which makes theoretical sense. It is unlikely that governors left off United Russia's list can systematically outperform those who made the list in terms of vote delivery. A more reasonable expectation of the gubernatorial vulnerability hypothesis is for longer-serving governors left off of United Russia's list to perform as well as other governors who did make the list. Only the longest-serving governors left off the list have a chance of outperforming governors on the list.

While table 6.1 examines the impact of a region's share of non-Russians on United Russia's regional vote share alongside the gubernatorial list placement variables, figure 6.2 considers differences between ethnic regions and other regions. Specifically, it presents the 19 governors left off of United Russia's 2007 list, their respective regions, type of region (e.g., okrug, republic, etc.), the governors' tenure in office, and United Russia's share of the regional vote in 2007. The cases are sorted from United Russia's lowest vote share (49.7 percent in Nenets Okrug) to its highest (98.8 percent in Ingushetia). To differentiate between "overachievers" and "underachievers," I use the 50th percentile for United Russia's vote share among regions where governors made United Russia's list; that figure is 62.3 percent, indicated by the vertical line in figure 6.2. Note that, of the 19 regions where governors were left off United Russia's 2007 list, just over half (10) qualify as overachievers by this measure. In addition, as the preceding analysis reveals, gubernatorial tenure alone is not the sole determinant of vote delivery. While several long-serving governors pass the threshold in question, so too do governors with tenures below the 75-month mark, while vote delivery in regions with some long-serving

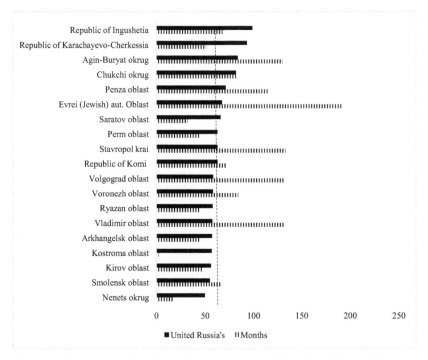

Figure 6.2. Comparison of regions without governors on United Russia's 2007 list

governors, particularly those in the oblasts of Vladimir and Volgograd, fall short. Among the ethnic regions with governors left off of United Russia's 2007 list, all three of the republics and two of the three okrugs emerge as overachievers, despite their governors holding office for significantly fewer months than the governors of Vladimir and Volgograd and fewer months than the overall average (87) at the time. The only ethnic region that fails to emerge as an overachiever is Nenets, where the governor had the second-shortest tenure (18 months) among the 19 cases under consideration.

In sum, the results so far present a fuller picture of how Russia's use of locomotives operated in 2007: While the conventional locomotive hypothesis holds, it emerges empirically only when examined alongside the gubernatorial vulnerability hypothesis. According to the latter, capable governors responded to list exclusion by demonstrating their electoral value to the Kremlin during the 2007 elections in an effort to extend their career prospects under the gubernatorial appointment system. The next part of the analysis considers the effectiveness of locomotives in the 2011 Duma elections. Support for the gubernatorial vulnerability hypothesis will be bolstered if the relationship identified in 2007 disappears as governors with longer tenures are replaced with appointees lacking electoral experience.

While United Russia dominated regional politics between the 2007 and 2011 Duma elections, its position across the Russian Federation was far from uniform. For example, Panov and Ross (2013, 750) identify "hidden divisions" and "competition between regional elites" affiliated with United Russia despite the fact that United Russia's candidates clearly dominated the 43 regional assembly elections held between 2008 and 2011. Within the Duma, United Russia faced few political obstacles, thanks to a constitutional majority and conspicuously little opposition from the other parties represented: A Just Russia, the Communist Party of the Russian Federation, and the Liberal Democratic Party of the Russian Federation. In fact, March (2012, 241) observes that interparty politics among parties represented in the Duma appeared surprisingly tranquil during this period, especially given that the Russian economy suffered from one of the severest collapses of any country in the Organization for Economic Cooperation and Development: a 7.9 percent drop in GDP in 2009. For him, this outcome is surprising because the three parliamentary parties besides United Russia claimed to be genuine opposition parties, possessed real voters, real funding, and real elected representatives, and yet not one used the post-2008 economic crisis in Russia to challenge the regime.[16] Of course, Russia's 2011 parliamentary elections dramatically altered Russia's political landscape: United Russia's vote share of 49 percent constituted a 15-percentage point decrease when compared to its performance in 2007. More startling were the unanticipated and large public protests as Russian citizens challenged the legitimacy of the election results that allowed United Russia to keep its majority in the Duma. Popular dissatisfaction with United Russia specifically featured prominently in both the election campaign and the protests that followed. Most notable was the labeling of United Russia as "the party of swindlers and thieves" by the anticorruption activist Alexei Navalny in February 2011.[17]

Looking at United Russia's 2011 list reveals substantial changes in its composition relative to the previous elections. In 2011, the number of governors on United Russia's list dropped (from 65 to 53). So too did the average tenure of Russia's governors. In 2007, the mean gubernatorial tenure was 87 months, making the start of the average governor's term well before the 2005 cessation of gubernatorial elections. In 2011, the mean tenure was under 73 months, putting the average governor's first month in office well into the appointment period. Thus, while governors' tenures still varied, the institutionalization of the appointment system dramatically reduced the number of governors who had won elections themselves and who had held office during more competitive national contests. Although an analysis of the correlates of candidate selection is a separate question and beyond the scope of this chapter, it is notable that, out of the ten overachievers identified in figure 6.2, governors from only three of these regions landed on United Russia's 2011 list. All three regions were republics: Ingushetia, Karachayevo-Cherkessia, and Komi.[18] In none of these cases, however, was the governor the same as in 2007. This pattern suggests that United Russia's leadership doubled down on the use of large ethnic regions in 2011 by adding republics that had emerged as overachievers in 2007. Meanwhile, the Kremlin's willingness to replace the sitting governors in these three regions suggests a belief that an appointed governor could assume control of these existing regional networks.[19]

TABLE 6.2. Correlates of regional support for United Russia in 2011

	Equation 1	Equation 2
Off 2011 List	−0.23	−2.13
	(1.86)	(2.93)
Tenure, 2011	1.42E-3	−6.16E-3
	(0.02)	(0.02)
Off 2011 List X Tenure, 2011	—	0.03
		(0.03)
Vote for Medvedev, 2008	1.13*	1.12*
	(0.16)	(0.16)
Regional Democracy Index, 2006–2010	−0.65*	−0.63*
	(0.19)	(0.19)
Percent non-Russian, 2010	0.10	0.10
	(0.06)	(0.06)
Percent with higher education, 2010	0.05	0.07
	(0.21)	(0.21)
Change in real income (2011–2007)	0.03	0.04
	(0.15)	(0.15)
Change in regional unemployment (2011–2007)	−0.64	−0.61
	(0.41)	(0.41)
Percent Rural, 2011	0.10	0.10
	(0.10)	(0.10)
Constant	−6.94	−6.50
	(14.23)	(14.22)
R^2	0.81	0.81
N	82	82

Note: Coefficients are unstandardized while the numbers in parentheses are standard errors.
* indicates significance at the .05 level or better. All tests are two-tailed.

Table 6.2 again uses robust regression analysis to estimate United Russia's regional vote share in 2011 using two models that closely resemble those in table 6.1. As before, the first equation tests only the conventional locomotive hypothesis, while the second tests it alongside the gubernatorial vulnerability hypothesis, which again relies on an interaction term that multiplies gubernatorial tenures and a dichotomous variable where a score of one indicates that a governor was left off the ruling party's list in 2011. As in table 6.1, the components of the interaction term are included in the equation, as are updated measures controlling for presidential coattails (i.e., Medvedev's regional vote shares in 2008), regime type, economic conditions, and differences in regional demography.

Once again, tenure and the dummy variable for the conventional locomotive hypothesis are not statistically significant in the first specification.[20] The only two variables correlated with regional support for United Russia in 2011 (both at the .001 level for two-tailed tests) are Medvedev's vote share in 2008 and the region's democracy scores from 2006 to 2010. Looking at the unstandardized coefficients, the model predicts a greater than 1 percent increase in United Russia's vote share for each 1 percent increase in Medvedev's regional vote share in 2008, all else being equal. A one-point increase in the Petrov-Titkov democracy index is associated with a decline of a little more than 0.6 percent in United Russia's regional vote share, all else being equal. Neither the percentage of non-Russians in the regions nor changes in real income since the previous elections reach standard levels of significance in 2011. In other words, ethnic composition and economic performance failed to influence cross-regional variation in United Russia's 2011 vote shares when controlling for regional support for Medvedev in 2008 and regional regime type. Equation 2 reveals that neither the dichotomous variable estimating the conventional locomotive hypothesis nor the interaction between gubernatorial tenure and list exclusion prove statistically significant in 2011. As expected, conventional locomotives fail to matter in 2011, while governors left off the United Russia's 2011 list failed to compensate for their exclusion by delivering votes.

Taken together, tables 6.1 and 6.2 reveal that the electoral payoffs from the practice of locomotives came from motivating regional elites with electoral experience to deliver votes. While a conventional view of this practice is to focus on those governors who made United Russia's list, table 6.1 reveals that an important part of the dynamic involves the behavior of governors left off the list, since empirical support for the conventional locomotive hypothesis in 2007 emerges only when one controls for the gubernatorial vulnerability hypothesis. In addition, neither dynamic significantly influences United Russia's regional vote shares during the 2011 Duma elections, most likely because governors experienced with delivering votes had been removed from office.

A Closer Look at United Russia's Narrow 2011 Majority

Although the 2003 and 2007 legislative elections may be interpreted as consolidating United Russia's position in Russian politics, the 2011 elections provided the first real test of the party's resilience—and United Russia passed. It won 49 percent of the vote, which translated into a bare majority of seats. While the performance may have relied on as many as 15 million fraudulent votes (Lyubarev 2012, 4), such estimates merely confirm United Russia's status as the ruling party in an electoral authoritarian regime, one where incumbents win elections to stay in power, at least in part, by stealing votes. In other words, United Russia lived up to expectations: It tilted the playing field as much as it needed to win.

Given the previous analysis, however, one might conclude that Russia's PR-only rules played no role in this outcome or, worse, worked against the party. However, in separate work, Aidan Klein and I investigate whether experiences with the PR-only rules in 2007 encouraged regional actors to the deliver votes in United Russia's direction in 2011 (Klein and Moraski 2020). Specifically, we contend that regions that benefited from PR-only rules in 2007 with greater legislative representation via the ruling party than they possessed in the 2003 elections, which were governed by the mixed-member system, were more likely to deliver votes in United Russia's direction in 2011. We find support for this hypothesis. Since the variables used in that article differ somewhat from those used in this chapter, I re-run the robust regression model presented above in table 6.2 while adding the primary explanatory variable from the analysis with Aidan Klein: the percent change in United Russia deputies between 2003 and 2007 per region.

Table 6.3 presents the results. The models confirm that the electoral system effect identified by Klein and Moraski (2020) also holds, if more modestly, in this analysis: United Russia's regional vote share in 2011 is higher in regions that experienced an increase in the number of United Russia deputies in 2007 (i.e., under the first PR-only election) relative to 2003. The effect is significant at the .10 level for a two-tailed test.[21] The effect is slightly better in the reduced model (equation 2), which

TABLE 6.3. Correlates of regional support for United Russia in 2011 with change in regional representation added

	Equation 1	Equation 2
Percent change in United Russia deputies (2007–2003)	1.54+	1.50+
	(0.91)	(0.81)
Off 2011 List	−1.09	—
	(2.98)	
Tenure, 2011	−9.82E-3	—
	(0.02)	
Off 2011 List X Tenure, 2011	0.02	—
	(0.03)	
Vote for Medvedev, 2008	1.08*	1.10*
	(0.16)	(0.15)
Regional Democracy Index, 2006–2010	−0.72*	−0.71*
	(0.20)	(0.18)
Percent non-Russian, 2010	0.11+	0.12*
	(0.06)	(0.05)
Percent with higher education, 2010	0.07	—
	(0.20)	
Change in real income (2011–2007)	7.88E-3	—
	(0.15)	
Change in regional unemployment (2011–2007)	−0.57	−.55+
	(0.40)	(0.30)
Percent rural, 2011	0.08	0.06
	(0.09)	(0.08)
Constant	−4.02	−6.00
	(13.99)	(12.44)
R^2	0.82	0.84
N	82	83

Note: Coefficients are unstandardized while the numbers in parentheses are standard errors.
+ indicates significance at the .10 level. * indicates significance at the .05 level or better. All tests are two-tailed.

excludes the most insignificant variables from equation 1. Note that the amount of variance explained in equation 2 also increases, likely because of the addition of a previously excluded case that had missing data for a variable that is not included in the second specification. On the whole, the models yield support for the assertion that the Russia's PR electoral system helped United Russia squeak out enough votes during the 2011 elections to receive a bare majority of seats in the Duma.

Conclusion

This chapter examines the Russian practice of placing regional governors on the ruling party's regional sub-list, a practice that was noted (but not explored) in chapter 3. While spillover effects across levels of government are not new, most works investigate them in democratic settings, as the role of electoral manipulation in more authoritarian contexts complicates matters. In Russia, the regime relies on regional officials, such as governors, to deliver votes for its preferred presidential candidate and party. Although regional politicians may deploy a variety of administrative resources to demonstrate their utility, this chapter evaluates the effectiveness of a national-level electoral practice that binds governors explicitly to the ruling party: gubernatorial locomotives.

The practice of locomotives expanded dramatically in 2007 following Russia's shift to appointed governors and the adoption of an entirely closed-list PR electoral system. This development is notable given Huntington's (1968, 89) contention that the "only potential rival to the party as the distinctive institution of the modern polity is federalism." While the sovereignty of the political units composing the Russian Federation has been reined in substantially by the Putin regime, this process has not merely coincided with the rise of United Russia, as this chapter illustrates; it has been used to complement and bolster the party's electoral performance in national legislative elections. These developments, combined with the manipulation of Russia's legislative electoral system, constitute rule changes analogous to those Schedler (2006) identifies as foundational to the nested game of electoral authoritarianism. Moreover, while the conventional wisdom holds that the expansion of gubernatorial locomotives between 2003 and 2007 bolstered the ruling party's regional vote shares, the preceding analysis reveals that regions where long-serving governors were left off United Russia's 2007 list performed as well as regions where the conventional practice was used. This dynamic appears to reflect the leverage that the Kremlin possessed over governors thanks to the replacement of direct gubernatorial elections with a system of presidential appointments.

In addition to varying across space, the dynamics of locomotive effects on United Russia's electoral performance varied over time. By 2011, the institutionalization of the appointment system largely removed the variation in electoral experience that had permitted some governors left off the party's list in 2007 to distinguish themselves. Thus, by 2011, the synergistic relationship between tenure in office and list exclusion disappears. The outcome may have even indicated a loss in the utility of the appointment system, which has since been eliminated, making the PR system less effective and more of a liability. I return to this topic in the book's conclusion.

This chapter also finds that the proregime effects of Russia's PR-only electoral system did not rest solely on the existence of well-established governors in the regions and the stick of gubernatorial replacement. As Klein and Moraski (2020) contend, the shift from a mixed electoral system to PR-only also offered a carrot to regional actors: regions that delivered more votes in the ruling party's direction were allocated more seats from United Russia's list. This dynamic should have incentivized the delivery of votes for United Russia in 2011 out of a desire to increase regional levels of representation given the results of the 2007 Duma elections. Adding this possibility to the analysis of United Russia's performance in the 2011 Duma elections finds modest support and helps to explain United Russia's slim 2011 majority, which is no small contribution. Thus, while the Kremlin is clearly using both the ruling party and the country's federal institutions to organize and control political participation in Russia—as Huntington (1968) might expect—changes to the latter worked together with the adoption of PR rules to establish and preserve the electoral position of the former.

The Consequences of Party Nominations in Ukraine

Ukraine's first proportional representation (PR)–only elections were held in the aftermath of an electoral revolution that was largely seen as liberalizing, if not democratizing, the country's political system (Aslund and McFaul 2006; Bunce and Wolchik 2011; D'Anieri 2005; McFaul 2007; McFaul and Youngs 2013; Wilson 2005). In this context, the pro-presidential party Our Ukraine struggled to capitalize on its new position.[1] Both during and after the 2006 elections, Our Ukraine faced stiff competition from a former ally, the Tymoshenko Bloc, as well as from the Party of Regions. In other words, Our Ukraine's status differed markedly from that of United Russia.

As chapter 2 notes, Russia's first PR-only elections were held during an important juncture in the authoritarian regime's development: the presidential transition from one handpicked successor to another. The ruling party, United Russia, dominated those elections and faced no formidable challenges within the resulting legislature. In the nomenclature of many observers of Russian politics, United Russia emerged as the latest and most successful "party of power."[2] While the country witnessed several events in the years following the 2007 Duma elections that would have tested party discipline in a more competitive setting (e.g., economic recession and a natural disaster in the form of widespread wildfires in 2010), United Russia faced little systemic opposition, as other parliamentary parties proved conspicuously compliant (Hutcheson 2013; March 2012).

As chapters 3–5 make clear, differences between Russia and Ukraine complicate the comparative analysis. Thus, while competitive politics in Ukraine may be a good juxtaposition to Russia's authoritarian regime when seeking to identify commonalities across how parties adapt to new electoral systems, it is far from a perfect comparison, since we cannot know with certainty whether the differences identified across the two countries are products of differences in regime type or of other country-specific explanations, particularly Russia's federal institutions. Nevertheless, I take the position that, while Russia's federal framework provided valuable opportunities for delivering more votes in United Russia's direction (see chapter 6), the practices under investigation attest more to the authoritarian nature of the regime than to the presence of federalism in Russia. For example, the potency of locomotives appears to have hinged on the Kremlin's decision to temporarily cease gubernatorial elections. Indeed, one might contend that the cessation of gubernatorial elections actually eliminated a critical difference between Russia's federal system and Ukraine's unitary system, where governors have also been appointed.[3]

Despite this convergence, it was rare to see sitting governors serve on a party list during Ukraine's PR-only experiment. Of Ukraine's 27 regions, including the two cities of special status (Kyiv and Sevastopol), only three sitting regional chief executives were legislative candidates during the 2006 Verkhovna Rada elections: Bul'ba of Poltava and Tsushko of Odesa were ranked 11th and 12th on the Socialist Party's list, while Zeinalov of Kirovohrad was a modest 65th on Our Ukraine's list.[4] As a result, this chapter does not investigate gubernatorial list placement and party consolidation in Ukraine. Instead, it focuses more directly on questions of party discipline and party cohesion, which were two major concerns for Ukrainian parties prior to the move to PR-only rules.

To explore the incidental effects of party nominations in Ukraine, this chapter examines whether Our Ukraine's position was helped or hindered by the tactics it pursued while navigating the move to PR-only rules. Since an emphasis on co-opting formerly unaffiliated deputies could reasonably be interpreted as an attempt to broaden Our Ukraine's political base, and thus its electoral prospects, I begin there. As outlined in chapter 4, this tactic also introduces risks to party discipline. While existing research has noted Our Ukraine's difficulties in this regard following the 2006 Rada elections (e.g., D'Anieri 2007), those challenges have not been linked, theoretically or empirically, to the tactics that Our Ukraine used to navigate the new PR-only electoral system. With that in mind, this chapter asks: Among those nominated by Our Ukraine during the 2006 elections, which deputies were more likely to defect from the party following the elections?

From Electoral Motives to Party Discipline

In chapter 4, I examined the likelihood of two of Ukraine's largest parties, Our Ukraine and the Party of Regions, to use the first PR-only elections to co-opt deputies who had not previously affiliated with them. The two parties are an interesting pair because of their relationships with the two candidates who contested the second round of the 2004 presidential election in Ukraine, the outcome of which spawned the Orange Revolution. It is notable that Viktor Yushchenko went on to become Ukraine's president, winning a repeat of the second round of the 2004 presidential election. As a result, Our Ukraine emerged as a pro-presidential party going into the 2006 legislative elections, the first to be held under PR-only rules.

The analysis in chapter 4 finds that Our Ukraine did co-opt some Party of Regions members by nominating them as candidates in 2006. However, deputies who were Party of Regions members in 2002 received significantly worse ranks than deputies who were members of Our Ukraine in 2002. In contrast, independents and deputies who were members of parties other than the Party of Regions (or Our Ukraine) in 2006 received positions on Our Ukraine's 2006 list that were on par with deputies who had been Our Ukraine members in 2002. Perhaps more striking, deputies nominated by For a United Ukraine— the 2002 electoral coalition to which Party of Regions members often belonged—actually received significantly better list positions than 2002 Our Ukraine nominees. Taken together, these findings suggest that Our Ukraine's leadership was willing to pay a reasonably high price for some previously unaffiliated deputies, ranking them as high or higher than previously affiliated deputies. However, this approach did not extend to those deputies who could be understood as the riskiest investments: those more committed to the Party of Regions.

While a prevailing view in the study of legislative behavior is that parties and deputies care intensely about reelection, scholars also realize that legislators are not single-minded individuals: "If reelection is not at risk, [legislators] are free to pursue other goals, including enacting their own visions of good public policy or achieving influence" within the legislature (Arnold 1990, 5). With this point in mind, this chapter changes its focus away from candidate nominations (i.e., decisions that are more likely to be driven by electoral motives) to the study of how those decisions affect legislative behavior and thus the development of parties as legislative organizations. Specifically, this chapter investigates which incumbent deputies, among those nominated by Our Ukraine during the 2006 elections, were more likely to defect from the party following the elections.

The notion that elected deputies nominated by one party who had previously competed under another party's banner will be more likely to break party discipline than deputies who were not recently co-opted (and, presumably, are more ideologically inclined toward the party in question) is commonsensical. Indeed, the foundational literature on legislative politics and political parties often begins with the observation that parties shape how legislatures are organized (e.g., Aldrich 1995; Cox and McCubbins 1993), determine the prospects for majority or coalition governments, and are responsible for holding governments to account (e.g., Dodd 1976; Laver and Schofield 1990; Schofield and Sened 2006). This literature also outlines the logic underpinning a party's desire to preserve disciplined voting among those deputies it nominates. As Laver and Shepsle (1996, 24) point out:

> If individual party politicians were permitted to pursue their own private desires at every opportunity, then their party's reputation in the wider political process would constantly be at risk. People would not know what the party stood for, so that voters, interest groups, and others who might see the party as acting on their behalf would have nothing to rely on. As a consequence, the party would be severely hampered in its ability to attract support.

Although Laver and Shepsle use this logic to justify an assumption of strong party discipline in established parliamentary democracies, which in turn facilitates their analysis of government formation, the assumption does not hold in countries with weakly institutionalized parties (and neither would the authors expect it to). As outlined in chapter 2, a lack of party discipline, stemming in part from the election of deputies competing as independents, plagued legislative politics in Ukraine prior to the adoption of PR-only rules. While one might have hoped that the electoral system change would ameliorate the situation, there are grounds for skepticism. For example, it is possible that, in the short-term at least, party decisions about whom to nominate may have undermined this outcome. Specifically, a decision to expand the party's electoral appeal by nominating previously unaffiliated deputies risks relying on candidates who will more likely prove disloyal when serving as party deputies in the months and years to come.

While party decisions to award these deputies with better list ranks might be understood as an attempt to buy the politicians' loyalty by addressing their electoral concerns, the prospects for defection increase as the question of electoral uncertainty associated with the move from one electoral system to another recedes and the politicians' personal, policy, and prior ideological motives resurface once they are in office. Just as periods of electoral system change may introduce significant amounts of electoral uncertainty (Andrews and Jackman 2005), politicians should feel more comfortable with the new system once they have had an opportunity to observe how the rules interact with voters' party preferences and the number of parties competing. Put differently, once politicians have been elected to office, they should be more confident in their abilities to successfully navigate the new system in place. As a result, those who behaved opportunistically during the period of uncertainty that accompanied the implementation of new electoral rules will likely be less bound by the electoral motive after that uncertainty dissipates.

Like the decision to co-opt previously unaffiliated deputies, the decision to improve on, or at least preserve, a party's organizational presence by nominating district deputies may undermine discipline among a party's legislative delegation. In theory, the move from district contests, which are more candidate-centered, to closed-list PR rules could improve party discipline among legislators, since their reelection prospects in future contests will depend on internal party decisions about list placement (see, e.g., Carey 2007). In practice, however, this outcome is far from guaranteed. For example, Tavits's (2009) analysis of legislative voting in five European democracies finds that politicians with stronger local ties are more likely to emerge as legislative mavericks—that is, they are more likely to violate party discipline than other deputies. Similarly, Olivella and Tavits's (2014) study of legislative voting behavior in Hungary finds that, while legislators who go from being elected under PR rules to being elected in single-member-district (SMD) contests are, as expected, more likely to subsequently defect from the party line, the change from a district mandate to a party list mandate fails to significantly influence the legislators' voting behavior. The former district deputies continue to be more independent-minded.

Drawing on these insights, I expect deputies nominated by Our Ukraine in 2002 to be significantly less likely to defect from the party line compared to those not affiliated with the party in 2002 but co-opted by it in 2006. To the extent that deputies who were affiliated with Our Ukraine during the 2002 elections defected from it after the 2006 elections, any attempt by the party to renominate these deputies as a way to preserve cohesion can be viewed as falling short of the mark. Likewise, if co-opted deputies prove more likely to have defected than deputies who had already affiliated with the party in 2002, then attempts to expand the candidate pool in 2006 may be interpreted as having not been worth the risk. I also expect that, all else being equal, former district deputies will be more likely to defect than former list deputies.

The 2006 Rada Elections and Our Ukraine's Support for Yanukovych

Although Ukraine's Orange Revolution led to widespread optimism that the country might be on the path toward consolidating a democratic political regime, political polarization and institutional gridlock dashed the hopes of Ukrainian citizens and foreign observers alike (Allina-Pisano 2010; Berenson 2010; D'Anieri 2010). In the March 2006 Rada elections, the two parties most closely identified with the Orange Revolution—Our Ukraine and the Tymoshenko Bloc—outpolled the Party of Regions, but neither attained a decisive victory. In fact, it was the Party of Regions that received the largest share of the popular vote, with more than 32 percent. Second place went to the Tymoshenko Bloc, which garnered more than 22 percent, leaving Our Ukraine in a distant third with slightly less than 14 percent. The only other parties to pass Ukraine's 3 percent legal threshold in place at the time were the Socialist Party of Ukraine (5.7 percent) and the Communist Party of Ukraine (3.7 percent) (Official Website of Ukraine's Central Election Commission, www.cvk.gov.ua). According to Kuzio (2006, 479), not only was Our

Ukraine's share of the vote a sizable drop from the 23 percent received in 2002; Our Ukraine's inability to hold on to coalition members who had joined the bloc in 2002 meant that the party was less centrist and less "nation-democratic" than it was previously.[5] Meanwhile, the rising fortunes of the Tymoshenko Bloc, which was historically more combative in its dealings with the former president, Leonid Kuchma, contributed to Ukraine's political polarization (Kuzio 2006, 480).

These election results make it difficult to contend that the co-optation of formerly unaffiliated deputies helped Our Ukraine's electoral performance in 2006. While it is plausible that Our Ukraine simply failed to co-opt deputies who could effectively drive votes in Our Ukraine's direction, it is also not likely that a different decision—that is, a decision to emphasize cohesion over co-optation—would have improved the party's electoral prospects.[6] Rather, the outcome seems to reflect the competitive nature of Ukraine's electoral environment at the time, which granted unaffiliated deputies a wide range of party options, including the opportunity to join a rival but ideologically proximate organization: the Tymoshenko Bloc.

As D'Anieri (2019, 141) emphasizes, the political alliance between Yushchenko and Tymoshenko leading into Ukraine's 2004 presidential election rested on shaky ground. While Tymoshenko agreed to back Yushchenko in exchange for the post of prime minister, the decision also reflected a fear that the Kuchma regime would divide and conquer the opposition, thereby ensuring a Yanukovych victory. However, once this outcome had been averted, the rivalry between Tymoshenko and Yushchenko not only reemerged; it was exacerbated by the 2004 constitutional compromise that granted Ukraine's prime minister the power to appoint some cabinet ministers. As the months progressed, institutional divisions within the executive fueled competition over economic assets and spurred accusations of corruption. In September 2005, Yushchenko dismissed Tymoshenko as prime minister with the two sides "at barely disguised war with one another" (D'Anieri 2019, 142). Under these conditions, it is not surprising to learn that the Tymoshenko Bloc managed not only to draw a couple of Our Ukraine deputies into its ranks but also to attract a large number of independents and self-nominated deputies to its 2006 list (see the analyses of district deputy list placement in chapters 2 and 4).

Our Ukraine was not the only coalition from 2002 to compete with a former ally in 2006. The Party of Regions was forced to contend with Lytvyn's People's Bloc (discussed in chapters 2 and 4), as well as Labor Ukraine and the People's Democratic Party, both of which were part of For a United Ukraine in 2002. None of these parties passed the legal threshold in 2006, however.[7] Looking at the Lytvyn Bloc in particular, it is evident that the Party of Regions succeeded for the most part in preserving ties with Party of Regions members, losing only two district deputies to the Lytvyn Bloc. The Party of Regions fared less well when it came to holding on to deputies who had merely been nominated by For a United Ukraine in 2002, as 18 of these district deputies competed on the list of the Lytvyn Bloc in 2006. Thus, if one were to contend that the tactic of cohesion worked to the electoral benefit of the Party of Regions, the argument would likely rest on the electoral shortcomings of the Lytvyn Bloc, which failed to pass a relatively low legal threshold of 3 percent.

For D'Anieri (2007, 44), the 2006 election results provide little cause to expect parties to consolidate and monopolize the electoral arena in Ukraine. While the new electoral system was certainly intended as a crucial step in establishing a lasting national party system, there were reasons to doubt the system's ability to overcome the legacy of ad hoc alliances and personal resources that had defined Ukrainian elections since independence. D'Anieri points to the difficulty that Ukrainian parties encountered when forming a governing coalition following the elections as evidence supporting his position that Ukraine's party system would remain unstable, though his reasoning focuses primarily on the legal threshold: with each party reaching 3 percent receiving at least 13 seats in parliament, "the temptation to abandon parties rather than invest in them will remain" (D'Anieri 2007, 247).

Government formation in Ukraine following the 2006 elections differed from government formation after previous elections. Prior to 2006, Ukraine's president appointed the prime minister, who was merely confirmed by parliament. In addition, the president's approval was needed for ministerial appointments, and the president could dismiss ministers. Under the new constitutional arrangement, which was agreed to as part of the deal to repeat the second round of Ukraine's 2004 presidential election, the president would still formally nominate the prime minister, but that nomination was to take place in consultation with the ruling majority in parliament. Since the new system also gave parliament the power to confirm the prime minister, the parliamentary majority was, in practice, given control over who the new prime minister would be (D'Anieri 2007, 244–45). Given this change and the level of political polarization in Ukraine at the time, the process of government formation serves as a critical moment in Ukraine's post-Orange politics, and the vote for Ukraine's new prime minister provides a special opportunity for considering the consequences of the decisions that the major parties made while constructing their 2006 party lists.

With no clear winner in the March 2006 Rada elections, Ukraine's major parties set out to establish a majority coalition. The largest, the Party of Regions, could either join forces with the Communists and Socialists or put differences aside and work with Our Ukraine. Meanwhile, Our Ukraine's options were working with the Party of Regions or forming a coalition with the Tymoshenko Bloc and the Socialist Party. Our Ukraine's position was complicated further by internal divisions: business interests within the party supported a coalition with the Party of Regions betting that the resulting government would prove to be an advocate for big business. Others within the party viewed the proposal as a "betrayal of the Maidan"—a reference to Independence Square in Kyiv where the Orange Revolution began (Wolowski 2008, 27).

In June 2006, a reunited Orange coalition emerged that included Our Ukraine, the Tymoshenko Bloc, and the Socialist Party. Under this arrangement, Tymoshenko was expected to become prime minister; however, the Socialists withdrew before the coalition could create a government because of Our Ukraine's unwillingness to accept the Socialists' choice for parliamentary speaker. The withdrawal of the Socialists created an opportunity for the Party of Regions, which joined with Socialists and the Communists to form an "anti-crisis" coalition.[8] The resulting coalition of the Party of Regions, the Socialists, and the Communists included 240 of the 450 deputies, which was enough for Yanukovych to become prime minister without having to compromise with Our Ukraine.[9] Officially, then, Our Ukraine opposed the governing coalition. However, when the vote for prime minister was finally held, 30 out of Our Ukraine's 80 deputies broke with the party and backed Yanukovych's candidacy (Kuzio 2006, 482–83).

Given these developments, I use the vote on Yanukovych's nomination for prime minister as an opportunity to examine the consequences of the list decisions that Our Ukraine made while navigating the move from a mixed-member electoral system to the PR-only rules that governed the 2006 elections. As a reminder, chapter 4 uses the nomination of deputies previously not affiliated with Our Ukraine as an indicator of the party's willingness to co-opt a new cadre of experienced, but possibly unreliable, members. With that in mind, the following analysis of the parliamentary vote for Yanukovych narrows the lens to only those members of Our Ukraine at the time of the vote (August 4, 2006) who also served in the Rada's Fourth Convocation (2002–2006). These conditions reduce the number of deputies under investigation to 42.

To examine the variation in the willingness of these 42 members of Our Ukraine's legislative faction to toe the party line and oppose Yanukovych's nomination as prime minister, the dependent variable is a dichotomous variable where a score of one indicates that the deputy in question voted in favor of Yanukovych's nomination and a score of zero indicates that a deputy voted against, abstained, did not vote, or was absent.[10] In other words, the higher value signals defection. To the extent the characteristics that determined whether Our Ukraine would place deputies from the Fourth Rada on its list in 2006 (e.g., having been nominated by Our Ukraine in 2002) are negatively correlated with this dependent variable, one can contend that the traits favored party loyalty and that the decision to nominate deputies with such characteristics was a successful utilization of list placement in terms of maintaining party cohesion. By contrast, if deputies who were affiliated with Our Ukraine during the 2002 elections defected, then the party's presumed attempt to nominate these deputies in 2006 as a way to preserve cohesion following the elections fell short of the mark. Similarly, if co-opted deputies were significantly more likely to defect compared to deputies who had already affiliated with the party in 2002, then the risks that one might associate with attempts to increase the pool of candidates in 2006—presumably out of a desire to improve the party's electoral prospects—will have come home to roost.

As these dynamics suggest, it is challenging to contend with much confidence that every observed effect reflects good (or bad) decision-making on the party's part. To begin making the case, one must control for other factors that might explain defection. Since the same factors also may have determined the deputies' list placements, instrumental variable analysis would be the preferred method of analysis. However, since the small number of cases under investigation precludes this option, I instead employ logistic regression analysis and construct three models: one baseline model without indicators of the deputies' prior affiliations with Our Ukraine, a second model that adds whether the deputies were nominated by Our Ukraine or were Our Ukraine party members in 2002, and a third model that also controls for the deputies' ranks on Our Ukraine's 2006 list. This approach provides one means of determining whether adding, say, the deputies' ranks on Our Ukraine's 2006 list affects the likelihood of defection (with, for example, better ranked candidates less likely to defect) or alters the performance of other variables in the equation. The independent variables composing the baseline model resemble those used in chapter 4: a dichotomous variable for a 2002 nomination by Our Ukraine; a second for a 2002 membership in Our Ukraine; a third dichotomous variable capturing prior incumbency (i.e., deputies in the Fourth Convocation who had served in the Third Convocation); a fourth dichotomous variable indicating that a deputy held a position of leadership in the Rada's Fourth Convocation; the number of factions a deputy had joined prior to the start of the campaign for the 2006 elections; and a final dummy variable for legislative mandate with a score of one indicating that the deputy in question was a district deputy (with a zero signifying a list deputy).

Before presenting the analysis, it is worth noting that party leaders going into the 2006 Rada elections may have actually had cause to believe that party discipline would be higher in the Fifth Convocation than it had been previously. The primary reason for this expectation was the adoption of the "imperative mandate," which also was adopted as part of the agreement to repeat the second round of Ukraine's 2004 presidential election. As D'Anieri (2007, 187) notes, under the imperative mandate, seats won via proportional representation (PR) belong to the party rather than to the individual deputy, so if a deputy leaves the party, she also loses her seat. D'Anieri (2007, 247) describes the imperative mandate as a "logical extension of proportional representation" because, at least in theory, party leaders should be in the position to more reliably deliver votes that they promise, which will in turn facilitate the formation of governing coalitions and allow other deals to be struck. In practice, however, the anticipated effects of the imperative mandate were less certain, since it did not require deputies to vote the party line on every bill and since, as noted, deputies could keep their seats as long as they did not formally leave the party. D'Anieri (2007, 248) points to voting for Yanukovych as prime minister as a case in point: "Having engineered a new coalition to take control of parliament, the Party of Regions found it difficult to assemble sufficient votes in that coalition to elect Yanukovych prime minister, because several Socialist deputies did not follow their leader, Moroz, when he switched his support from Yushchenko to Yanukovych." For purposes of the current analysis, the notion that Socialist Party discipline was not guaranteed highlights the degree to which party discipline within Our Ukraine could have blocked Yanukovych's rise, making the defections from Our Ukraine in favor of Yanukovych all the more important to the final outcome.

Table 7.1 presents the results of a reduced model analyzing voting for Yanukovych as prime minister, one that leaves out the primary variables of interest: prior affiliation with Our Ukraine and rank on Our Ukraine's 2006 list. This model provides a comparative baseline for the more fully specified models presented in table 7.2. The first equation in table 7.2 adds the dichotomous variables for a 2002 Our Ukraine nomination and membership in Our Ukraine in 2002, which were intentionally left out of the baseline model presented in table 7.1. The second equation in table 7.2 includes these two variables and also adds the variable indicating a deputy's rank on Our Ukraine's party list. For the most part, I am agnostic about the direction of the effect of rank. On the one hand, better-placed deputies may have received those placements precisely because they were party loyalists. On the other, since Our Ukraine used list construction to co-opt previously unaffiliated deputies, higher list placement may have been awarded to deputies with questionable levels of party loyalty, possibly out of a hope that better placement would translate into greater loyalty. However, given their ability to ascertain higher list ranks, better-placed deputies might feel more empowered to defy the party on critical votes. In other words, even when controlling for factors that influenced inclusion on Our Ukraine's party list, there are theoretical reasons for why better-ranked politicians might be more (or less) likely to violate party discipline in the period following the institution of PR rules.

TABLE 7.1. Correlates, excluding party variables, of votes in favor of Yanukovych as prime minister from 2002 deputies elected via Our Ukraine in 2006

	Odds ratio (p value)	95% Confidence interval	
Incumbent, 2002	4.025 (.115)	0.713	22.710
Rada or committee leader, 2002–2006	0.209 (.068)	0.039	1.123
Number of factions prior to July 7, 2005	**1.744 (.032)**	1.050	2.895
SMD deputy	1.474 (.625)	0.311	6.981
Constant	0.161 (.061)	0.024	1.091
Pseudo R^2	0.184		
Likelihood ratio χ^2 (significance)	10.06 (.038)		
Number of cases	42		

Note: Numbers in bold indicate significance at the .05 level for a two-tailed test.

Comparing tables 7.1 and 7.2 reveals that the addition of variables capturing previous ties to Our Ukraine and 2006 list rank improves the overall performance of the model, evidenced by higher pseudo-R^2s and more significant likelihood ratio χ^2s. Also, in the reduced model, only one variable significantly influences the likelihood of voting for Yanukovych: the number of factions that deputies belonged to in the previous convocation of the Rada. As would be expected, those deputies who belonged to more legislative factions were more likely to break from the party and vote in favor of Yanukovych. The effect is significant at the .05 level for a two-tailed test. Besides this variable, only the dichotomous variable indicating that a deputy held a leadership position in the previous parliament appears to have affected the likelihood of voting for Yanukovych. Those deputies who held such positions were almost five times less likely to support Yanukovych (1/.209 = 4.78) than other deputies, though the effect holds only at the .10 level for a two-tailed test.

As table 7.2 illustrates, adding the variables for prior affiliation with Our Ukraine to the model (equation 1) changes the findings in meaningful ways. First, of the 42 deputies, only one was a party member of Our Ukraine in 2002, and that deputy, Mikhailo Polyanchin, voted in favor of Yanukovych's candidacy for prime minister. Since this vote results in a value of zero for the corresponding variable and perfectly predicts a vote for Yanukovych when included in the model, the statistical software package STATA drops the observation, reducing the total number of observations to 41. With this change, and after one controls for a 2002 Our Ukraine nomination, the number of legislative factions that a deputy belonged to no longer matters. Instead, the only variable to attain significance at the .05 level for a two-tailed test is the dichotomous variable indicating that a deputy held a leadership position in the previous convocation of the Rada. In this specification, these deputies are eight times less likely to support Yanukovych compared to other deputies under investigation. Deputies who had longer affiliations with Our Ukraine, captured by a 2002 nomination, were also eight times less likely to vote for Yanukovych as prime minister, although the effect of this variable holds only at the .10 level for a two-tailed test. Interestingly, the first equation

TABLE 7.2. Correlates, including party variables, of votes in favor of Yanukovych as prime minister from 2002 deputies elected via Our Ukraine in 2006

	Equation 1		Equation 2	
	Odds ratio (p value)	95% Confidence interval	Odds ratio (p value)	95% Confidence interval
Our Ukraine rank, 2006	—		0.102 (.297)	0.989 1.074
Our Ukraine nomination, 2002	0.120 (.053)	0.014 1.031	**0.115 (.050)**	0.013 0.999
Our Ukraine member, 2002	—		—	
Incumbent, 2002	7.934 (.051)	0.993 63.361	**9.998 (.038)**	1.135 88.064
Rada or committee leader, 2002–2006	**0.122 (.043)**	0.016 0.933	0.219 (.182)	0.024 2.039
Number of factions prior to July 7, 2005	1.449 (.191)	0.831 2.527	1.522 (.159)	0.848 2.731
SMD deputy	0.525 (.534)	0.069 4.003	0.610 (.634)	0.080 4.677
Constant	1.052 (.973)	0.056 19.950	0.227 (.482)	0.004 14.113
Pseudo R^2	0.281		0.303	
Likelihood ratio χ^2 (significance)	14.79 (.011)		15.93 (.014)	
Number of cases	41		41	

in table 7.2 indicates that Our Ukraine legislators who were already incumbent deputies in 2002 were more likely to vote for Yanukovych as prime minister in 2006. While the effect is also only at the .10 level, it suggests that longer-serving legislators—all else being equal—were, if anything, more likely to defect from the party. Since the effect emerges while controlling for party affiliations, the outcome hints at a tendency for long-serving legislators to behave more like political survivors who recognize the importance of compromise.

Equation 2 in table 7.2 repeats the analysis once more, this time adding the control variable for list rank. With this modification, the impact of a 2002 Our Ukraine nomination increases, as does the effect of prior incumbency, both of which become significant at the .05 level for a two-tailed test. In other words, the second equation in table 7.2 suggests that 2006 deputies whom Our Ukraine had also nominated as candidates in 2002 were significantly less likely to vote for Yanukovych as prime minister compared to deputies nominated by the party for the first time in 2006. At the same time, deputies who were incumbents going into the 2002 elections and still in office after the 2006 elections continued to be more likely to defect from Our Ukraine on this issue compared to less experienced legislators. Under this latest specification, the effect of a prior parliamentary leadership position no longer proves significant. This outcome likely reflects the degree to which committee chairs and vice chairs in the previous Rada enjoyed better placements on Our Ukraine's 2006 list (see chapter 4) and the inclusion of list rank as an independent variable. Nevertheless, list rank itself proves insignificant. This finding suggests that list rank did not have a universal effect on Our Ukraine's deputies, which makes sense to the extent that it was used to reward party loyalists as well as co-opt previously unaffiliated deputies (see chapter 4). One notable null finding across all of the models is that district deputies were no more likely to defect during the vote compared to list deputies. This outcome, however, may simply reflect the question at hand (i.e., Who should become prime minister?), which is not one that will necessarily divide legislators on the basis of whether or not they see politics through a regional or local lens.

Looking deeper into the types of nominations among the 2006 Our Ukraine deputies under investigation, a couple of differences merit discussion. First, of the four deputies nominated by For a United Ukraine in 2002, three supported Yanukovych as prime minister. Of the ten deputies who were self-nominated or nominated by a party other than Our Ukraine or For a United Ukraine, five voted for Yanukovych. While these (unreported) results comport with expectations, the effects are not large enough to produce statistical significance when analyzed alongside the other variables included in the model.

In sum, the preceding analysis suggests that deputies nominated by Our Ukraine in 2002 were significantly less likely to defect from the party line—and support Yanukovych—than those not affiliated with the party in 2002 but co-opted by it in 2006. While we cannot know whether the deputies who were co-opted would have proven more loyal than those whom Our Ukraine did not nominate via its 2006 party list, the finding that those who were co-opted proved less disciplined than those who had already been affiliated with the party emphasizes the political risks of co-optation. From the perspective of party development, Our Ukraine's use of co-optation appears to have yielded few electoral benefits (discussed above) while failing to produce strong party discipline. By contrast, it is not surprising that support for Yanukovych's candidacy for prime minister in 2006 was nearly unanimous among Party of Region deputies: Of the 186 members, 184 voted yes, one did not vote, and another is recorded as absent (Official Web Portal of the Verkhovna Rada, http://rada.gov.ua). Not only did the party rely heavily on existing party members as candidates in the 2006 elections; the question is itself one largely destined to favor party discipline within the Party of Regions.

Of course party discipline matters more often than only when the composition of the government is at stake, and roll-call voting records are commonly used to determine the degree to which legislators toe the party line (e.g., Morgenstern 2003; Poole and Rosenthal 1985). However, in contexts such as Ukraine, roll-call voting data may prove to be unreliable (or even misleading) indicators of party unity. As Herron et al. (2019) highlight, Ukrainian media, civil society groups, and partisan actors have lamented the absenteeism of Ukraine's national legislators over the years and leveled allegations that the votes of absentee deputies are often cast by proxy even though parliamentary regulations and statutes do not permit such a practice.[11]

Although the practice of proxy voting in Ukraine means that one may need to take the results of the preceding analysis with a grain of salt, it is likely that the vote was early enough in the convocation and important enough to individual deputies to have reduced the likelihood of proxy voting in that case. Unfortunately, the practice raises serious concerns about any attempt to draw inferences about patterns of legislator behavior on the basis of more routine votes. To substantiate this point, Herron et al. (2019) capitalize on data from the Eighth Convocation of the Rada, which began after Ukraine's October 2014 parliamentary elections, the first to provide full registration records that could be used to evaluate the votes of each deputy alongside whether she was personally present. Their analysis not only documents the existence of proxy voting; it also reveals that the practice presents a false sense of party cohesion: "[G]overning parties generally use it as a tool to garner affirmative votes and opposition parties use it, albeit less frequently, to oppose legislation" (Herron et al. 2019, 56).

While party discipline captures the degree to which legislators affiliated with a party regularly accept and enact the commands of the party leadership (Özbudun 1970, 305), Giollabhuí (2013, 595) observes that "a high level of resignations, defections, splits and, in the worst case, the complete breakdown or collapse of the party" also signal low levels of party cohesion. With this point in mind, and the validity of roll-call voting records being called into question, the remainder of this chapter considers two alternative indicators of party cohesion. First, since the practice of legislators changing party factions not only plagued Ukrainian politics but also partially motivated the move to the closed-list PR-only system (see chapters 2 and 4), changes in faction membership warrant particular attention.

Second, the legality of faction defections in the Rada became a source of contention in the spring of 2007, with President Yushchenko asserting that Yanukovych's ruling coalition was seeking to enhance its legislative influence by pursuing defectors from the opposition, including the president's party. In April 2007, arguing that Ukraine's revised constitution permits only factions, and not individual deputies, from changing sides, Yushchenko called for new parliamentary elections (*BBC News* 2007; D'Anieri 2019, 144). Despite these developments, there were no instances of defection, such as those observed in the previous convocation, among the 42 Our Ukraine deputies under investigation. According to the Rada's online archive (Official Web Portal of the Verkhovna Rada, http://rada.gov.ua), only two of the 42 deputies left Our Ukraine's faction during the period in question: Yurii Orobets, who died in a car accident in October 2006 ("Zaginuv Narodnii Deputat Yurii Orobets" 2006), and Roman Zvarich, who left the Rada to become the minister of justice in September 2006 ("Zvarich Roman" n.d.).

Given this lack of variation and the fact that an *absence* of legislative defectors from a party's faction signifies at best a minimal level of cohesion, I consider a second, more stringent indicator of party cohesion, one that again emerges from the particularities of Ukrainian politics at the time: the level of legislative support for President Yushchenko's decree calling for new elections. After some discussion about the decree's constitutionality, a path for dissolution was identified in May 2007: new elections would be necessary if the composition of the 450-member Rada fell below 300 members. To fulfill this stipulation, 169 opposition deputies were expected to submit their resignations on June 1. To prevent the replacement of those who resigned with other candidates farther down on their party lists, both Our Ukraine and the Tymoshenko Bloc adopted resolutions to invalidate their 2006 party lists en masse. On June 12, 2007, however, the parliamentary speaker, Oleksandr Moroz, announced that the Verkhovna Rada had received only 79 reliable statements of resignation, which required the leadership in both parties to renew their efforts to persuade deputies to give up their legislative mandates in the quest to initiate the new elections (Maksymiuk 2007). While the parties were, in the end, able to meet this goal, I use the variation among legislators to voluntarily cut short their terms in office as another litmus test of the individual deputies' willingness to toe the party line.

To determine whether the factors driving Our Ukraine's 2006 list construction may be correlated with its deputies' decisions to resign from office, which is a pretty tough sell, I again utilize logistic regression analysis, focusing on the returning 42 members of parliament. Table 7.3 presents two models that parallel those presented in table 7.2, except that the dependent variable in table 7.3 is a dichotomous variable where a one indicates that a deputy is recorded as having left the Rada (i.e., resigned from office) on or before June 12, 2007, and a zero indicates that a deputy remained in office. As a reminder, the number of observations decreases for this analysis, since it comes after two members left Our Ukraine's Rada delegation (noted above). Of the 40 Our Ukraine

TABLE 7.3. Correlates, including party variables, of resignations (on or before June 12, 2007) by 2002 deputies elected via Our Ukraine in 2006

	Equation 1			Equation 2	
	Odds ratio (p value)	95% Confidence interval		Odds ratio (p value)	95% Confidence interval
Our Ukraine rank, 2006	—			1.003 (.899)	0.963 1.043
Our Ukraine nomination, 2002	1.437 (.713)	0.208 9.907		1.425 (.719)	0.208 9.782
Our Ukraine member, 2002	—			—	
Incumbent, 2002	0.177 (.055)	0.030 1.037		0.179 (.058)	0.030 1.063
Rada or committee leader, 2002–2006	3.006 (.182)	0.597 15.137		3.238 (.247)	.443 23.658
Number of factions prior to July 7, 2005	0.746 (.342)	0.407 1.366		0.747 (.345)	0.408 1.369
SMD deputy	1.886 (.461)	0.350 10.166		1.864 (.471)	0.343 10.126
Constant	0.615 (.735)	0.037 10.290		0.533 (.730)	0.015 19.005
Pseudo R^2	0.138			0.138	
Likelihood ratio χ^2 (significance)	7.03 (.218)			7.05 (.317)	
Number of cases	39			39	

deputies under investigation, 15 resigned on or before June 12. Although the number of resignations among these deputies grows to 29 by June 19, 2007, I report results using June 12 as the cutoff because this date sets a higher threshold for compliance and because the results using a dependent variable that differentiates deputies who left the Rada at any time in June 2007 from those who did not leave the Rada performs even more poorly than the one presented below.

As table 7.3 illustrates, the variables used to predict a deputy's placement on Our Ukraine's 2006 list do a poor job of predicting whether a deputy resigned from the Rada on or before June 12, 2007, so as to initiate new elections, as desired by President Yushchenko and the party leadership. Neither model reports statistically significant likelihood ratio χ^2s. At the same time, the only variable to attain significance (and then only at the .10 level for a two-tailed test) is the dummy variable identifying deputies who were already incumbents prior to Ukraine's 2002 legislative elections. According to both models, these longer-serving legislators were nearly six times less likely to resign from office; this result supports previous evidence that depicts these deputies as political survivors. None of the other variables—a 2002 Our Ukraine nomination, a deputy's rank on Our Ukraine's 2006 list, whether a deputy held a leadership position in the previous convocation, the number of faction memberships that a deputy possessed in the previous convocation, or legislative mandate—matters.

It is likely that the null findings in table 7.3 reflect the exceptional nature of the issue under investigation: toeing the party line by resigning from office so as to initiate new elections is fundamentally different from voting with the party for or against a particular government or policy. While all of these decisions may have implications for one's political career, resigning from office early threatens it most directly. As a result, individual deputies may not only be more reluctant to take such a step; those who do may also be more likely to request assurances from the party that, if they do resign early, then they will be rewarded for their compliance. Moreover, it seems like the most equitable compensation for such a step would be placement on the party's list for the newly initiated elections. In fact, 14 of the 15 deputies who resigned on or before June 12 received spots on Our Ukraine's 2007 list, while 26 of the 29 deputies who left the Rada before the end of June received spots. By contrast, none of the eleven deputies who failed to resign were renominated by the party.

Conclusion

This chapter examines the effect of party nomination decisions on party cohesion by focusing primarily on parliamentary voting for Viktor Yanukovych's candidacy as prime minister, the first prime minister to be elected following Ukraine's implementation of a closed-list PR electoral system. The Rada's appointment of Yanukovych as prime minister was a decisive moment in Ukrainian politics because it allowed the losing candidate in Ukraine's 2004 presidential election—the candidate whose eventual defeat rested solidly on popular protests in the country's capital—to establish himself as a legitimate and influential player in the executive branch of the country's government. While the post of prime minister was certainly not the presidency, constitutional changes in Ukraine had elevated the status of the office. In fact, upon assuming office in 2006, Prime Minister Yanukovych and his cabinet pushed the limits of the prime minister's powers. In September, Yanukovych declared that Ukraine would not pursue NATO membership, sparking a rebuke from President Yushchenko. Then, in January 2007, the Rada passed a bill strengthening the prime minister's authority, one that Yushchenko vetoed for violating constitutional divisions of power (Herron 2008, 551). As discussed above, growing tensions between Prime Minister Yanukovych and President Yushchenko led Yushchenko to call for early elections, and as a result Ukrainian parties, politicians, and voters experienced two PR-only elections in a span of less than two years.

Ukraine's 2007 Rada elections provide some indication that Ukrainian parties and politicians were quick studies of the country's newly instituted electoral rules: between 2006 and 2007, the percent of wasted votes was cut in half, with only 10 percent casting an "against all" ballot or voting for parties that failed to pass the legal barrier, compared to 22 percent in 2006 (Herron 2008, 554).[12] Representation among the three major parties in 2007, meanwhile, resembled that in 2006, with the Party of Regions once again coming in first with 34 percent of the vote (compared to 32 percent in 2006), followed by the Tymoshenko Bloc (31 percent in 2007 versus 22 percent in 2006), and the renamed coalition Our Ukraine–Self Defense in third (with approximately 14 percent in both contests).[13] Two major differences between the two elections, however, were the ability of the Lytvyn Bloc to pass the legal threshold, with nearly 4 percent of the vote, and the inability of the Socialist Party to do so (Official Website of Ukraine's Central Election Commission, available at www.cvk.gov.ua).

Looking at the 2007 construction of Our Ukraine's party list suggests little fallout from the vote on Yanukovych's appointment as prime minister in 2006. Of the 42 Rada deputies in office prior to the 2006 elections and nominated to Our Ukraine's 2006 party list, a Pearson χ^2 test fails to indicate any significant difference in the likelihood of the 15 deputies who defected from the official party line on the vote that elected Yanukovych and the 27 deputies who did not support Yanukovych when it came to landing on Our Ukraine's 2007 party list: 10 (or 67 percent) of the former made the list and 16 (or 59 percent) of the latter, yielding a Pearson χ^2 of .22.

On the whole, this chapter questions whether electoral rule changes in competitive regimes characterized by weakly institutionalized parties can overcome existing practices and behavior, at least in the short term. It takes time for electoral systems to produce consistently observable effects on party systems. Only by repeatedly holding elections under the same framework—with no real expectation for the rules to change—can voters, candidates, and party leaders anticipate how the rules will operate and, in turn, develop the kinds of consistent behavior that institutionalizes parties as both electoral and legislative organizations. From this perspective, one of the main culprits responsible for party instability in Ukraine may not be the type of electoral system in place at one particular point in time; rather it may be the frequency of electoral system change that has occurred in Ukraine over time. As I discuss in the conclusion, we cannot know the potential long-term effects of PR rules in Ukraine because the country's 2012 parliamentary elections were once again conducted under a different electoral system with the return of a mixed-member system.

Conclusion

This book is a study of how parties navigate major electoral system changes. However, since electoral rule changes can take a variety of forms and move in different directions, the work constitutes only a first step toward understanding this phenomenon. Out of an effort to capitalize on a rare empirical opportunity, I investigate the consequences of two strikingly similar electoral system changes that occurred at roughly the same time in two neighboring states with a shared, if complicated, history and diverging regime trajectories: the replacement of independent, mixed-member electoral systems in Russia and Ukraine with closed-list proportional representation (PR) systems. As I note in the introduction, the electoral system changes are notable because the adoption of closed-list PR rules using a single national district is not something that scholars interested in advancing the cause of democracy would prescribe; neither is it a system that scholars who study the consolidation of authoritarian rule would expect. The electoral system changes are inherently intriguing. At the same time, the transition from systems where half of the legislative seats were allocated via geographic districts and permitted the election of independent candidates to one where candidacy on a party list constitutes the only pathway to elected office allows me to interrogate the consequences of electoral system change from a new direction: candidate selection. Thus, while the book's overarching question centers on how parties respond to electoral rule changes such as the adoption of closed-list PR that grant them control over the nomination process, chapters 1–5 tackle the topic by investigating how parties choose among prospective candidates during the implementation of these new rules.

The work begins with a review of existing literature on the evolution of the electoral systems and party systems in general and in Russia and Ukraine in particular to develop the proposition, presented in chapter 1, that electoral system change can serve as a catalyst for party change and that the adoption of closed-list PR in Russia and Ukraine constituted a potential means for improving party institutionalization, regardless of the countries' regime trajectories. With this in mind, I present the politics of candidate selection as a substantively important process that offers insight into party goals and tactics as incumbent legislators and major parties seek to advance their electoral prospects under new the rules.

Chapter 2 compares how different parties in Russia and Ukraine responded to the elimination of single-member-district (SMD) seats by examining their relationships with those deputies whose mandates were the subject of reform: district deputies. It finds that Russia's ruling party, United Russia, reinvested in those district deputies whom it had previously nominated at a rate much higher than Ukrainian parties and that it seemed to be better positioned to co-opt district deputies who had not affiliated with the party in the past. One explanation for this difference is United Russia's decisive victory during the 2003 Duma elections (i.e., the last one governed by a mixed-member system prior to the institution of PR-only rules) and its status as the party of President Vladimir Putin, a highly popular politician who faced little organized opposition to his rule. Neither party in Ukraine enjoyed such advantages. However, chapter 2 also finds that a desire to utilize both co-optation and cohesion may be a common party preference, one tempered more by constraints than actual desire. While this study cannot speak to party behavior beyond Russia and Ukraine, some generalizability seems plausible to the extent that parties, as political organizations, are commonly depicted as seeking to simultaneously concentrate and expand their power and that party nominations themselves serve as expressions of power. Chapter 2's analysis suggests that the ability of parties to both preserve party cohesion—by renominating large numbers of previously affiliated district deputies—and benefit from co-optation—by recruiting a cadre of previously unaffiliated district deputies—may depend on the level of electoral competition in place. Naturally, ruling parties in authoritarian states enjoy sizable advantages. The motivations governing such parties' actions, however, do not appear unique to authoritarianism.

While chapter 2 considers the relationships between parties and district deputies in Russia and Ukraine, it does not control for the multitude of factors that shape party decisions about whom to nominate as legislative candidates. For example, that chapter does not test whether the parties under investigation were more likely to nominate district deputies than other (i.e., party list) deputies. Moreover, the discussion in chapter 2 focuses only on whether a candidate is nominated. It does not identify the characteristics—from electoral records to legislative experience—that may improve a nominee's electoral chances, which parties essentially control in closed-list PR systems such as those under investigation. Chapter 3 addresses these issues by narrowing the analytical lens to Russia's ruling party (United Russia) and by casting a wider theoretical net so that it may answer more questions about the priorities and tactics that United Russia used to capitalize on the country's PR system.

Chapter 4 focuses on two Ukrainian parties: Our Ukraine and the Party of Regions. Like the analysis of United Russia in chapter 3, chapter 4 uses multivariate analyses to compare the range of factors that the parties likely considered when selecting among incumbent deputies during Ukraine's first PR-only elections and investigates the characteristics that influenced the nominees' electoral prospects. In addition, chapter 4 discusses differences in the data available for Ukrainian deputies and those available for Russian deputies to emphasize the importance of analyzing the two countries separately prior to any effort to combine them into a single analysis.

On the whole, chapter 3 finds that United Russia not only preserved its relationship with deputies who had already committed to it but also was more likely to co-opt independent politicians and politicians from minor parties than politicians affiliated with the Communist Party, the Liberal Democrats, and Rodina in 2003. In fact, the patterns uncovered are indicative of a stabilizing party system. The incumbent deputies with no national party ties or with ties to electorally weak parties were ripe for co-optation, while the likelihood of co-optation for the parties with better electoral prospects (i.e., those having passed the legal threshold in the previous legislative elections and complicit in the consolidation of Putin's authoritarian regime) varied in accordance with these parties' post-Soviet trajectories. Deputies from the Communist Party were least likely to receive a United Russia nomination, deputies from Rodina (widely seen as a Kremlin project) were most likely, while the odds of deputies from the historically pro-Kremlin Liberal Democratic Party fell in between. It is worth noting that chapter 3's analyses also suggest that United Russia was more likely to nominate district deputies than list deputies. To the extent that parties in Russia nominated candidates in the PR-only elections via regional sub-lists, a reliance on politicians with more regional ties makes sense. However, this outcome was not preordained given the widely held belief that the elimination of district mandates was designed to guarantee party discipline in the legislature and that the district deputies specifically had undermined party discipline. This finding supports the expectation that United Russia, with greater control over the candidate selection process, found value in the local ties that district deputies possessed, such as their connections to regional electoral machines or the financial-industrial groups that had previously functioned as party substitutes.

Chapter 4 uses multivariate analyses to compare the range of factors that two Ukrainian parties may have considered when selecting among incumbent deputies during that country's first PR-only elections. Although the results presented in chapter 4 also support the expectation that parties may use the move from a mixed-member system with district mandates to closed-list PR as a way to improve party control over candidates from geographically defined constituencies, the results illustrate how the mechanism by which this occurs may differ by party. Specifically, chapter 4 reveals how Our Ukraine was more likely to nominate district deputies than list deputies but did not systematically discriminate between mandates when ranking incumbent legislators. The Party of Regions, meanwhile, did tend to reward district deputies with better list ranks, even though no mandate effect emerged when it came to the likelihood of landing on this party's 2006 list.

With separate investigations of party behavior under PR rules in Russia and Ukraine completed, chapter 5 moves on to an empirical analysis that directly compares party nominations in the two regimes. Chapter 5 begins by discussing the necessary modifications to the data used in chapters 3 and 4 to enable the cross-case comparisons before presenting the analyses and discussing the findings. Chapter 5 finds that political parties, at least in less institutionalized party systems, can be expected to reinvest in a core of seemingly loyal and experienced deputies during periods of electoral system change and that this occurs regardless of the regime in which they operate or the parties' relationship with the executive. In practice, however, what constitutes prior party affiliation depends on context and may, in fact, be party-specific: although prior party membership mattered to United Russia and the Party of Regions, prior party nomination was enough for Our Ukraine, which was itself an electoral bloc as opposed to a more conventional party.

Chapter 5 also identifies a potentially important country effect, finding that United Russia was significantly more likely to nominate district deputies than either of the two Ukrainian parties under investigation. This outcome is notable because it highlights the value of the cross-national analysis. Only with this comparison can one observe that the difference between the Ukrainian parties when it comes to nominating district deputies (see chapter 4) is less impactful than the difference across parties operating in the two regimes. While a likely explanation for this country effect is the reliance of Russia's PR-only rules on regional sub-lists, which themselves predate the move to the PR-only system, future research should continue to explore a possible regime effect, which cannot be ruled out and has some theoretical grounding (see chapter 2).

Finally, although chapter 5 does not compare the correlates of list rank across the three parties under investigation, it does assess the extent to which considerations that are largely unobservable—such as bribery—biased the results presented in chapters 3 and 4. Specifically, chapter 5 ends by comparing the actual list ranks of the deputies nominated by each party to their predicted ranks in an effort to identify cases that would qualify as "overachievers" or "underachievers" from the perspective of the statistical models. While the presence of overachievers on the lists of United Russia and the Party of Regions, and their absence on Our Ukraine's list, may lead one to conclude initially that the former two organizations were more susceptible to illicit behavior, closer inspection reveals that these placements could often be explained in ways that complemented the extant logic underpinning the statistical analyses.

With these findings in hand, the next two chapters take the book in a different direction. Specifically, while chapters 2 through 5 look for similarities across the two countries in terms of how parties and politicians responded to the move from mixed-member electoral systems to closed-list PR, chapters 6 and 7 highlight differences in how the new rules operated. Chapter 6 considers how authoritarian regimes may combine the use of PR with other institutional changes to consolidate power. Admittedly, this topic merits more attention than a single chapter. Since electoral system reform may be part of a larger set of institutional changes designed to consolidate the regime, just as it was in Putin's Russia, how the new system operates will likely interact with those other reforms. From this perspective, then, chapter 6 only scratches the surface of how electoral system change may interact with other institutional reforms. Nevertheless, the contribution of chapter 6 is its ability to uncover and illustrate such interactions, which may easily go unnoticed.

Since a reliance on PR-only rules proved to be short-lived in both Russia and Ukraine, the analyses presented in chapters 6 and 7 matter because they expose the degree to which the return to mixed-member electoral rules in both cases were themselves grounded in two different sets of experiences. In other words, just as Russia's and Ukraine's paths to closed-list PR rules varied from one another (see the introduction), so too have their paths back to mixed-member electoral rules. Understanding the differences between Russia and Ukraine is important if political scientists wish to avoid drawing false equivalences about the relationship between electoral systems and party systems, especially in cases that are culturally and geographically proximate. For example, it is difficult to contend that the electoral system changes in Ukraine have helped address the country's inchoate party system (see also Herron 2018). In fact, one may even assert that a failure to commit to a specific set of electoral institutions is symptomatic of Ukraine's democratic shortcomings. As Linz and Stepan (1996, 4) note, "[i]t is, therefore, disagreement not only about the value of democracy but also about the specific institutions of a democracy that might make consolidation difficult." In Russia, by contrast, incumbent politicians have concentrated power to a much greater extent compared to their peers in Ukraine, and the country's PR experiment has helped established a stable party system—it just happens to be one where United Russia emerged as the dominant party in an increasingly authoritarian regime. From this perspective, Russia constitutes a prototypical "adaptable" authoritarian regime, one where rulers pursue "reforms" as a way to stay in power and to avoid more radical changes in years to come (Stacher 2012, 21). Specifically, the electoral system change, along with other tactics by the Kremlin—such as the elimination of gubernatorial elections and decisions about whom to anoint as Putin's successor as well as when (see Hale 2014, 278–82)—helped Putin's regime avoid the kinds of elite defection that had been instrumental in bringing down other authoritarian systems (Langston 2006), including other postcommunist dictatorships (Bunce and Wolchik 2011). From this perspective, the adoption of PR-only rules constitutes an example of the kind of authoritarian innovation that Beissinger (2007) anticipated from those incumbents who were astute enough to take proactive measures in an effort to cope with the existential paradox of using a façade of competitive elections to legitimize their terms in office (see also Golosov 2017).

In the pages that remain, I use insights from the previous chapters to place the cessation of Russia's and Ukraine's PR experiments in comparative perspective. In doing so, I submit that investigating the manner in which parties utilized previous electoral system changes, such as the institution of closed-list PR, may help us understand the longevity—or, as in these two case studies, the brevity—of those systems. In other words, the remainder of this conclusion serves as a reminder that political institutions and electoral rules are reflections of how power is configured at the time they are implemented. Similar rules may constrain power— giving hope to political pluralism and electoral competition—in one context and consolidate power and facilitate authoritarian rule in another. As such, scholars must tread cautiously when attributing the prospects for democracy or authoritarianism to certain institutional arrangements. In other words, while institutionalists may hope that "getting the rules right" can produce attitudinal and behavioral changes amenable to democratic outcomes, it is more prudent to express expectations that are a more proportional reflection of the consequences that institutional changes may actually have, given the particular contexts in which they operate.

The Restoration of District Mandates in Ukraine

As chapter 3 highlights, parties as well as candidates took steps to adapt to Ukraine's new PR-only rules, with many deputies who previously competed as independents or as candidates nominated by smaller parties subsequently nominated by one of Ukraine's two largest parties: Our Ukraine and the Party of Regions. However, chapter 7 reveals that Ukraine's second PR-only elections differed from Russia's in at least two important ways. First, in Ukraine, the second PR elections occurred less than two years after the first. Second, it was clear by Ukraine's 2007 elections that no single party had established majority control in the legislature, let alone a monopoly on power across the branches of government. The situation changed with Ukraine's 2010 presidential election: Viktor Yanukovych's victory not only increased the political profile of the Party of Regions; it also put electoral system change back on the country's political agenda.

In 2011, Ukrainians once again witnessed a major change in the rules governing elections to the Rada as the national legislature voted to replace the closed-list PR system with one that resembled the system used in 1998 and 2002. For Ukraine's 2012 Rada elections, 225 legislators would again be elected on the basis of 225 single-member-district constituencies governed by plurality rule, while the other 225 would be elected in a national PR tier with a 5 percent legal threshold.[1] A casual observer of Ukrainian politics might explain the return to a mixed-member electoral system as reflecting a desire on the part of the Party of Regions and President Yanukovych to maximize the ruling party's seat shares in 2012. As Herszenhorn (2013), for example, points out, the disproportionality associated with Ukraine's mixed-member system in general and the reintroduction of district mandates in particular seemed designed to help the Party of Regions preserve its position in the Rada given its declining support in opinion polls.[2] According to Kortukov (2019, 495), for example:

> For the Party of Regions and its coalition partners, the reintroduction of SMD seats was the obvious seat-maximizing option, given the previous patterns of electoral support for the pro-regime forces. SMD seats also enabled the unfair use of patronage and governmental connections (also known as the "administrative resource") to ensure the victory of pro-regime candidates. The first year of his presidency showed no signs that Yanukovych's regime would hesitate to use these tools.

In other words, Yanukovych's electoral system changes, which also raised the legal threshold to 5 percent and prohibited electoral blocs (i.e., preelectoral coalitions among parties), were designed to increase the electoral chances of proregime parties while impeding those of the opposition. While this conclusion is logical, Thames (2017) depicts it as overly simplistic.

According to Thames (2017), seat-maximization and policy-based explanations for electoral system change generally assume that parties behave like unitary actors. Although this assumption can often prove useful, it also fails to recognize that electoral systems have different implications for intraparty behavior. As I have noted elsewhere in the book, where voters choose among individuals and campaigning is personalized, as in SMD-plurality systems, tensions inherently emerge between a deputy's needs to satisfy both constituency demands and demands from her party, which often seeks to represent a broader cross-section of the population. For the most part, parties operating in an SMD system tend to tolerate weaker party discipline among their deputies, since doing so increases the likelihood that their nominees will win district contests and, by extension, improve the organizations' prospects for controlling the legislature. By contrast, in closed-list PR systems, party leaders rank incumbent deputies on party lists, which makes an individual deputy's reelection prospects dependent on party decisions and her party's electoral performance. This difference results in greater incentives for individual legislators elected in closed-list PR systems to toe the party line while in office.[3]

With similar points in mind, Thames (2017, 617) observes that "there is no *a priori* reason to assume that all members of a party, in particular legislators, will view electoral alternatives similarly. Legislators elected in one system may not view a shift to another system as being in their personal interest if the shift could potentially undermine their own electoral fortunes." When it comes to Ukraine, Thames (2017, 619) accepts the explanation that Ukrainian parties preferred PR as a system that could increase party discipline in the Rada. However, his analysis of legislative voting on proposed electoral system changes also reveals that Ukrainian parties were internally divided on electoral system reform, with district deputies more supportive of majoritarian options and list deputies more supportive of proportional representation (Thames 2017, 632).

Turning to the restoration of Ukraine's mixed-member electoral system, Thames (2017) notes that the 2010 presidential election dramatically changed Ukrainian politics. Thames points out that Tymoshenko's narrow defeat in 2010 meant that the victors of the Orange Revolution no longer controlled the executive branch. Following the 2010 election, the Party of Regions capitalized on defections from both Our Ukraine and the Tymoshenko Bloc to pass a no-confidence vote in the Tymoshenko government, which paved the way for a new government headed by Mykola Azarov of the Party of Regions.[4] With these changes in place, the bill reforming Ukraine's legislative electoral system moved quickly through the Rada (Thames 2017, 633–34). Particularly notable, however, is the level of support that the return to a mixed-member system enjoyed from parties besides the Party of Regions, especially from Our Ukraine and the Tymoshenko Bloc. While Thames acknowledges that these deputies may have supported the bill because it would have likely passed without them—something that Kortukov (2019, 495) similarly observes—Thames also suggests that deputies who were previously elected in SMD contests also may have preferred the restoration of a mixed-member system because they saw the change as increasing their prospects for reelection. The evidence supports this conclusion:

> On the vote to reintroduce the mixed-member majoritarian system, 99 deputies who previously served in the Rada as single-member district deputies took part: 41 of these deputies were in the Party of Regions, 43 were in BYuT [the Tymoshenko Bloc] and Our Ukraine. In the majority that voted for the bill, 38 of the 41 Party of Regions and 33 of the 43 right party former single-member district deputies voted to reintroduce the mixed-member majoritarian system. (Thames 2017, 636)

Thames's work highlights how the resurrection of Ukraine's mixed-member electoral system should not be understood solely as a political ploy by the executive and ruling party to maintain control over the electoral arena by altering the rules of the game. When given the choice, incumbent legislators who were not affiliated with either the executive or the ruling party had cause to support the reintroduction of district mandates. Specifically, former district deputies—even those who seemed to have successfully adapted to PR-only rules—preferred the old system. These dynamics highlight the extent to which Ukrainian politicians across a range of parties continued to see electoral system change as means that could be used to serve their own interests.

The End of Russia's PR-Only System

In previous work, I contend that the adoption of closed-list proportional representation in Russia could be understood as part of a larger effort by the Putin regime to develop a lasting ruling party in Russia, one that could provide a degree of organizational continuity while President Putin observed the constitutional term limit that existed in Russia at the time (Moraski 2007). I point out that, while it was unlikely that adopting closed-PR would have substantially changed the number of seats that United Russia won in the 2007 legislative elections, it would grant United Russia greater control over those seeking and winning legislative office, which is something that the Kremlin cared about (see also Remington 2006). At the same time, since the Russian constitution did not explicitly bar a president from serving more than two terms as long as the additional terms were nonconsecutive, I note that a lasting ruling party could prove to be a useful vehicle for preserving control over the political arena should Putin wish to seek the presidency again in 2012 (Moraski 2006; 2007), which he did. This rationale underpins the analyses presented in chapters 2 and 3, where I consider United Russia's nomination of incumbent legislators following the electoral system change. However, as chapter 6 notes, while United Russia appeared electorally unassailable during the 2007 Duma elections with more than 64 percent of the vote, this was no longer the case in 2011. In those elections, United Russia squeaked out a majority of seats, officially with less than 50 percent of the popular vote. These results, and the popular protests that followed, set the stage for Russia's return to a mixed-member electoral system.

While developments in Russia prior to the 2011 elections exhibited some warning signs that would concern ruling parties in democratic regimes, most in Russia expected a continuation of the status quo during the 2011 elections. After all, as Gel'man (2015, 117) notes, "all the systemic parties remained loyal to the authorities, the degree of public support for the regime had decreased only slightly, analysts' concerns about rising public discontent were not taken seriously, and the Russian economy had recovered after the 2008–2009 global crisis." In retrospect, scholars contend that United Russia fell victim to changes in public opinion as well as shortcomings within Russia's electoral authoritarian regime itself. Hale (2014, 283), for example, observes that, while President Dmitri Medvedev, Prime Minister Putin, and United Russia remained more popular than potential alternatives, multiple polling agencies reported declining support for all of them over the course of 2011. Although

Hale links these declines to slowing economic growth in the wake of the global financial crisis and leadership fatigue among voters, he also contends that statements by Medvedev and Putin made matters worse. Specifically, on September 24, 2011, at United Russia's 12th party congress, President Medvedev announced that he would not seek a second term and that Prime Minister Putin instead would compete in the upcoming presidential election. Putin himself indicated that this arrangement had been decided in secret four years prior—that is, when Putin anointed Medvedev as his chosen successor.[5]

For United Russia, the problems confronting the ruling tandem of Medvedev and Putin were compounded by the decision for Medvedev, not Putin, to head the ruling party's list (Hale 2014, 285). Since United Russia uses its support for Putin to define itself in the minds of voters, any dip in Putin's popularity or any indication that Putin might be distancing himself from the party would undermine United Russia's electoral prospects. By November 2011, even the state-contracted polling agency, the Public Opinion Foundation, reported that only 36 percent of respondents planned to vote for United Russia in the upcoming elections (Hale 2014, 283–84). As cracks in United Russia's veneer of invincibility began to emerge, opposition to the party ticked up. With the anticorruption blogger Alexei Navalny characterizing United Russia as the "party of swindlers and thieves" and calling for voters to vote for any party other than United Russia, even systemic opposition parties such as A Just Russia and the Liberal Democratic Party of Russia began to rally against the ruling party in the hopes of capitalizing on its declining fortunes (Gel'man 2015, 118).

With United Russia's majority status in jeopardy, the authoritarian component of Russia's electoral authoritarian regime appears to have become an increasingly important determinant of the 2011 elections. According to Gill (2016), however, the regime's electoral management apparatus suffered from a variety of shortcomings, some of which related to how United Russia itself had developed over time. Specifically, Gill notes that, while membership within United Russia is widely seen by Russian politicians as critical for career advancement, party membership cannot be equated with loyalty to United Russia, since the party lacks any clear ideational outlook or independent identity. In other words, while United Russia emerged as the dominant electoral party in the 2003 and 2007 Duma elections, party members typically joined for instrumental reasons and likely feel bound to the party only as long as Putin supports it. Equally problematic, Gill contends that United Russia, despite its national presence, lacked the level of organizational capacity and internal coordination in 2011 that is commonly associated with dominant parties in other authoritarian regimes. By his count, few local officials are actively involved in the party, while party membership itself plays only a limited role in guiding the official activities of local politicians. In the end, Gill contends that United Russia's key function in 2011 was to serve as the primary vehicle for candidates seeking a path into politics (Gill 2016, 364–65). In the context of this work, it is notable that this function was accomplished in large measure thanks to the closed-list PR system that had been put into place in 2007 and 2011.

As chapter 6 highlights, one critical development that undermined United Russia's organizational capacity in the electoral arena was President Medvedev's removal of governors who had headed several of the most effective political machines in Russia's regions. In many cases, the governors were replaced by appointees with weak local ties and little to no electoral experience. While these traits were not necessarily detrimental to the regime when United Russia's popularity was high, they proved more problematic in 2011 when electoral conditions were less favorable. As Hale (2014, 284) notes, local officials not only "scrambled to find ways to pump up official ballot counts"; their "panicky efforts to manufacture or falsify a strong official vote total for United Russia were therefore often sloppy and careless, sometimes captured on video that was posted on the Internet for all to see." Making matter worse, in 2011 the independent Russian election monitoring organization, Golos, partnered with Gazeta.ru to publicize reported electoral violations online.[6] It was within this context that United Russia's performance not only appeared dubious but also spurred popular protests that challenged the elections' legitimacy.

Seemingly uncertain about the effects that the use of violence against the protesters would have, the Kremlin adapted by proposing a number of electoral reforms. The proposals included installing webcams in polling stations for the March 2012 presidential election, easing party registration requirements so that only 500 party members would be required (instead of 40,000), and permitting the return of direct gubernatorial elections (Hale 2014, 286).[7] As Gel'man (2015, 120) points out, these changes were not reforms as much as they were "half-measures" designed to stem the tide of collective action against the regime. From Golosov's (2012b) perspective, a careful examination of President Medvedev's announcement of a package of political reforms on December 22, 2011, highlights the degree to which observers cannot take statements from government officials at face value. For example, although government representatives asserted that the program of reforms had been in the works prior to the protests, the electoral system reform in particular was revised twice following Medvedev's initial announcement, with the bill that was sent to the Duma bearing "almost no relation to the initial proposal" (Golosov 2012b, 4).

An important change in the 2012 presidential campaign was the Kremlin's decision to appeal to conservative Russian voters by depicting Putin's regime as one that would guarantee stability and protect traditional values. In the past, such an approach might have been seen as unnecessarily alienating potential voters.[8] However, since the controversy surrounding the 2011 election results had already alienated these voters, the Kremlin seemed free to build on these stronger ideational ties (Hale 2014, 287). Just as important, the Kremlin took pains to make sure its administrative apparatus would be mobilized in a more coherent and consistent manner than it had been just a few months before:

> It developed a more aggressive media campaign based on vicious attacks against opposition leaders, who were accused of being Western agents. It intimidated voters with threats of a new color revolution in Russia and presented the status quo as the only way to preserve "stability." It fired lower-level officials, ranging from regional governors to chiefs of electoral commissions, who had produced poor results for United Russia in December 2011. Finally, it organized an aggressive campaign of counter-mobilization of hundreds of thousands of peripheral voters for pro-Putin meetings, which aimed to demonstrate wide public support for the incumbent. (Gel'man 2015, 121)

With these changes in place, Prime Minister Putin once again became President Putin, winning more than 63 percent of the vote in 2012.[9]

Despite Putin's victory, United Russia's position proved more tenuous than it had been prior to his departure from the presidency in 2008. In fact, Reuter (2016, 2) contends that, after the 2012 election, Putin's relationship with United Russia waned along with the party's popularity. For example, while Putin became United Russia's party chairman in 2008 and frequently participated in party functions as prime minister, President Putin rarely met with party leaders in 2012 and 2013. For Reuter (2016, 3–4), United Russia's falling approval ratings help explain the Kremlin's 2013 decision to resurrect the Duma's mixed-member electoral system. In his view, the Kremlin saw the disproportionality associated with single-member-district plurality elections as working in United Russia's favor (also see Herszenhorn 2013).[10] This position comports well with conventional wisdom on electoral systems and authoritarian politics. For example, Birch (2007) contends that electoral fraud is more efficient in SMD contests compared to PR systems because a few stolen votes can have a bigger payoff in the former than in the latter. United Russia's ability to win 90 percent of the SMD seats in 2016 appears to substantiate Reuter's (2016) assessment. Yet this explanation may be only part of the story.

SMD-plurality systems are certainly well known for having the potential to convert modest electoral victories into decisive legislative seat totals, since a marginal increase in the form of a few thousand stolen votes may grant the ruling party a share of legislative seats that greatly outstrips its vote share when those victories are aggregated across districts.[11] No less important is the system's focus on individual candidates. In single-member-district contests, individual politicians gain directly from election fraud, and the particularistic benefits to the victors make the chances of getting caught committing fraud worth the risk.[12] Thus, as Birch (2007) notes, electoral fraud is more efficient and more likely in SMD systems because in PR systems evidence of election fraud undermines a party's reputation, giving party leaders greater incentive to enforce compliance with electoral laws. In other words, a ruling party can more easily portray instances of election fraud in an SMD system as disparate acts by self-interested politicians rather than a coordinated effort on the part of the ruling party to buoy its vote share. In closed-list PR contests, by contrast, the number of fraudulent votes needed to guarantee victory is not only much higher; greater coordination is also required, and acts of electoral fraud threaten the elections' legitimacy and the legitimacy of the party itself. It is precisely this lesson that United Russia learned firsthand in 2011.[13]

In sum, the 2011 Duma elections revealed that Russia's closed-list PR system had served its purpose and outlived its usefulness.[14] With regard to the former, the PR rules allowed United Russia—and, by extension, the Kremlin—to rein in unruly and more independent-minded deputies who had occupied many legislative seats following elections governed by the original mixed-member electoral system. It also helped United Russia establish itself as the primary vehicle for entering the national legislature (see chapters 2 and 3), thereby guaranteeing a degree of continuity while Medvedev was president and setting the stage for Putin's return in 2012. The Russian experience illustrates how electoral reforms that change the calculations of incumbent politicians help explain how regimes that draw legitimacy from multiparty elections may consolidate authoritarian rule. However, as chapter 6 illustrates, the 2011 elections also revealed that the PR system was less effective in delivering votes in United Russia's direction following the removal of long-serving governors who had previously oversaw many of the country's most capable political machines. Worse yet, United Russia's drop in popular support meant that the regime needed to rely heavily on election fraud, and doing so while utilizing closed-list PR-only rules undermined United Russia's legitimacy in a manner that had detrimental effects for the regime itself.

While these conditions help explain the decision to change the electoral system once again, they do not explain why the regime returned to a mixed-member system. In fact, President Medvedev's initial proposal was "to strengthen the ties of deputies with voters" by introducing a system that utilized 225 two-member districts ("Poslanie Prezidenta Federal'nomu Sobraniyu" 2011). It is notable, however, that electoral systems with such low magnitudes actually risk producing results that are even less proportional than SMD-plurality systems (see, e.g., Barkan 1995, 115). Thus, as Golosov (2012b, 7) notes, Russia's authorities abandoned the option in favor of a system that, once again, combined PR and SMD-plurality.[15] Initially, the return to a mixed-member system included a provision that only parties could nominate candidates (i.e., a key feature of the PR-only system). The eventual bill, however, largely reinstituted the system that had preceded the closed-list PR system, including the lower 5 percent threshold.[16]

A logical expectation that one might have when it comes to the restoration of mixed-member systems in Russia and Ukraine is that these rules could once again allow independent-minded politicians greater access to legislative office. In Russia, in particular, one might have anticipated the mixed-member system's return to threaten the efficient majorities enjoyed by United Russia that had previously eluded parties of power. As Reuter (2016) points out, Russia's district deputies, thanks to their strong regional ties, might be the first to distance themselves from the regime should it falter. Such a development "could be especially perilous for the Kremlin given that 59% of UR faction members" were SMD deputies (Reuter 2016, 3). However, a lot changed in Russia between 2003—the last Duma contests that elected district deputies—and 2016, and the Kremlin seems to have wagered that its control over the electoral process was enough to handle any potential risks associated with a return to a mixed-member system. Indeed, using United Russia's national vote share in the PR tier of the 2016 elections as an indicator of the party's support across the country, the mixed-member system clearly worked to the ruling party's advantage. With only 54.2 percent of the vote, United Russia won 62 percent of the list mandates and 90 percent of the district mandates, or more than 76 percent of the total (Official Website of the Central Election Commission of the Russian Federation, www.cikrf.ru).

It is also noteworthy that most of the legislators elected in 2016 entered parliament after the implementation of the PR-only system: in 2016, only 68 of the 450 mandates (or about 15 percent) were filled with deputies who had also been elected in Russia's December 2003 Duma elections. Of these, 43 were members of United Russia's faction following the 2016 elections. While 42 of these deputies were elected via district mandates in 2016, which in theory would encourage more independent behavior, nearly all of these deputies had either been nominated by United Russia in 2003 or had been co-opted by United Russia under the PR-only system. In fact, only two qualify as "prodigal deputies"—that is, deputies who failed to successfully navigate the move to closed-list PR, only to return to office with the restoration of the mixed system. One is Vladimir Plotnikov, who won a district election in 2016. Plotnikov was elected as an independent district deputy in 2003, did not join a faction in the Fourth Convocation of the Duma, and failed to win election in either of the 2007 or 2011 PR-only elections.[17] The other is Mikhail Bugera, who also won a district mandate in 2016. Bugera was elected in 2003 but failed to win reelection in 2007 or 2011. Unlike Plotnikov, however, Bugera was elected in 2003 via United Russia's party list and became a United Russia faction deputy in the Fourth Duma (Official Website of the State Duma, http://duma.gov.ru). In the end, United Russia not only dominated the 2016 SMD contests but also appears to have done so while continuing to marginalize former district deputies who had failed to win reelection under the PR-only rules.[18] To the extent that such deputies were deemed too independent in the past or, worse yet, may have felt scorned by United Russia or unjustly reformed out of office under the new system, keeping them out of the Duma would be an important step in preserving the efficient majorities that the PR system helped establish.

Of course, as existing research on electoral authoritarian regimes emphasizes, ruling parties in such systems can never be truly certain about the extent of elite loyalty (Schedler 2013). Vigilance matters, and United Russia seems to be tackling threats to party discipline head-on. In the summer of 2018, for example, Russia witnessed large public protests against a proposal to raise the retirement age of men from 60 to 65 by 2028 and of women from 55 to 63 by 2034 (see, e.g., Kozlovsky 2018). Despite these protests, and nearly 2.8 million people signing a petition against the reform on Change.org, the measure still passed the first of three readings in the Duma, with all of the votes in favor of it coming from United Russia ("Protesters Challenge Pension Reform . . ." 2018). Out of United Russia's 337 deputies in office at the time, 328 voted on the measure, including Bugera and Plotnikov (Official Website of the State Duma, http://duma.gov.ru). Of the eight deputies who were absent, one, Sergei Zheleznyak, subsequently resigned, and the only deputy to vote against the proposal, Natalya Poklonskaya, faced pressure from the party's leadership to resign as well ("Lone United Russia Deputy Defies Leadership . . ." 2018). While this vote highlights the importance of United Russia's oversized legislative majority, it also provides some modest support for the assertion that, if United Russia were to have a problem with party discipline in the future, the problem may come from its renewed reliance on district deputies. Although Poklonskaya was elected in 2016 as a list deputy, seven of the eight absent deputies, including Zheleznyak, were district deputies (Official Website of the State Duma, http://duma.gov.ru).[19]

Conclusion

The adoption of proportional representation systems to govern elections to national legislatures in interwar Europe represents an institutional change that has garnered significant attention in political science (e.g., Andrews and Jackman 2005; Boix 1999; Calvo 2009; Cusack et al. 2007). One reason for this attention may be that scholars of electoral systems have identified proportional electoral systems as more favorable to democracy and as more responsive to society, making their origins in established democratic cases of particular interest. Although scholars of electoral system change would not contend that the adoption of PR rules indicates a regime's commitment to democratization, such reforms do indicate that those in power needed to adapt to changing economic, political, and social contexts: from the expansion of Europe's working class via industrialization and the rise of socialist parties, to the establishment of universal suffrage. In other words, the adoption of these rules may be seen as important moments in the development of Western democracies. From this perspective, the study of electoral system change anticipated Capoccia and Ziblatt's (2010, 940) call for scholars to view European democratization less as wholesale regime transitions at single moments in time and to focus more on key episodes in the process during which "the institutional building blocks of democracy emerged *asynchronically*" (emphasis in original).

Although Capoccia and Ziblatt (2010) are primarily interested in historical cases of democratic institutional design and reform, the need to unpack the institutional components of political regimes applies as much to studies of authoritarianism—contemporary and historic—as to studies of democratization. In fact, scholars interested in such episodes would benefit from comparing episodes of institutional changes across regime types, as I do in this book, if they wish to better understand the origins and effects of those changes on regime development. In other words, authoritarian regimes are also "built one institution at a time" (Capoccia and Ziblatt 2010, 945), and it is important to understand when and why similar institutions operate differently across the two regime types.

While scholars of comparative party systems have a long tradition of focusing on the consequences of electoral systems, which includes efforts to explore the generalizability of these consequences to aspiring democracies (e.g., Bochsler 2010; Moser and Scheiner 2012), the study of electoral systems in authoritarian settings remains relatively underdeveloped (but see Golosov 2006; 2016; Lust-Okar and Jamal 2002; Stroh 2010). This imbalance may exist because of a mistaken assumption that in authoritarian settings—that is, once levels of political rights and civil liberties fall below a certain level—election outcomes are deemed to be manufactured from above and immune to the independent effects of the rules. Alternatively, perhaps a prevailing normative interest in how to nurture democracy has led scholars to concentrate on the ability of politicians to convert liberalizing moments into democratic breakthroughs rather than on how members of an authoritarian regime respond to a changing environment so that they may maintain their hold on power. Regardless, electoral systems in the postcommunist region, at least, have been far from static, and the changes have not been limited to the years immediately following the communist collapse. Although continued experimentation (or manipulation) of legislative electoral rules in the post-Soviet region may undermine the ability of scholars to identify patterns comparable to the generalizations drawn between electoral system design and party system development in advanced industrial democracies,[20] these rule changes will also continue to demand investigation. How parties and politicians adapt to the new rules will reflect, if not play a decisive role in, how regimes operate.

ACKNOWLEDGMENTS

In July 2013, I was in Washington, DC, for a Fulbright orientation, looking forward to a spring semester in Kyiv working on a new book project. The primary aim of the research was to compare the consequences of Russia's recently discarded proportional representation system to a similar system that had been implemented and replaced in Ukraine. I had planned to spend January through March of 2014 gathering data that could be utilized in quantitative analyses of party nominations; April and May would be spent collecting qualitative information on former legislators from Ukraine's Russian-speaking regions in the east. As one might surmise, the timing of the award was not ideal. Ukraine's Euromaidan, or Revolution of Dignity, greatly complicated research in Kyiv. Not only did many of the clashes between antigovernment protesters and riot police take place outside the National Parliamentary Library; the International Red Cross had set up a field hospital inside it. Then, right as the situation in Kyiv began to stabilize, the travel restrictions that accompanied Russia's annexation of Crimea in March and the outbreak of war in Ukraine's Donbas put an end to my plans to conduct research there.

While the Fulbright experience was quite different from the one anticipated, it still contributed to this book project. I would like to thank the J. William Fulbright Foreign Scholarship Board, the Council for International Exchange of Scholars, and the US Department of State's Bureau of Educational and Cultural Affairs for the grant, in addition to the National University of Kyiv–Mohyla Academy (NaUKMA), the Fulbright Office in Kyiv, and the University of Florida for institutional support during the award period. I am also grateful to Paul D'Anieri for putting me in touch with some of his Ukrainian contacts prior to the award period and to Oleksander Demyanchuk for hosting me at NaUKMA, as well as Serhiy Kudelia, Anatoliy Romanyuk, Yuriy Shveda,

Serhiy Tereshko, and Andreas Umland for their insights into Ukrainian politics.

As readers will notice, the final incarnation of the project is predominantly quantitative, and a lot of work went into converting information from the sources identified into usable datasets. Fortunately, I received valuable research assistance over the years from a number of talented students, both graduate and undergraduate, at the University of Florida. I thank Alexandra Chopenko, M.K. King, Daria Kirilenko, Aidan Klein, Junseok Lee, Arina Martemyanova, Steven Minegar, Anna Mwaba, Sarah Rickner, Marianna Tuninskaya, Saskia van Wees, Stanislav Veremeychik, and Jon Whooley for assisting me at various stages in the project.

The book also benefited greatly from the comments and suggestions of numerous colleagues, including discussants and audience members at various professional conferences. Those colleagues include Jorge Alves, Enrique Desmond Arias, Gavril Bilev, Elizabeth Carlson, Matthew Caverly, Larry Dodd, Amanda Edgell, Agustina Giraudy, Magda Giurcanu, Nicholas Knowlton, Amie Kreppel, Edmund Malesky, Michael Martinez, Eduardo Moncada, Conor O'Dwyer, Suhas Palshikar, William Reisinger, Daniel Smith, Richard Snyder, Dragana Svraka, Michelle Taylor-Robinson, Frank Thames, and Lily Tsai. I would like to offer a special thanks to Michael Bernhard, who provided detailed comments on an initial draft of the entire manuscript. Their comments and criticisms, as well as those from several anonymous reviewers, pushed me to produce a better, if still imperfect, work for final publication. Finally, I am grateful to my editor at New York University Press, Sonia Tsuruoka, for her encouragement, suggestions, and support.

Chapters 3 and 4 significantly expand on articles previously published in *Party Politics* (Moraski 2015) and the *Journal of Elections, Public Opinion, and Parties* (Moraski 2017), respectively. Chapter 6 is derived in part from an article, "Reverse Coattails Effects in Undemocratic Elections: An Analysis of Russian Locomotives," published in *Democratization* on August 30, 2016, available online at https://doi.org/10.1080/13510347.20 16.1222373. I am grateful for permission from Taylor & Francis (www.tandfonline.com) to reprint portions of that work here.

In addition to expressing my gratitude to my wife, Jayne, and our two daughters, Blaire and Joslyn, for persevering through some challenging weeks in Kyiv, I would like to dedicate this book to my parents, Jim and

Rosella Moraski. Not only did my childhood as an Air Force brat spark my interests in travel and comparison; my time in Kyiv gave me a greater appreciation of their fortitude as parents, especially given the parallels to the months that we spent in Tehran leading up to the 1979 Iranian Revolution.

NOTES

INTRODUCTION

1. Ukraine's score dropped from 2.5 to 3 on the Freedom House scale, which ranges from 1 for "most free" to 7 for "least free" ("Ukraine, Freedom in the World 2011" https://freedomhouse.org).
2. Interested readers may wish to consult, among others, Koshkina (2015), Kudelia (2014), Moraski (2016), Portnov (2014), Sakwa (2016), Shevtsova (2014), and Shore (2018).
3. Single-member-district-plurality systems divide the country into a number of electoral districts equal to the number of seats to be filled. One representative is elected per district, with the seat awarded to the candidate who wins more votes than any other candidate. These systems are also commonly referred to as "first-past-the-post," or FPTP. Conventionally, proportional representation systems that allocate all seats in one countrywide district are conceptualized as anchoring the opposite end of the electoral system spectrum. Ukraine's mixed-member system, then, split the difference, allocating half of the seats one way and half of them the other.
4. On this point, see also Remmer (2008).
5. For example, they note that where a party is institutionalized on the basis of ethnic or cultural exclusivity, the institutionalization of a competitive party system becomes problematic (Randall and Svåsand 2002, 24).
6. Scholars generally expect legislators in democratic settings to pursue policy that will benefit their constituents. Specifically, incentives to appease voters in corresponding geographic districts help to explain the behavior of legislators elected in single-member districts. While legislators elected via PR also seek to appease constituents, those constituents are not necessarily geographically determined. In their study of legislative behavior in Germany, Stratmann and Baur (2002) find that deputies elected via district seats in that country's mixed-member electoral system are significantly more likely to serve on committees that allow them to deliver policy that can service their geographically based constituents. PR legislators not only avoid such committees but are also more likely to hold seats on committees that influence the distribution of funds that can benefit their party's national constituencies (i.e., those that span geographic regions).
7. Moreover, to the extent that regional sub-lists might preserve a degree of vertical accountability that democracy advocates would recommend, the consequences of

regional sub-lists in an increasingly authoritarian Russia merit closer investigation (see chapters 2, 3, and 6).

8. According to Duverger (1954, 223), SMD-plurality systems promote two-party competition at the district level (i.e., within each individual constituency) even if the parties in competition with one another are different in different regions of the country.

9. Hutcheson (2018, 76) reiterates this point after considering how both the 2003 and 2007 elections unfolded.

10. Herron (2009, chapter 2) identifies three stages of Soviet elections: The first stage occurred during the consolidation of the Soviet system (1917–1936), the second stage lasted from Stalin's purges to the start of Gorbachev's tenure as General Secretary of the Communist Party (1937–1984), and the third stage accompanied Gorbachev's reforms and ended with the Soviet Union's dissolution (1985–1991).

11. Although both Russia and Ukraine trace their historical origins to Kievan Rus, placing too much emphasis on these shared experiences risks sounding like Russian politicians, including President Vladimir Putin, who discount Ukraine's independence and statehood. For examples, see D'Anieri (2019, 162–64). Although much of contemporary Ukraine was indeed part of the Russian Empire and subjected to policies of Russification, this common history does not necessarily translate into a shared destiny. According to Pipes (1997), for example, the formation of a separate Ukrainian nation was an open question during the eighteenth and nineteenth centuries (9), with demands for Ukrainian autonomy surging as the Russian Empire disintegrated (53–61). Moreover, in the three years that followed the Bolshevik Revolution, at least nine different governments sought to establish control over Ukraine, with Ukrainian nationalists and Russian communists emerging as the main protagonists. Although the latter managed to establish control over Ukraine, elements of Ukraine's national movement also succeeded in penetrating the Communist Party (Pipes 1997, 148–50).

12. During the period under investigation, both Russia and Ukraine may be categorized as "semipresidential" systems, thanks to the presence of a prime minister who operates alongside a popularly elected president (Duverger 1980; Elgie 1998). However, not everyone agrees with this categorization. In both countries, the presidents appoint the cabinet, including the prime minister, which means that executive-legislative arrangement more closely resembles a presidential system, like that of the United States, than a semipresidential system, like the one in France, where the balance of power among parliamentary parties determines the government. Shugart and Carey's (1992) semipresidential subtypes of president-parliamentarism and premier-presidentialism help differentiate the former, where the president possesses more leverage over the government, from the latter. (For more thorough discussions of these considerations as they apply to Russia, see Clark 2010 and Remington 2000.) Indeed, the amount of constitutional power allocated to Russia's president under the 1993 constitution led some scholars in the 1990s to argue that the system was, in fact, "super-presidential" (Clark 1998;

Fish 1997; Holmes 1994). Putin's decision to leave the presidency and assume the post of prime minister from 2008 through 2012 challenged this position, however. If anything, the presidency of Dmitri Medvedev seemed to reveal that, in Putin's Russia, the man makes the office, the office does not make the man. And, in 2020, Putin remade the office of the presidency through a series of constitutional changes that better reflected political practice (see, e.g., Von Gall and Jäckel 2020). Like Russia's 1993 constitution, Ukraine's 1996 constitution established a semipresidential system that gave Ukraine's president dominion over the government. While Ukraine's second president, Leonid Kuchma, took steps to expand presidential power in Ukraine, arguably in pursuit of his own super-presidential system, an institutional tug-of-war between branches of government not only impeded this development but also fomented division within the executive branch (Kudelia 2013). Sedelius and Mashtaler (2013, 115), in particular, find that Ukraine actually experienced more intraexecutive conflict than any other postcommunist president-parliamentary system.

13. However, Brudny and Finkel (2011, 827) also acknowledge that Yanukovych's 2010 election moved Ukrainian politics in a more authoritarian direction, indicated by the judicial prosecution of his political opponents, restrictions on media freedoms, and attempts to assert executive control over the judiciary.

14. Way's account (2016, chapter 3) supports this assertion, suggesting that national divisions limited the control that Ukraine's first president, Leonid Kravchuk, had over regional governments, which in turn yielded a more democratic presidential election in 1994 than what would have occurred otherwise. However, the state under Leonid Kuchma, Ukraine's second president (1994–2004), possessed a greater capacity to repress dissent and engage in electoral fraud thanks to Kuchma's ability to capitalize on regional and economic networks that he had maintained from the Soviet period (Way 2016, chapter 3, "Rapacious Individualism . . .").

15. While Brudny and Finkel (2011, 817–18) highlight the historical differences between western Ukraine, which was not fully incorporated into the Soviet Union until after World War II, and eastern and southern Ukraine, which had been part of the Russian Empire for centuries, they also remind readers that "one should not confuse the Eastern Ukrainian identity with a Russian one" (818). At the time of Ukraine's 1991 referendum, for example, large majorities in Ukraine's west, south, and east supported independence, albeit for different reasons. In western Ukraine, "the main motivation was to create an independent Ukrainian state for the Ukrainian nation," while in eastern and southern Ukraine support for independence was more economically motivated, shaped by the belief "that the economic strength of Ukraine would bring affluence deliberately blocked by Moscow" (825). Both positions, then, may be interpreted as "anti-imperial."

16. On the Kremlin's relationship with previous propresidential parties, including Unity, see Reuter (2017, chapter 3).

17. For an overview and analysis of this event, see Javeline and Baird (2011) and Tuathail (2009).

18. According to White and Kryshtanovskaya (2011, 557), the move to closed-list PR had been in the works for months, with Putin having proposed the change in a previous address to Russia's Central Election Commission.

19. As White and Kryshtanovskaya (2011, 558) caution, interviews of this kind raise methodological questions (e.g., how were the subjects selected) and complicated issues about the material itself (e.g., to what extent are the first-person narratives partial or self-serving?).

20. As Turovsky (2011, 203) notes, entirely proportional systems were adopted not only in Russia and Ukraine but also in Kazakhstan and Kyrgyzstan.

21. While one could reasonably expect the electoral prospects for smaller parties to be better in Ukraine than in Russia thanks to the difference in the two system's legal thresholds, the different threshold levels themselves may be seen as reflections of the two countries' diverging regime trajectories. In Russia, the threshold was raised after the merger of Unity and Fatherland–All Russia, and it was a change that would benefit the newly formed United Russia as well as other, more established parties in Russia, from the Liberal Democrats to the Communists. The more drastic change of eliminating district elections, by contrast, occurred after United Russia's decisive victory in 2003 and the legislative bandwagon that would grant Putin a constitutional majority as he began his second term in office. In Ukraine, meanwhile, the reduced threshold reflects the legislative parties' feelings of uncertainty about how they might fair in competitive elections governed by PR-only rules. In other words, the lower threshold in Ukraine constitutes a necessary accommodation to parties operating in a competitive electoral environment, while the increase in Russia more closely resembles an early step in a series of reforms that signaled the desire and ability of those in power to reduce the level of electoral competition.

22. For an analysis of a mandate effect on legislative behavior in Ukraine, see Thames (2016).

23. As Reisinger and Moraski (2017, 4) note, in the 2000s, scholars were increasingly more likely to describe Russia's political regime as authoritarian—that is, as "competitive authoritarian" (Levitsky and Way 2002), "electoral authoritarian" (e.g., Ross 2005; 2011), or even fully authoritarian (e.g., Levitsky and Way 2010, 371).

24. In comparative perspective, however, the effects of electoral protests, such as those associated with the Orange Revolution, on democratization are questionable, especially relative to the impact of international influences (see Kalandadze and Orenstein 2009).

1. ELECTORAL SYSTEMS, POLITICAL PARTIES, AND CANDIDATE SELECTION

1. For a discussion of how competitive authoritarianism and electoral authoritarianism relate to one another, see Howard and Roessler (2006, 367).

2. For an analysis of party-switching in Ukraine, see Thames (2007)

3. Harasymiw (2005, 200) notes that Ukraine's mixed-member system, which was first used in its March 1998 elections, also defied expectations: "An outstand-

ing feature in the outcome of these elections was that the two components of the electoral mechanism apparently operated contrary to their conventionally accepted manner in established liberal democracies. The proportional representation half of the system actually produced *fewer* parties in the legislature, while the single-member, simple plurality (SMSP) half actually created *more* parties: eight *versus* 22!" (emphasis in original). Like Moser and others, Harasymiw identifies the ability of local notables to win election in SMD contests "without the support or endorsement of a major national party" as a cause.

4. In fact, Svolik (2012, 4–5) finds that more than two-thirds of dictators who held office for more than a day between 1946 and 2008 and lost power by nonconstitutional means did so as a result of actions taken by regime insiders.

5. See Blaydes (2010) for a discussion of how authoritarian elections aid in the distribution not only of rents but also of coveted positions within the regime, thus making them a means for controlling intraelite conflict. On the prevalence of patronage politics in former Soviet countries, including Russia and Ukraine, see Hale (2014).

6. While institutions may improve an autocrat's ability to co-opt potential rivals, Gerschewski (2013) notes that authoritarian stability also relies on legitimation and repression. Rivera (2017), meanwhile, finds that the reliance on authoritarian legislatures not only improves the ability of these regimes to manage political conflict but also reduces their need to rely on repression. Although Rivera also finds that the likelihood of repression increases as the influence of opposition parties increases, manipulating the electoral system may function as an effective means of suppressing those parties.

7. According to Svolik (2012, 10), repression and co-optation complement one another in an authoritarian regime and cannot be examined in isolation, especially if one moves beyond a focus on elites to an investigation of the population at large. As he notes, the state's repressive capacity not only shapes the regime's ability to expand its influence into the economy and society; such an expansion is also more likely to make party membership and related service essential to career advancement (165).

8. While problems associated with power-sharing and control may drive authoritarian politics (Svolik 2012, 196), the motives of political parties in authoritarian regimes that derive legitimacy from competitive, if unfair, elections are still likely to reflect electoral concerns, including the desire to preserve an image of invincibility from one election to the next (Magaloni 2006).

9. However, as I note below, in Russia candidates with better list placements can decline their mandates, which allows the next person on the party list to be elected.

10. As Lupu and Riedl (2013) note, studies of party institutionalization in developing democracies focus on a variety of indicators, from party volatility to voter attachments and programmatic appeals. Indeed, research on voter attachments in Russia and Ukraine during the 1990s was relatively optimistic about the prospects for party development there (Brader and Tucker 2001; Colton 2000; Evans and

Whitefield 1998; Klobucar, Miller, and Erb 2002; Miller et al. 2000; Miller and Klobucar 2000).

11. Russia's legislative candidates had the option of competing as district candidates, list candidates, or both district and list candidates in the 1993, 1995, 1999, and 2003 Duma elections (Smyth 2006, 132). Although Russian candidates could win district contests while simultaneously holding electable positions on a party list, they could also decline the list mandate, which would then go to the next person on the party's list. Ukrainian politicians could run as district, list, or both district and list candidates during the 1998 Rada elections but not in 2002 (Herron 2018, 919). Throughout this book, then, "district" or "list" refers to a deputy's *legislative* mandate as opposed to her candidacy. For example, if a victorious district candidate in Russia also held a prime spot on a party list only to decline the list mandate in favor of the district mandate, the deputy is categorized as a "district deputy." Theoretically speaking, differences between electoral mandate and legislative mandate for Russian politicians enjoying both district and list nominations involve questions about electoral prowess (i.e., can a politician nominated both as a district candidate and list candidate actually win the district contest?), party affiliation (since district candidates who are also nominated on a party list should be more closely affiliated with the party of that list), and constituency once in office (i.e., deputies who accept their positions on the basis of a district victory may be less likely to toe the party line than those elected via the party list). The analyses in chapter 3 capture these differences by using indicators that not only identify the characteristics of individual politicians, which likely influenced their prospects of making United Russia's 2007 party list but are also more generalizable than a reliance on Russian-specific dummy variables that differentiate district, list, and dual electoral mandates from one another.

12. Like Randall and Svåsand (2002), this work distinguishes between individual party institutionalization and party system institutionalization. For Randall and Svåsand, however, a major sticking point is not only that individual party institutionalization and party system institutionalization are not the same thing but also that the two phenomena are not always mutually compatible from a democratization perspective (6). As they note, the institutionalization of a party that exacerbates ethnic or other cultural divisions can jeopardize the institutionalization of a competitive party system (24). While one can say the same thing about the institutionalization of a party intent on consolidating authoritarian rule, such a development may in fact prove to be crucial to the system's institutionalization. It would just happen to be a noncompetitive party system.

13. Levitsky's (1998) work, which unpacks party institutionalization as a concept, illustrates the degree to which Russian and Ukrainian parties were underinstitutionalized prior to their first closed-list PR elections. For Levitsky, party institutionalization consists of both "value infusion" and "behavioral routinization" (i.e., the entrenchment of the rules of the game making political behavior regularized and predictable) (79–80). As noted above, prior to the adoption of closed-list PR,

a significant number of national legislators had yet to find that party affiliation was necessary for gaining access to the national legislature, let alone value a particular party for its own sake. Moreover, the electoral system changes themselves emphasize the extent to which the rules of the game remained in flux, even if those changes were intended to increase the predictability of political behavior in the years to come.

14. Perhaps the most secretive aspect of list placement relates to rumors that individuals may rely on bribes to secure party nominations. (On the pervasiveness of corrupt informal practices in Russia and Ukraine, see Chashin 2009; Cheloukhine and King 2007; Herron 2020; Holmes 2008; Kuzio 2014; Solomon and Foglesong 2000; Zhdanov 2002.) While questions about how illicit acts such as bribery shape electoral politics are beyond the scope of this work (but see, on Russia, Maksimov 1999; Nisnevich 2014), the analysis establishes some control for these factors by focusing on incumbent legislators (discussed more in the following chapter). By concentrating on incumbent deputies, all the potential candidates under investigation have already paid any initial "entry costs" associated with successfully competing for office (see Smyth 2006, 78–79) and arguably should have been well-positioned and sufficiently motivated to continue to "pay to play." At the end of chapter 5, I delve more deeply into this topic and present an approach that future scholars may use to identify cases of suspicious list placement.

15. At a subsequent press conference, Yanukovych provided no clear answers as to why a former general prosecutor, Svyatoslav Piskun, made the list, noting only that the decision was made collectively by the party leadership ("Yanukovych ne boitsya Akhmetova . . ." 2005).

2. CLOSED-LIST PROPORTIONAL REPRESENTATION AND THE DYNAMICS OF CANDIDATE SELECTION

1. For a discussion of the mechanisms through which Russian business influences political campaigns, from investing in to sponsoring candidates, including independents, see Barsukova and Zviagintsev (2006).

2. For work on using diminished subtypes to conceptualize parties that do not meet expectations associated with democratic representation, see Luna et al. (2021).

3. As Oversloot and Verheul (2006, 394) note, parties of power are typically created by politicians who wield power in the executive branch with the goal of establishing legislative support for the regime's policies. While the organization may formally be called a "party" or "political bloc," Oversloot and Verheul submit that parties of power do not have a life of their own—that is, beyond their dependency on the executive—and therefore are "neither 'ruling' nor much of a party at all." Despite these considerations, I refer to these organizations as "propresidential parties" or "ruling parties," which are terms more commonly used in the general literature on political parties. For an argument in favor using party of power— despite its "defects"—as a concept that describes a phenomenon specific to the post-Soviet region, see Makarenko (2012, 64) in addition to Laverty (2015).

4. On the Kremlin's relationship with previous propresidential parties, including Unity, see Reuter (2017, chapter 3).

5. This approach, however, does not resolve concerns about where real power resides in Russia (see Makarenko 2012).

6. In fact, Reuter (2017, 173) points out that affiliating with United Russia eased the process of registering as a candidate, which is no simple task given Russia's onerous registration process and the capriciousness of regional authorities who use their influence over electoral officials to keep undesirable candidates off the ballot: "Carrying a United Russia affiliation eliminates the need to gather voter signatures—the most common method used to disqualify candidates—and provides some insurance against the unpredictable actions of regional authorities." See also Nisnevich (2014, 72–73).

7. On the importance of personal connections as well as the incentives and conflicts associated with them in Russia, see Huskey (2005), Lynch (2005), Pain (2011), Robinson (2007; 2012; 2017), Van Zon (2008), and Whitmore (2010). Reisinger and Moraski (2017) submit that informal patron–client ties not only structure contemporary Russian politics at the regional level but also played a critical role in the Kremlin's ability to consolidate control over the electoral arena.

8. Wright and Escribà-Folch (2012) find that, while legislatures may sustain authoritarian rule by making the dictator's promises appear more credible, the establishment of ruling parties that are capable of protecting the interests of autocratic elites—should a democratic transition occur—may in fact destabilize the regime.

9. Way (2016, chapter 3, "Party and State Strength") describes Kuchma's supporters as "a centrally coordinated but highly fragmented 'multi party ruling party' that consisted of competing political parties and patronage networks that all depended for their survival on the president's support."

10. Yanukovych emerged as the status quo candidate in the 2004 presidential election since a constitutional term prevented President Kuchma from seeking reelection.

11. According to Diuk and Gongadze (2002, 163), most of the independent deputies who joined For a United Ukraine after the 2002 elections "came from central and eastern Ukraine, where the presidential forces had reportedly spent large sums to manipulate or simply to buy votes. These candidates were not in all cases set up by the regime, but were businessmen who thought it would serve their own best interest to join the presidential faction once in parliament." A geographic divide characterized the list results as well, with For a United Ukraine and the Communist Party performing best in two of Ukraine's eastern regions, Luhansk and Donetsk. The Communists received almost 40 percent of the list vote in Luhansk and close to 29 percent in Donetsk, while For a United Ukraine gained more than 14 percent in Luhansk and almost 37 percent in Donetsk. By comparison, Our Ukraine tended to dominate in western Ukraine, garnering more than 74 percent of the vote in Ivano-Frankivsk, 69 percent in Ternopil, and almost 64 percent in Lviv Oblasts (Meleshevich 2007, 90).

12. Meleshevich (2007, 71–72) notes that, while the Yanukovych cabinet was to a large extent dependent on parliamentary support, the coalition government is best understood as an alliance of nonideological parties of power representing clans from the Donbas, Dnipropetrovsk, and Kyiv that agreed to set their differences aside so as to sideline the largest political force in Ukraine at the time: Yushchenko's Our Ukraine.

13. The winners in all cases were registered officially as independents (Central Election Commission of the Russian Federation, www.cikrf.ru).

14. Since the March 2004 by-elections were held following United Russia's clear victory in December, these three independents were particularly susceptible to this bandwagon effect, which probably explains why Clark (2005) lists United Russia with a total of 106 SMD seats. It also means that these deputies were operating in a fairly different political climate than those who competed in the initial round of the 2003 elections, which is why I exclude them from the analysis.

15. These deputies are Vladimir Litvinov (District 144), Ivan Zhdakaev (160), Yurii Losskii (187), and Valerii Kuzin (220). I used online biographies and news reports on the individual deputies, such as those at *Monitoring Zakonoproektov RF GD* (https://lawmon.ru) and *Rossiiskii Professional'nii Portal o Lobbizme i GR* (http://lobbying.ru) to determine whether politicians were alive at the end of the 2003–2007 legislative session and therefore could have competed as candidates in the 2007 elections. The multivariate analyses in subsequent chapters consider other factors that may have influenced the likelihood of a United Russia nomination. Note, however, that the statistical results of preliminary analyses of the nomination of all deputies elected in the December 2003 elections differed only marginally from those when the deceased persons are excluded, yielding the same substantive and seemingly robust findings.

16. Note that Russia's 2005 election law required that parties create regional sub-lists, with the total list not exceeding 600 names. Thus, United Russia could have easily placed all 103 district deputies on its 2007 list.

17. Of United Russia's 103 district deputies, almost 10 percent (10) were female. The mean winning percentage of these deputies was 44, with a range of 19 percent to 82 percent. The KPRF's elected district deputies, meanwhile, included two women, or almost 17 percent of its total. The average winning percentage of its deputies was 38, with a range of 19 percent to 73 percent. The similarities across these figures are striking given that the 2003 results were the worst for the KPRF since the country's first post-Soviet legislative ballot in 1993. The statistics for deputies from parties and electoral blocs that would come to comprise A Just Russia also closely resemble those for United Russia's deputies. About 7 percent (or two out of 20) of the deputies from these parties were women, and the average winning percentage is 43, with a range of 19 percent to 79 percent. These data suggest that United Russia and A Just Russia had strikingly comparable pools of district deputies in terms of quality, though certainly not in terms of quantity, to draw from in the construction of their 2007 party lists.

18. Here, 154 made a party list—any party list—in 2007. And 144 of the 154 landed on one of the three lists examined in figures 2.1–2.3. The other 10 were distributed across the lists of the Union of Rightist Forces, the Patriotic Party, the Agrarian Party, and Citizens Strength.

19. The exclusion of district deputies who were nominated by United Russia in 2003 could reflect a decision by the party leadership to punish deputies who broke ranks with the party during their time in office. Indeed, the logic behind the move to a PR-only system was that United Russia would use a more centralized electoral process to preserve party discipline in the Duma. However, existing literature suggests not only was voting cohesion higher among United Russia's deputies relative to those of previous pro-presidential parties (Kunicova and Remington 2008) but also that after the 2003 elections "the 300-plus-member United Russia faction . . . exercised ironclad discipline over its members" (Reuter and Remington 2009, 507).

20. These districts were numbers 18, 35, and 201 (Official Website of Ukraine's Central Election Commission, available at www.cvk.gov.ua). Repeat elections were held on July 14, 2003.

21. In Ukraine, district deputies are listed as party members or not party members (*bezpartiinii*) in their candidate biographies. However, district deputies in Russia are listed as nominated by a party or as self-nominated (*samovydvizhenie*) as opposed to nonpartisan (i.e., *bespartiinii*). I consider the differential effects of party membership as opposed to party nomination in chapters 3 and 4.

22. In some cases, Ukrainian candidates competed as independents even though they are listed on the Ukrainian Central Election Commission's website as members of a party. In other cases, the listed party affiliation differs from that of the party nominating the candidate. Since such deviations are precisely the kinds of behavior that the move to closed-list PR was intended to eliminate, and my goal is to differentiate deputies according to the degree of party commitment, this initial analysis categorizes deputies based on the source of each candidate's *official* nomination.

23. Nonpartisan exit polls indicated that Yushchenko enjoyed a commanding lead during the presidential runoff election, with 52 percent of the vote compared to 43 percent for Kuchma's chosen successor, Viktor Yanukovych. However, official results announced that Yanukovych had defeated Yushchenko by 2.5 percent of the vote. As the tally was challenged, increases in voter turnout figures from eastern Ukraine added to the furor. "The eastern Donetsk region—Yanukovich's home base—went from a voter turnout of 78 percent to 96.2 percent overnight, with support for Yanukovich at around 97 percent. In neighboring Luhansk, turnout magically climbed from 80 percent at the time the polls closed to 89.5 percent the next morning, with Yanukovich winning 92 percent or more of the votes" (Karatnycky 2005, 35–36).

24. Since these institutional changes resulted from the Orange Revolution, they are also part and parcel of Ukraine's regime trajectory, outlined in the introduction. For work correlating the strength of a country's national legislature and its democratic prospects, see Fish (2005; 2006) and Barkan (2008).

25. Kudelia and Kuzio (2014, 273), for example, find that a key distinction between the Party of Regions and Our Ukraine as well as Tymoshenko's party, Fatherland, was that the former actually offered groups within its alliance—which consisted of regional *nomenklatura* elites and Donetsk-based oligarchs—more voice in internal discussions. By comparison, Our Ukraine and Fatherland relied more heavily on the personal appeal of their leaders, who also tended to dominate internal party politics. As a result, even though all three parties had their origins in the politics of patronage, Kudelia and Kuzio find that the Party of Regions over time proved better at absorbing rivals and also exhibited greater unity and more party discipline than Our Ukraine and Fatherland, both of which suffered from defections as the political influence of their leaders diminished.

26. For example, while Lytvyn headed the list of For a United Ukraine, he was officially an independent during the 2002 elections. Similarly, 28 of the 40 district deputies nominated by Our Ukraine were not party members. While such deputies may be less committed compared to party members in 2002, they also represented viable candidates for list placement following the move to PR-only rules. Still, since party nominations were optional at this point in time, one could reasonably interpret those competing under, say, the Our Ukraine banner as signaling greater commitment to that coalition than those who did not (i.e., other party nominees and self-nominated candidates). I return to this issue in chapter 4.

27. I consider the possibility of differential effects from party nomination and party membership in chapter 4.

28. Volodimir Satsyuk from District 64 fled to Russia and became a Russian citizen after being suspected of involvement in the poisoning Yushchenko ("Dos'ye: Satyuk" n.d.). Meanwhile, Oleh Oleksenko from District 82 died in office prior to the end of the parliamentary session (Piskovii 2002), as did Ivan Chetverikov from District 151 ("Stenograma plenarnoho zasidanny" 2004).

29. The two Socialist district deputies populate the extremes: Stanislav Nikolay-enko (District 187, Kherson) held the best list placement among the eight, while Mikola Karnaukh (District 152, Poltava) received the worst. Of the eight district deputies on the Socialist Party's list, only Nikolayenko and Serhii Matviyenko—nominated by For a United Ukraine in 2002 and ranked 25th by the Socialists in 2006—ranked high enough to win election in 2006.

30. Of the 22 not renominated by Our Ukraine, four landed placements with parties that ultimately won seats in 2006: two on the Party of Regions list, and two on the list of the Tymoshenko Bloc. Of the remaining 18, eight were not candidates in 2006, leaving 10 on the lists of other minor parties.

31. Deputies formerly nominated by For a United Ukraine also made appearances on the lists of the three parties winning seats in 2006 besides the Party of Regions: Our Ukraine (three), the Socialist Party (two), and the Tymoshenko Bloc (one). Of the remaining 16 district deputies nominated by For a United Ukraine in 2002, seven were not candidates in 2006 and nine were candidates on minor party lists.

3. MANAGING THE MOVE TO PROPORTIONAL
REPRESENTATION IN RUSSIA

1. Other scholars have argued that, while United Russia may enjoy party system dominance, it lacks genuine *political system* dominance (Roberts 2012b), particularly since the Kremlin has the power to destroy United Russia should it become a threat to the regime (Sakwa 2012).

2. According to Golosov (2012a, 8–9), by the end of 2006 party registration was so arduous that practice demonstrated how "creating a new party in Russia was impossible." Such restrictions, however, were eased following the 2011 Duma elections and the mass protests that accompanied these races (see, e.g., Hale 2014, 286).

3. Deputies also may choose to seek another office. Below I discuss why this is not necessarily problematic for a study of Russia in 2007.

4. This group includes the 21 deputies who did not join a faction in the Duma following the 2003 elections. These politicians appear to constitute deputies who were the least willing to bind their fates to a particular party, even United Russia.

5. In addition to diluting votes for the opposition, Gel'man (2015, 90) argues that the inherent uncertainty that rulers in competitive authoritarian regimes face contributed to the rise of Kremlin-sponsored alternatives that could serve as a potential substitute for the party of power if necessary. Roberts (2012a, 40) seems to echo this position when he describes both Rodina and A Just Russia as possessing "an uncertain party of power status."

6. Fish (2006, 194), for example, argues that the LDPR "does little more but collect bribes from the presidential administration in exchange for unstinting support."

7. In the following analysis, "mandate" refers to legislative mandate rather than electoral mandate. Among the characteristics examined, which may have influenced the prospects of different deputies making United Russia's 2007 party list, are those that would also be used to differentiate district, list, and dual electoral mandates from one another, such as electoral prowess and party affiliation. Moreover, focusing on legislative mandate captures the politicians' supposed constituencies once in office.

8. As noted in chapter 2, I used online biographies and news reports on the individual deputies, such as those published at *Monitoring Zakonoproektov RF GD* (https://lawmon.ru) and *Rossiiskii Professional'nii Portal o Lobbizme i GR* (http://lobbying.ru), to determine whether politicians were alive at the end of the 2003–2007 legislative session and therefore could have competed as candidates in the 2007 elections. The statistical results of previous analyses with all deputies elected in the December 2003 elections differed marginally from those when the deceased persons are excluded, yielding similar substantive findings.

9. These data come from Official Website of the State Duma of the Russian Federation. Although the site has been revised, the version used is archived at http://old.duma.gov.ru.

10. As I note above, while Russia's incumbent deputies may have competed as dual candidates (i.e., district-and-list candidates) in 2003, the fundamental distinction in the extant literature on party discipline and legislative behavior, including attempts to assemble a propresidential majority in the Duma (i.e., Remington 2006), emphasizes the importance of party affiliation, including whether or not deputies are independents. Moreover, to the extent that mandate matters, the approach that permits the greatest comparability is to focus on legislative mandate— that is, simply district or list (see, e.g., Sieberer 2010; Stratmann and Baur 2002).

11. For additional research on party affiliation in Russia that considers both those who formally affiliated with a party and those who did not affiliate with a party, but acted as if they did, see Kynev and Liubarev (2011).

12. Data on list rank come from the Central Election Commission of the Russian Federation (www.cikrf.ru).

13. Bushway et al. (2007, 166) identify the Heckman model as an option for cases of incidental selection such as judicial sentencing (i.e., when a judge first decides whether to incarcerate an individual and then decides sentence length).

14. The second-stage equations presented in table 3.2 were also estimated using robust regression analysis. The results of the robust regression model were substantively similar to those from the second stage of the Heckman selection model for the transformed dependent variable. The results were less consistent across estimation techniques for the model estimating list rank without the transformation.

15. All of the deputies received spots on a regional sub-list as opposed to the national list, which contained only the name of Vladimir Putin in 2007.

16. According to Bushway et al. (2007, 172–73), utilizing the same predictors in a Heckman analysis to model both the selection process and the substantive outcome breeds substantial multicollinearity, as the correction term is often strongly correlated with the included variables. To address this issue, they recommend employing exclusion restrictions, or variables that influence the first stage but not the second.

17. Russian gubernatorial data come from the dataset of Reisinger and Moraski (2017).

18 All statistical analyses were conducted using version 13.1 of the statistical software package STATA. For the Heckman models, the package estimates the first stage using probit (which is commonly used for estimating models where the dependent variable is dichotomous), as recommended by Bushway et al. (2007).

19. The powerful effect of this variable emphasizes the need for its inclusion so as to avoid an omitted variable bias.

20. These data come from Official Website of the State Duma of the Russian Federation. Although the site has been revised, the version used is archived at http://old .duma.gov.ru.

21. The Pearson $\chi2$ for the relationship is 62.0, which is significant at the .001 level for a two-tailed test.

22. I use the term "opposition party" in the sense that these parties were not United Russia and at least asserted that they were opposition parties. These parties are commonly referred to as the "systemic" opposition as a way to indicate their willingness to work within, even benefit from, the political system in place; they are to be distinguished from those organizations that genuinely oppose the regime (among others, see Atwal and Bacon 2012; Gel'man 2005; 2015; March 2009; 2012).

4. CONTENDING FOR POWER UNDER PROPORTIONAL REPRESENTATION IN UKRAINE

1. It is worth noting that party membership among list deputies nominated and elected by Our Ukraine and the Party of Regions in 2002 was even scarcer than for district deputies. Since both Our Ukraine and For a United Ukraine were electoral alliances, it is probably not surprising that only one list deputy elected by Our Ukraine was an Our Ukraine party member. For a United Ukraine, meanwhile, six of the elected list deputies identified as Party of Regions members.
2. Data come from Official Website of the Ukraine's Central Election Commission (www.cvk.gov.ua).
3. According to D'Anieri (2007, 170), this status reflected, to a large extent, the party's ties to elites in Donetsk Oblast and the financial support of the oligarch Rinat Akhmetov.
4. On March 5, 2005, Party of Regions members officially voted to become an opposition party during its seventh congress ("Partiya Regionov" n.d.).
5. Data for these variables come from Official Website of Ukraine's Central Election Commission (www.cvk.gov.ua).
6. Data come from Official Web Portal of the Verkhovna Rada (https://rada.gov.ua/).
7. This coding complements domestic observations of legislative behavior. I thank Anatoliy Romanyuk and Yuriy Shveda at the Ivan Franko National University of L'viv who underscored that the start of election campaigns constituted moments when Ukrainian deputies were most likely to change faction memberships.
8. As chapter 2 notes, three district deputies were excluded for having won their seats in by-elections, while three more deputies were unavailable to compete as candidates in 2006, yielding a total of 444 possible candidates.
9. While I focus primarily on how specific parties navigate the transition to PR-only rules, future research may wish to investigate more closely how individual politicians navigated the new rules, possibly by identifying similarities and differences in their professional backgrounds and legislative experiences beyond those used in the following multivariate models (e.g., party affiliation, faction-switching, and committee positions).
10. Although the analysis examines the entire population rather than a sample, I report significance levels as indicators of relationship strength.
11. As a reminder, in the models for this chapter, the variable "independent" corresponds to the party membership at the time of the elections, which is explicitly available for all Rada deputies. For the analysis of United Russia's list construc-

tion, however, the data are more opaque. As a result, I operationalize independence as "self-nominated" candidates, which applies only to district deputies, as well as a measure of nonpartisanship that includes list deputies without an explicit party affiliation alongside self-nominated district deputies (see chapter 3).

12. The only category that does not travel across both halves of the mixed-member electoral system is "self-nominated." While district deputies could be self-nominated, list deputies, by definition, could not be, which is why the analysis does not account for this possibility.

13. The winning percentages in the 2002 district elections ranged from a low of 12.7 percent to a high of 84.4 percent. Data come from Official Website of Ukraine's Central Election Commission (www.cvk.gov.ua).

14. Data for list ranks come from Official Website of Ukraine's Central Election Commission (www.cvk.gov.ua).

15. SMD deputies were differentiated from PR deputies with a value of zero on this variable, making this approach preferable to other options that create zero values for some PR deputies (such as 0–1 scaling and z-score scaling, the latter of which creates a mean of zero). I was then able to test models using (1) only the standardized list rank measure in place of the mandate; (2) only the vote shares of the district deputies with list deputies receiving scores of zero; and (3) both of the variables together without the mandate variable. These different specifications did not substantially alter the findings.

16. As in chapter 3, the Heckman models use probit to estimate the first stage, as recommended by Bushway et al. (2007).

17. As with the analysis in chapter 3, I also conducted robust regression analyses along with the Heckman selection models. Like the Heckman model in this case, the robust regression yields significance at the .05 level for electability and legislative leadership. However, the variables attaining significance at the .10 level in the Heckman model (i.e., age and prior incumbency) fell short of this mark in the robust regression model.

18. Party of Regions membership and electability are also significant at the .05 level when robust regression is used instead of the Heckman model. The effect of faction membership, however, is only significant at the .10 level, while the mandate effect observed in the Heckman model falls short of this mark.

5. COHESION AND CO-OPTATION IN RUSSIA AND UKRAINE

1. Members of the Rodina bloc, which was newly established for the 2003 elections, nicely illustrate the range. The list of elected deputies includes those who identify themselves as members of parties (from the Socialist United Party to the Communist Party of the Russian Federation), those who report their positions within specific party organizations (e.g., the People's Will and the Party of Regions), as well as those who do not report any party ties (Central Election Commission 2004, 263–64).

2. Data come from the sources previously identified in chapters 2–4.

3. Given the results from equation 2, the significant finding for nominating experienced legislators across all three parties should be taken with a grain of salt, as it likely reflects the practices of United Russia and Our Ukraine outweighing that of the Party of Regions when aggregated.
4. Regional sub-lists were also used during Russia's mixed-member elections. In 2003, four candidates appeared on United Russia's national (or general) list: Minister of Internal Affairs Boris Gryzlov; Minister of Emergency Situations Sergei Shoigu; the mayor of Moscow, Yurii Luzhkov; and the president of the Republic of Tatarstan, Mintimer Shaimiev. In 2007 and 2011, United Russia's general lists contained only one name, Vladimir Putin and Dmitri Medvedev, respectively.
5. For United Russia, I used the second model from table 3.2, which logs list rank to capture the diminishing marginal utility of placements as one falls lower on a regional sub-list.
6. Such traits could be added to future statistical models to the extent that the attempt to capture the multitude of potentially relevant characteristics can avoid multicollinearity. For example, legislative leadership positions could be weighted so that incumbents such as Gryzlov are given greater value than those holding less important posts.

6. PROPORTIONAL RULES AND MAJORITARIAN OUTCOMES IN RUSSIA

1. For the larger story, readers may consult a wide range of works on the topic that emphasize the role of Putin personally (Gessen 2012; Dawisha 2014); the economic and institutional shortcomings of the post-Soviet regime (Fish 2005; Gel'man 2015); economic and political developments outside of Moscow's Ring Road (Reisinger and Moraski 2017; Remington 2011); and the practice of patronage politics (Hale 2014).
2. As Roberts (2012a, 186–87) points out, a party that appears to be dominant in the party system is not necessarily the source of dominant-power politics.
3. It is notable that another aspect of Russia's electoral law—the so-called sleeping mandate—may have made placement on United Russia's list desirable for Russian governors. This provision permitted elected deputies to refuse a seat in the Duma but reclaim it down the road (McAllister and White 2008, 936). According to Turovskii (2010, 65), some experts expected that certain governors would be "'asked' not to reject mandates" following the 2007 Duma elections.
4. Technically, not all of Russia's regional executives are called "governors." For example, Russia has two cities of federal status, Moscow and St. Petersburg, where the regional chief executives are mayors. Still, scholars of Russia as well as Russian media commonly use the term "governors" for simplicity's sake.
5. Future research might seek to explain variation in the number of locomotives over time in Russia by focusing on which governors the Kremlin trusts, with more trustworthy governors left off the list and less trustworthy ones on it. From this perspective, an increase in the use of gubernatorial list placement, as between

2003 and 2007, would indicate that the Kremlin trusted fewer governors, while the decrease in the number of locomotives in 2011 relative to 2007 would suggest that the Kremlin trusted more governors, possibly thanks to the appointment era. Substantiating this argument, however, requires correlating an indicator of presidential trust with list placement. It also changes the question to why governors made the list as opposed to what effect list placement had on United Russia's regional vote shares, especially since a trust-based approach struggles to explain patterns across the regions. For example, as the analysis reveals, short-tenured governors left off the list performed significantly worse than comparable governors on the list. For a trust-based explanation, this outcome would suggest that the Kremlin trusted a set of short-tenured governors that they should not have, which is an ad hoc correction to the trust hypothesis (i.e., one that rests on the belief that the Kremlin made mistakes in list placement) rather than the predicted expectation of the locomotive hypothesis. Shortcomings of the trust hypothesis also emerge for the 2011 elections. The current work expects a lack of significance for the locomotive and gubernatorial vulnerability hypotheses in 2011. A trust-based explanation of list placement, however, produces no insight into how or why these variables might perform differently in 2011 than they did in 2007.

6. Prior to the 2007 elections, it was publicized that United Russia's list would be determined by internal party primaries. The primaries were not public affairs, however (Petrov 2007), and neither were they decisive, since six of the governors on United Russia's party list are documented as not participating in them ("List of Snubbed Governors" 2007, 11).

7. One alternative would be to employ a two-stage model, with the first stage predicting the likelihood of a governor making United Russia's list and the second stage investigating the effect of that list placement on United Russia's vote share. However, this approach would require two differently specified models that would severely tax the degrees of freedom, which are already limited due to the relative small number of observations (n = 82). Indeed, the sample size of the current analysis falls short of the recommended number of cases to produce reliable results using a two-stage model. Kline (2015, 16), for example, recommends a sample-size-to-parameter ratio of 20:1, meaning that an analysis with just five variables should have a sample size of 100 cases.

8. Chechnya is not included in the analysis due to missing data (discussed below).

9. Data on gubernatorial list placement come from the Russian Central Election Commission (www.cikrf.ru). Data on tenure come from the dataset of Reisinger and Moraski (2013).

10. Although Matsuzato (2004) identifies variation among republics in their ability to establish authoritarian rule and insulate their politics from Moscow, Myagkov et al. (2009, 90) find that, on average, republican governors in the early 2000s had greater control of their regions and more opportunities to influence election results, including the falsification of ballots.

11. Also see Saikkonen (2016).

12. Since several okrugs merged with other regions during President Putin's second term (Oracheva 2009), the number of Russian regions dropped over time from 89 to 83. Still, the analysis in table 6.1 uses data from one of these regions, Agin-Buryat Okrug, which does not merge with Chita Oblast until March 2008.

13. Unemployment data include registered and nonregistered unemployment. Since nonregistered unemployment provides a fuller picture of the economic conditions in the region, I use it. Due to missing data for real income in 2003 and 2007, I exclude Chechnya from the multivariate analysis. This reduces the number of cases under investigation in table 6.1 to 83 and in table 6.2 to 82. Data come from the Russian Federal State Statistics Agency (2005; 2007; 2008; 2012).

14. Regression diagnostics failed to reveal collinearity problems. No independent variable in the model has a variable-inflation factor near, let alone above, 10. At the same time, the statistical results without the regional support for Putin in 2004 also support the hypotheses under investigation. Since including this variable is the more difficult test, I report equations that include it.

15. The results are similar when tenure is logged. Logging tenure makes sense to the extent that the difference between being in office for 203 months (the maximum value in 2007) and 153 months should not be as important as the difference between being in office for 53 months (still long before the beginning of the appointment era) and the minimum value of two months (not only an appointed governor but one with relatively little time in office). Since this transformation produces similar results while only complicating the interpretation of the findings, I report the results without logging tenure.

16. March (2012) does not argue that the parliamentary "opposition" parties stood idly by during this period: all three proposed anticrisis measures and criticized both international and domestic actors, including United Russia. Rather, he contends that the parties muted their criticism, avoiding direct attacks on the prime minister and president at the time (Putin and Medvedev, respectively), and that this self-limiting behavior by these parties helped prevent the economic crisis from becoming a political crisis. In a similar vein, Hutcheson (2013, 918) submits that interparty collusion prevailed, with Russia's parliamentary opposition agreeing to the same barriers to entry that empowered United Russia because such collusion would ensure those parties' long-term survival.

17. Since the leader of Russia's Liberal Democratic Party, Vladimir Zhirinovskii, described United Russia in a remarkably similar way in October 2009 (i.e., as the party of "swindlers, thieves, villains and scam-artists"), March (2012, 251) cites the development as an example that might demonstrate how rhetoric from the parliamentary "opposition" about the economic crisis could have undermined Russia's regime.

18. Note that only one of the two okrugs that emerged as overachievers in 2007 still existed in 2011 due to the merger of the Agin-Buryat Okrug with Chita Oblast to form Zabaikalskii Krai.

19. Future research may wish to consider potential relationships between the personal characteristics of appointed governors and United Russia's performance across the regions in 2011.
20. Like equation 1 in table 6.1, regression diagnostics failed to reveal collinearity problems.
21. The significance of the effect is above the .05 level in the analysis presented by Klein and Moraski (2020), which uses the percent of eligible voters as the dependent variable.

7. THE CONSEQUENCES OF PARTY NOMINATIONS IN UKRAINE

1. Propresidential parties in Ukraine have also been described as "parties of power"; see, for example, D'Anieri's (2007, 211–12) discussion of Ukrainian power politics.
2. Roberts (2012a, 184) questions the accuracy of the description "party of power," especially since it has been applied to previous, and ultimately ephemeral, parties that were affiliated with the Kremlin, such as Our Home Is Russia. He argues that such parties, including United Russia, have actually been characterized by a "relative lack of power." Since Roberts (2012a, 185) also finds little comparative utility in the description, he prefers Gunther and Diamond's (2003) category of "personalistic party."
3. Kudelia (2013, 164), for example, notes that President Kuchma, following the adoption of Ukraine's 1996 constitution, used the system of appointed governors to subordinate the regional executives to the central government. While Ukraine's first president, Leonid Kravchuk, also formally possessed the power to appoint regional executives, Way (2006, 178–79) argues that Kravchuk was less adept at overcoming the regional differences that divided the country and as a result struggled to assert control over regional governments, especially those in eastern Ukraine.
4. Data on Ukraine's governors were assembled in September 2013 and May 2014 from the internet directory *Ofitsiina Ukraina S'ogodni* (available at http://dovidka.com.ua) and cross-referenced with data on Rada candidates available from Official Website of Ukraine's Central Election Commission (www.cvk.gov.ua).
5. Adding to parliamentary polarization was the fact that the new coalitions formed by more moderate deputies (e.g., the Reforms and Order/Pora coalition and the Kostenko-Pliushch blocs) failed to pass the Rada's 3 percent threshold in 2006 (Kuzio 2006, 479).
6. The alternative—pursuing a tactic of cohesion—appears possible. As chapters 2 and 4 note, in 2006 the Tymoshenko Bloc nominated only two deputies who had been previously nominated by Our Ukraine. Two others were nominated by the Party of Regions. No Our Ukraine deputies from 2002 landed on the party lists for the Communists, the Socialists, or Lytvyn's People's Bloc.
7. The other coalition member, Anatoliy Kinakh's Party of Industrialists and Entrepreneurs, defected from For a United Ukraine in favor of Yushchenko during the second round of the 2004 elections and joined Our Ukraine for the 2006 elections (Kuzio 2006, 479).

8. After finishing third in the first round of Ukraine's 2004 presidential election, the Socialist Party's candidate, Oleksandr Moroz, agreed to support Yushchenko in the runoff, and in return Yushchenko would increase the role of the parliament and award ministerial posts to the Socialists in the new government. According to Zimmer and Haran (2008, 551), the failure of the Socialist Party to pass the 3 percent threshold needed to enter parliament in 2007 resulted from the party's decision to defect from this alliance in 2006 over its insistence that Moroz become parliamentary speaker.

9. Although Yushchenko and Our Ukraine were interested in joining an "anticrisis" coalition, they objected to the inclusion of the Communists (Kuzio 2006, 483).

10. Of the 80 Our Ukraine members in the Rada at the time, 30 voted in favor, six against, four abstained, 11 did not vote, and 29 were noted absent. Data come from Official Web Portal of the Verkhovna Rada (http://rada.gov.ua).

11. Herron et al. (2019, 59) cite a total of 102 instances over a two-year span, which the Ukrainian nongovernmental organization Chesno documented using video or photo evidence of the violations. They note that the most notorious cases occurred "when deputy Mykola Lisin registered as present at a plenary session 'based on presenting deputy ID and confirmation by [his] own signature' four days after he died in an automobile accident" (Herron et al. 2019, 44).

12. Herron (2008, 554) notes that Tymoshenko actively addressed the question of minor party representation during the campaign and urged voters to behave strategically and cast ballots for the Tymoshenko Bloc.

13. While the Party of Regions in 2007 again came out on top with the plurality of votes, the corresponding 175 mandates were fewer than in 2006, creating an opportunity for the namesake of the Tymoshenko Bloc, Yulia Tymoshenko, to become prime minister in December 2007. For D'Anieri (2019, 144–45), the "big winner" of the 2007 elections was Tymoshenko and the Fatherland party (i.e., the core of the Tymoshenko Bloc).

CONCLUSION

1. With a decade between these elections and the previous elections that used SMDs, the 2012 elections required reapportionment and redistricting to accommodate population changes. The eastern regions of Donetsk and Luhansk, for example, lost three districts compared to 2002, while Kyiv and the western region of Ivano-Frankivsk gained districts. In addition, the new electoral law also banned party blocs and eliminated the "against all" option from the ballot (see Herron 2014).

2. In 2012, the Party of Regions won 30 percent of the national PR vote, which translated into 72 PR mandates in addition to 113 district contests, for a total of 185 seats. This total closely resembled the seat share (186) that the Party of Regions possessed coming out of the 2006 elections (based on 32 percent of the vote) and 10 more mandates than it received following the 2007 elections (175) (in which it received slightly more than 34 percent of the vote) (Official Website of Ukraine's Central Election Commission, www.cvk.gov.ua).

3. In addition, Carey (2009) submits that more party-centered rules help centralize party leadership and electoral resources while spurring intraparty competition that further incentivizes party discipline.

4. Outside the Rada, the Party of Regions took steps to restore the constitutional system that was in place prior to the Orange Revolution, which included a more powerful president (Thames 2017, 633–34).

5. Many Russian voters—even those commonly understood to be core Putin supporters—took offense to the Kremlin's machinations. For example, Putin was publicly booed at a televised mixed martial arts event in Moscow (i.e., by an audience that most observers of Russian politics would have identified as traditionally quite friendly to him). For video of the event, see reporting by *Euronews* (available at www.youtube.com).

6. The online map is available at www.kartanarusheniy.org.

7. For a comprehensive review of the reforms and how the appearance of "party system pluralization" was expected to benefit Russia's electoral authoritarian regime, see Wilson (2016).

8. For example, in 2000 Putin proved to be something of a blank slate onto which Russians from all sides of the political spectrum could project their hopes and views, leading some scholars to wonder whether Putin would be a captive of opinion polls as he tried to be all things to all voters. See White and McAllister (2003).

9. In 2012, Putin defeated three candidates from the systemic opposition parties and the billionaire Mikhail Prokhorov. Although Prokhorov presented himself as an independent candidate, speculation swirled about the Kremlin's role in his candidacy (see, e.g., Ioffe 2012).

10. As I note above, the return to a mixed-member system for Ukraine's 2012 legislative elections appears to have helped the ruling party there, the Party of Regions, win more seats than it had in 2007 despite a drop in support for the party across the country.

11. From this perspective, it matters that United Russia had established itself as a primary vehicle for those seeking national legislative office and subsequent promotion (see also Reuter and Turovsky 2014). The last time district elections were used, in the 2003 Duma elections, United Russia simply had fewer opportunities to benefit from election fraud in these contests since it had nominated candidates in only 137 (or about 61 percent) of the 225 districts (Moraski 2006, 207). In 2016, United Russia nominated candidates in 207 districts (Official Website of the Central Election Commission of the Russian Federation, www.cikrf.ru).

12. Also important is the fact that many of the districts were gerrymandered to dilute the vote in large cities, since urban voters had become less supportive of United Russia over time (Reuter 2016, 4).

13. It is noteworthy that Reuter and Szakonyi (2021) find that the vast majority of Russians disapprove of electoral fraud. Moreover, while a large share of voters— especially those who support the regime—believe that Russian elections are

relatively free and fair, backers of the regime also withdraw their support when they learn about fraudulent acts by United Russia candidates.

14. Golosov (2012c) makes a similar point about Russia's strict party registration requirements and the system of gubernatorial appointments.

15. It is worth emphasizing that the primary focus of this work is on the consequences of the closed-list PR system and how those consequences likely motivated another round of electoral system change. How the Kremlin chose among the different options—from the two-member system initially proposed to the mixed-member system finally instituted—constitutes the "black box" of Russian political decision-making identified by White and Kryshtanovskaya (2011). While future research may wish to tackle the latter topic more directly, it is reasonable to suspect that the return to a mixed-member system reflected a decision to move in a more conservative direction due to the protests taking place at the time. For example, reinstituting this system could be framed as returning to the option that had previously governed more competitive elections in Russia. At the same time, the potential consequences of this option were not only well known; the regime also had successfully managed such elections in the past. From this perspective, the return to a mixed-member system represents a shrewd adjustment to the institutional and procedural process governing elections. According to Case (2006), such skillful maneuvering improves the ability of electoral authoritarian regimes to tamp down the opposition and to avoid an escalation of tensions that might facilitate regime change. A clumsier response would have been to refuse making any adjustment to how future elections were to be conducted or to have instituted reforms that would have more blatantly skewed future elections in the regime's favor, such as a two-member system.

16. As Golosov (2017, 202–03) notes, the reduced threshold should be viewed in conjunction with an easing of party registration requirements that dramatically increased the number of registered parties. As a rule, the newly registered parties were not genuine opposition parties but were instead "spoiler" parties that increased party-system fragmentation in a manner that benefited United Russia, especially at the regional level (see also Golosov 2015). Indeed, Russia's 2012 law on political parties preserved the regime's control over the party system to a large degree by explicitly prohibiting electoral coalitions and allowing parties to fill their lists only with party members or independents and not with members of other parties. More important, perhaps, the law left in place an array of mechanisms by which the regime could selectively control the competition. For example, the ability to deny registration to parties that exhibit irregularities when convening their inaugural congresses or possess platforms or charters that can be depicted as inconsistent with a particular law offers authorities enough leverage to keep organizations that may nominate unacceptable candidates off the ballot (Golosov 2012c, 7).

17. Aleksandr Zhukov was nominated by United Russia and elected as a district deputy in 2003, but he did not serve in the Duma following the 2007 elections.

However, Zhukov was elected on United Russia's 2007 list; he simply declined the mandate. Zhukov returned to the Duma following the 2011 elections, once again under United Russia's banner (Official Website of the State Duma, http://duma .gov.ru).

18. Of course, deputies elected in 2003 who were unable to win reelection in 2007 or 2011 may have also returned to the Duma in 2016 via a party other than United Russia. Aleksandr Kravets, for example, was elected as a KPRF list deputy in 2003, but he did not serve in the Duma following either the 2007 or 2011 elections. However, Kravets did return to the Duma as a list deputy after receiving the top spot on the KPRF's regional sub-list representing Omsk Oblast (Official Website of the State Duma, http://duma.gov.ru).

19. For a sweeping analysis of the topic of elite defection as it relates to United Russia in particular, see Reuter and Szakonyi (2019). Note that, in Ukraine, neither of the parties supporting President Yushchenko or President Yanukovych ever enjoyed majority status. Moreover, as chapter 7 notes, violations of party discipline continued despite the move to closed-list PR. From this perspective, it makes sense that questions about electoral benefits—to the ruling party and deputies previously elected in district contests—supplanted concerns about party discipline when it came to the question about changing Ukraine's electoral system back to a mixed-member system.

20. Changes include the decision in Moldova to move from a PR-only legislative electoral system to a mixed-member system for its 2019 elections (see "Venice Commission Criticises Changes to Electoral System" 2017; "Parliamentary Elections in the Republic of Moldova: Statement by Pre-Electoral Delegation of Europe" 2019).

REFERENCES

Aarts, Kees, and Jacques Thomassen. 2008. "Satisfaction with Democracy: Do Institutions Matter?" *Electoral Studies* 27 (1): 5–18.

Aldrich, John H. 1995. *Why Parties? The Origin and Transformation of Political Parties in America.* Chicago: University of Chicago Press.

Allina-Pisano, Jessica. 2010. "Legitimizing Facades: Civil Society in Post-Orange Ukraine." In *Orange Revolution and Aftermath: Mobilization, Apathy, and the State in Ukraine*, edited by Paul D'Anieri. Washington, DC: Woodrow Wilson Center Press. Pp. 229–53.

Ames, Barry. 1994. "The Reverse Coattails Effect: Local Party Organization in the 1989 Brazilian Presidential Election." *American Political Science Review* 88 (1): 95–111.

Andersen, Robert. 2008. *Modern Methods for Robust Regression.* Thousand Oaks, CA: Sage Publications.

Anderson, Christopher J., and Christine A. Guillory. 1997. "Political Institutions and Satisfaction with Democracy: A Cross-National Analysis of Consensus and Majoritarian Systems." *American Political Science Review* 91 (1): 66–81.

Andeweg, Rudy B. 2000. "Consociational Democracy." *Annual Review of Political Science* 3 (1): 509–36.

Andrews, Josephine T., and Robert W. Jackman. 2005. "Strategic Fools: Electoral Rule Choice under Extreme Uncertainty." *Electoral Studies* 24 (1): 65–84.

Apter, David Ernest. 1965. *The Politics of Modernization.* Chicago: University of Chicago Press.

Arnold, R. Douglas. 1990. *The Logic of Congressional Action.* New Haven, CT: Yale University Press.

Aslund, Anders, and Michael McFaul. 2006. *Revolution in Orange: The Origins of Ukraine's Democratic Breakthrough.* New York: Carnegie Endowment for International Peace.

Atwal, Maya, and Edwin Bacon. 2012. "The Youth Movement *Nashi*: Contentious Politics, Civil Society, and Party Politics." *East European Politics* 28 (3): 256–66.

Bacon, Edwin. 2012. "Electoral Manipulation and the Development of Russia's Political System." *East European Politics* 28 (2): 105–18.

Barkan, Joel. 1995. "Elections in Agrarian Societies." *Journal of Democracy* 6 (4): 106–16.

———. 2008. "Progress and Retreat in Africa: Legislatures on the Rise?" *Journal of Democracy* 19 (2): 124–37.

Barzachka, Nina S. 2014. "When Winning Seats Is Not Everything: Tactical Seat-Loss during Democratization." *Comparative Politics* 46 (2): 209–29.

Barsukova, Svetlana Iu., and Vasilii I. Zviagintsev. 2006. "Mekhanism 'politicheskogo investorvaniia' ili kak i zachem Rossiiskii biznes uchastvuet v vyborakh i oplachivaet partiinuiu zhizn." *POLIS: Politicheskie Issledovaniia* 2: 110–21.

BBC News. 2007. "Q&A: Ukrainian Parliamentary Poll," October 1. http://news.bbc .co.uk.

Beissinger, Mark R. 2007. "Structure and Example in Modular Political Phenomena: The Diffusion of Bulldozer/Rose/Orange/Tulip Revolutions." *Perspectives on Politics* 5 (2): 259–76.

Benoit, Kenneth. 2007. "Electoral Laws as Political Consequences: Explaining the Origins and Change of Electoral Institutions." *Annual Review of Political Science* 10 (1): 363–90.

Berenson, Marc P. 2010. "Less Fear, Little Trust: Deciphering the Whys of Ukrainian Tax Compliance." In *Orange Revolution and Aftermath: Mobilization, Apathy, and the State in Ukraine*, edited by Paul D'Anieri. Washington, DC: Woodrow Wilson Center Press. Pp. 193–228.

Berk, Richard A. 1983. "An Introduction to Sample Selection Bias in Sociological Data." *American Sociological Review* 48 (3): 386–98.

Bernauer, Julian, and Adrian Vatter. 2012. "Can't Get No Satisfaction with the Westminster Model? Winners, Losers and the Effects of Consensual and Direct Democratic Institutions on Satisfaction with Democracy." *European Journal of Political Research* 51 (4): 435–68.

Bernhard, Michael, and Ekrem Karakoç. 2011. "Moving West or Going South? Economic Transformation and Institutionalization in Postcommunist Party Systems." *Comparative Politics* 44 (1): 1–20.

Bielasiak, Jack. 2006. "Regime Diversity and Electoral Systems in Post-Communism." *Journal of Communist Studies and Transition Politics* 22 (4): 407–30.

Birch, Sarah. 2000. *Elections and Democratization in Ukraine*. New York: St. Martin's Press, Inc.

———. 2003. "The Parliamentary Elections in Ukraine, March 2002." *Electoral Studies* 22 (3): 524–31.

———. 2007. "Electoral Systems and Electoral Misconduct." *Comparative Political Studes* 40 (12): 1533–56.

Birch, Sarah, Frances Millard, Marina Popescu, and Kieran Williams. 2002. *Embodying Democracy: Electoral System Design in Post-Communist Europe*. New York: Palgrave Macmillan.

Bjarnegard, Elin, and Meryl Kenny. 2016. "Comparing Candidate Selection: A Feminist Institutionalist Approach." *Government and Opposition* 51 (3): 370–92.

Blakkisrud, Helge. 2011. "Medvedev's New Governors." *Europe-Asia Studies* 63 (3): 367–95.

Blaydes, Lisa. 2010. *Elections and Distributive Politics in Mubarak's Egypt*. New York: Cambridge University Press.

Bochsler, Daniel. 2009. "Are Mixed Electoral Systems the Best Choice for Central and Eastern Europe or the Reason for Defective Party Systems?" *Politics and Policy* 37: 735–67.

———. 2010. *Territory and Electoral Rules in Post-Communist Democracies*. New York: Palgrave Macmillan.

Bodian, Mamadou. 2016. "The Politics of Electoral Reform in Francophone West Africa" (Doctoral diss.). The University of Florida.

Bogaards, Matthijs. 2004. "Counting Parties and Identifying Dominant Party Systems in Africa." *European Journal of Political Research* 43 (2): 173–97.

———. 2008. "Dominant Party Systems and Electoral Volatility in Africa: A Comment on Mozaffar and Scarritt." *Party Politics* 14 (1): 113–30.

Boix, Carles. 1999. "Setting the Rules of the Game: The Choice of Electoral Systems in Advanced Democracies." *American Political Science Review* 93 (3): 609–24.

Boix, Carles, and Milan W. Svolik. 2013. "The Foundations of Limited Authoritarian Government: Institutions, Commitment, and Power-Sharing in Dictatorships." *Journal of Politics* 75 (2): 300–16.

Born, Richard. 1984. "Reassessing the Decline of Presidential Coattails: US House Elections from 1952–80." *Journal of Politics* 46 (1): 60–79.

Bowler, Shaun, Todd Donovan, and Jeffrey A. Karp. 2006. "Why Politicians Like Electoral Institutions: Self-Interest, Values, or Ideology?" *Journal of Politics* 68 (2): 434–46.

Brader, Ted, and Joshua A. Tucker. 2001. "The Emergence of Mass Partisanship in Russia, 1993–1996." *American Journal of Political Science* 45 (1): 69–83.

Brambor, Thomas, William Roberts Clark, and Matt Golder. 2006. "Understanding Interaction Models: Improving Empirical Analyses." *Political Analysis* 14 (1): 63–82.

Broockman, David E. 2009. "Do Congressional Candidates Have Reverse Coattails? Evidence from a Regression Discontinuity Design." *Political Analysis* 17 (4): 418–34.

Brownlee, Jason. 2007. *Authoritarianism in an Age of Democracy*. New York: Cambridge University Press.

Brudny, Yitzhak M. 2001. "Continuity or Change in Russian Electoral Patterns? The December 1999–March 2000 Election Cycle." In *Contemporary Russian Politics: A Reader*, edited by Archie Brown. New York: Oxford University Press. Pp. 154–78.

Brudny, Yitzhak M., and Evgeny Finkel. 2011. "Why Ukraine Is Not Russia: Hegemonic National Identity and Democracy in Russia and Ukraine." *East European Politics & Societies* 25 (4): 813–33.

Bunce, Valerie J., and Sharon L. Wolchik. 2011. *Defeating Authoritarian Leaders in Postcommunist Countries*. New York: Cambridge University Press.

Bushway, Shawn, Brian D. Johnson, and Lee Ann Slocum. 2007. "Is the Magic Still There? The Use of the Heckman Two-Step Correction for Selection Bias in Criminology." *Journal of Quantitative Criminology* 23 (2): 151–78.

Calvo, Ernesto. 2009. "The Competitive Road to Proportional Representation: Partisan Biases and Electoral Regime Change under Increasing Party Competition." *World Politics* 61 (2): 254–95.

Campbell, James E., and Joe A. Sumners. 1990. "Presidential Coattails in Senate Elections." *American Political Science Review* 84 (2): 513–24.

Capoccia, Giovanni, and Daniel Ziblatt. 2010. "The Historical Turn in Democratization Studies: A New Research Agenda for Europe and Beyond." *Comparative Political Studies* 43(8/9): 931–68.

Carey, John M. 2007. "Competing Principals, Political Institutions, and Party Unity in Legislative Voting." *American Journal of Political Science* 51 (1): 92–107.

———. 2009. *Legislative Voting and Accountability*. New York: Cambridge University Press.

Carey, John M., and Simon Hix. 2011. "The Electoral Sweet Spot: Low-Magnitude Proportional Electoral Systems." *American Journal of Political Science* 55 (2): 383–97.

Carothers, Thomas. 2002. "The End of the Transition Paradigm." *Journal of Democracy* 13 (1): 5–21.

Case, William. 2006. "Manipulative Skills: How Do Rulers Control the Electoral Arena?" In *Electoral Authoritarianism: The Dynamics of Unfree Competition*, edited by Andreas Schedler. Boulder, CO: Lynne Rienner Publishers. Pp. 95–112.

Caul, Miki. 1999. "Women's Representation in Parliament." *Party Politics* 5 (1): 79–98.

Central Election Commission of the Russian Federation. 2004. *Vybory Deputatov Gosudarstvennoi Dumy Federalnogo Sobraniya Rossiiskoi Federatsii 2003: Elektoral'naya Statistika*. Moscow: Ves' Mir.

Chaisty, Paul. 2005. "Party Cohesion and Policy-Making in Russia." *Party Politics* 11 (3): 299–318.

Chashin, Aleksandr Nikolaevich. 2009. *Korruptsiya v Rossii: Strategiya, Taktika i Metodi Bor'bi*. Moscow: Delo i Servis.

Cheloukhine, Serguei, and Joseph King. 2007. "Corruption Networks as a Sphere of Investment Activities in Modern Russia." *Communist and Post-Communist Studies* 40 (1): 107–22.

Clark, William A. 1998. "Presidential Power and Democratic Stability under the Russian Constitution: A Comparative Analysis." *Presidential Studies Quarterly* 28 (3): 620–37.

———. 2005. "The Russian Election Cycle, 2003–2004." *Electoral Studies* 3 (24): 511–19.

———. 2010. "Boxing Russia: Executive-Legislative Powers and the Categorization of Russia's Regime Type." *Demokratizatsiya* 19 (1): 5–22.

Claypool, Vicki Hesli, William M. Reisinger, Marina Zaloznaya, Yue Hu, and Jenny Juehring. 2018. "Tsar Putin and the 'Corruption' Thorn in His Side: The Demobilization of Votes in a Competitive Authoritarian Regime." *Electoral Studies* 54 (August): 182–204.

Colton, Timothy J. 2000. *Transitional Citizens: Voters and What Influences Them in the New Russia*. Cambridge, MA: Harvard University Press.

Coppedge, Michael. 1999. "Thickening Thin Concepts and Theories: Combining Large N and Small in Comparative Politics." *Comparative Politics* 31 (4): 465–76.

Coppedge, Michael, John Gerring, Carl Henrik Knutsen, Staffan I. Lindberg, Svend-Erik Skaaning, Jan Teorell, and David Altman et al. 2018. "V-Dem Country-Year Dataset 2018." Varieties of Democracy (V-Dem) Project.

Cox, Gary. 1997. *Making Votes Count: Strategic Coordination in the World's Electoral Systems*. New York: Cambridge University Press.

Cox, Gary W., and Jonathan N. Katz. 2002. *Elbridge Gerry's Salamander: The Electoral Consequences of the Reapportionment Revolution*. New York: Cambridge University Press.

Cox, Gary W., and Mathew D. McCubbins. 1993. *Legislative Leviathan: Party Government in the House*. New York: Cambridge University Press.

Cox, Karen E., and Leonard J. Schoppa. 2002. "Interaction Effects in Mixed-Member Electoral Systems: Theory and Evidence from Germany, Japan, and Italy." *Comparative Political Studies* 35 (9): 1027–53.

Crawford, Beverly, and Arend Lijphart. 1995. "Explaining Political and Economic Change in Post-Communist Eastern Europe: Old Legacies, New Institutions, Hegemonic Norms, and International Pressures." *Comparative Political Studies* 28 (2): 171–99.

Cusack, Thomas R., Torben Iversen, and David Soskice. 2007. "Economic Interests and the Origins of Electoral Systems." *American Political Science Review* 101 (3): 373–91.

Dahl, Robert A. 1971. *Polyarchy: Participation and Opposition*. New Haven, CT: Yale University Press.

D'Anieri, Paul. 2005. "What Has Changed in Ukrainian Politics? Assessing the Implications of the Orange Revolution." *Problems of Post-Communism* 52 (5): 82–91.

———. 2007. *Understanding Ukrainian Politics: Power, Politics, and Institutional Design*. Armonk, NY: ME Sharpe.

———. 2010. "Introduction: Civil Society in Ukraine—from Despair to Hope . . . and Back." In *Orange Revolution and Aftermath: Mobilization, Apathy, and the State in Ukraine*, edited by Paul D'Anieri. Washington, DC: Woodrow Wilson Center Press. Pp. 193–228.

———. 2019. *Ukraine and Russia: From Civilied Divorce to Uncivil War*. New York: Cambridge University Press.

Dawisha, Karen. 2014. *Putin's Kleptocracy: Who Owns Russia?* New York: Simon and Schuster.

Diuk, Nadia, and Myroslava Gongadze. 2002. "Post-election Blues in Ukraine." *Journal of Democracy* 13 (4): 157–66.

Dodd, Lawrence. 1976. *Coalitions in Parliamentary Government*. Princeton, NJ: Princeton University Press.

"Dos'ye: Satyuk Vladimir Nikolaevich." n.d. *PolitRada*. http://politrada.com.

Drury, A. Cooper, Richard Stuart Olson, and Douglas A. Van Belle. 2005. "The Politics of Humanitarian Aid: US Foreign Disaster Assistance, 1964–1995." *Journal of Politics* 67 (2): 454–73.

Dunleavy, Patrick, and Helen Margetts. 1995. "Understanding the Dynamics of Electoral Reform." *International Political Science Review / Revue Internationale de Science Politique* 16 (1): 9–29.

Duverger, Maurice. 1954. *Political Parties: Their Organization and Activity in the Modern State*. New York: John Wiley and Sons, Inc.

———. 1980. "A New Political System Model: Semi-presidential Government." *European Journal of Political Research* 8 (2): 165–87.

Elgie, Robert. 1998. "The Classification of Democratic Regime Types: Conceptual Ambiguity and Contestable Assumptions." *European Journal of Political Research* 33 (2): 219–38.

Elster, Jon, Claus Offe, Ulrich K. Preuss, Frank Boenker, Ulrike Goetting, and Friedbert W. Rueb. 1998. *Institutional Design in Post-Communist Societies: Rebuilding the Ship at Sea.* New York: Cambridge University Press.

Erikson, Robert S. 1972. "Malapportionment, Gerrymandering, and Party Fortunes in Congressional Elections." *American Political Science Review* 66 (4): 1234–45.

Evans, Geoffrey, and Stephen Whitefield. 1998. "The Evolution of Left and Right in Post-Soviet Russia." *Europe-Asia Studies* 50 (6): 1023–42.

Farrell, David M., and Ian McAllister. 1995. "Legislative Recruitment to Upper Houses: The Australian Senate and House of Representatives Compared." *Journal of Legislative Studies* 1 (2): 243–63.

Ferejohn, John A., and Randall L. Calvert. 1984. "Presidential Coattails in Historical Perspective." *American Journal of Political Science* 28 (1): 127–46.

Ferrara, Federico, and Erik S. Herron. 2005. "Going It Alone? Strategic Electoral Rules." *American Journal of Political Science* 49 (1): 16–31.

Fish, M. Steven. 1997. "The Pitfalls of Russian Superpresidentialism." *Current History* 96 (612): 326–30.

———. 2005. *Democracy Derailed in Russia: The Failure of Open Politics.* New York: Cambridge University Press.

———. 2006. "Creative Constitutions: How Do Parliamentary Powers Shape the Electoral Arena." In *Electoral Authoritarianism: The Dynamics of Unfree Competition*, edited by Andreas Schedler. Boulder, CO: Lynne Rienner Publishers. Pp. 181–97.

Flores-Macías, Gustavo A. 2012. *After Neoliberalism? The Left and Economic Reforms in Latin America.* New York: Oxford University Press.

Fleron, Frederic J. 2016. *Russian Studies and Comparative Politics: Views from Metatheory and Middle-Range Theory.* Lanham, MD: Lexington Books.

Freedom House. https://freedomhouse.org.

Freidenberg, Flavia, and Steven Levitsky. 2006. "Informal Institutions and Party Organization in Latin America." In *Informal Institutions and Democracy. Lessons from Latin America*, edited by Gretchen Helmke and Steven Levitsky. Baltimore, MD: The Johns Hopkins University Press. Pp. 178–97.

Frye, Timothy, Ora John Reuter, and David Szakonyi. 2014. "Political Machines at Work: Voter Mobilization and Electoral Subversion in the Workplace." *World Politics* 66 (2): 195–228.

———. 2019. "Hitting Them with Carrots: Voter Intimidation and Vote Buying in Russia." *British Journal of Political Science* 49 (3): 857–81.

Gaines, Brian J., and Christophe Crombez. 2004. "Another Look at Connections across German Elections." *Journal of Theoretical Politics* 16 (3): 289–319.

Gallagher, Michael, and Michael Marsh. 1988. *Candidate Selection in Comparative Perspective: The Secret Garden of Politics*. London: Sage Publications.

Gandhi, Jennifer. 2008. *Political Institutions under Dictatorship*. New York: Cambridge University Press.

Gandhi, Jennifer, and Ellen Lust-Okar. 2009. "Elections under Authoritarianism." *Annual Review of Political Science* 12 (1): 403–22.

Gandhi, Jennifer, and Adam Przeworski. 2007. "Authoritarian Institutions and the Survival of Autocrats." *Comparative Political Studies* 40 (11): 1279–301.

Gasiorowski, Mark J. 1995. "Economic Crisis and Political Regime Change: An Event History Analysis." *American Political Science Review* 89 (4): 882–97.

Geddes, Barbara. 1999. "What Do We Know about Democratization after Twenty Years?" *Annual Review of Political Science* 2 (1): 115–44.

Gelineau, Francois, and Karen L. Remmer. 2006. "Political Decentralization and Electoral Accountability: The Argentine Experience, 1983–2001." *British Journal of Political Science* 36 (1): 133–57.

Gel'man, Vladimir. 2005. "Political Opposition in Russia: A Dying Species?" *Post-Soviet Affairs* 21 (3): 226–46.

———. 2006. "From 'Feckless Pluralism' to 'Dominant Power Politics'? The Transformation of Russia's Party System." *Democratization* 13 (4): 545–61.

———. 2007. "Political Trends in the Russian Regions on the Eve of the State Duma Elections." *Russian Analytical Digest* 31: 6–7.

———. 2015. *Authoritarian Russia: Analyzing Post-Soviet Regime Changes*. Pittsburgh, PA: University of Pittsburgh Press.

Gerschewski, Johannes. 2013. "The Three Pillars of Stability: Legitimation, Repression, and Co-optation in Autocratic Regimes." *Democratization* 20 (1): 13–38.

Gessen, Masha. 2012. *The Man Without a Face: The Unlikely Rise of Vladimir Putin*. New York: Riverhead Books (Penguin).

Gill, Graeme. 2016. "Russia and the Vulnerability of Electoral Authoritarianism?" *Slavic Review* 75 (2): 354–73.

Giollabhuí, Shane Mac. 2013. "How Things Fall Apart: Candidate Selection and the Cohesion of Dominant Parties in South Africa and Namibia." *Party Politics* 19 (4): 577–600.

Gladdish, Ken. 1993. "The Primacy of the Particular." *Journal of Democracy* 4 (1): 53–65.

Golder, Matt, and Gabriella Lloyd. 2014. "Re-evaluating the Relationship between Electoral Rules and Ideological Congruence." *European Journal of Political Research* 53 (1): 200–12.

Golder, Matt, and Jacek Stramski. 2010. "Ideological Congruence and Electoral Institutions." *American Journal of Political Science* 54 (1): 90–106.

Golosov, Grigorii. 2004. *Political Parties in the Regions of Russia: Democracy Unclaimed*. Boulder, CO: Lynne Rienner Publishers.

———. 2006. "Disproportionality by Proportional Design: Seats and Votes in Russia's Regional Legislative Elections, December 2003–March 2005." *Europe-Asia Studies* 58 (1): 25–55.

———. 2011. "Russia's Regional Legislative Elections, 2003–2007: Authoritarianism Incorporated." *Europe-Asia Studies* 63 (3): 397–414.

———. 2012a. "Dmitry Medvedev's Party Reform." *Russian Analytical Digest* 115: 8–10.

———. 2012b. "Problems of the Russian Electoral System." *Russian Politics & Law* 50 (3): 18–39.

———. 2012c. "The 2012 Political Reform in Russia." *Problems of Post-Communism* 59 (6): 3–14.

———. 2015. "Do Spoilers Make a Difference? Instrumental Manipulation of Political Parties in an Electoral Authoritarian Regime: The Case of Russia." *East European Politics* 31(2): 170–86.

———. 2016. "Why and How Electoral Systems Matter in Autocracies." *Australian Journal of Political Science* 51 (3): 367–85.

———. 2017. "Authoritarian Learning in the Development of Russia's Electoral System." *Russian Politics* 2 (2): 182–205.

"Gorbal' Vasilii Mikhailovich." n.d. *Politrada*. http://politrada.com.

Greene, Kenneth F. 2007. *Why Dominant Parties Lose: Mexico's Democratization in Comparative Perspective*. New York: Cambridge University Press.

———. 2010. "The Political Economy of Authoritarian Single-Party Dominance." *Comparative Political Studies* 43 (7): 807–34.

Grzymala-Busse, Anna M. 2002. *Redeeming the Communist Past: The Regeneration of Communist Parties in East Central Europe*. New York: Cambridge University Press.

Gunther, Richard, and Larry Diamond. 2003. "Species of Political Parties: A New Typology." *Party Politics* 9 (2): 167–99.

Hain, Peter. 1986. *Proportional Misrepresentation: The Case against PR in Britain*. Guilford: Wildwood House.

Hale, Henry E. 2006. *Why Not Parties in Russia? Democracy, Federalism, and the State*. NY: Cambridge University Press.

———. 2007. "Correlates of Clientelism: Political Economy, Politicized Ethnicity and Post-Communist Transition." In *Patrons, Clients and Policies: Patterns of Democratic Accountability and Political Competition*, edited by Herbert Kitschelt and Steven I. Wilkinson. New York, NY: Cambridge University Press. Pp. 227–50.

———. 2014. *Patronal Politics*. New York, NY: Cambridge University Press.

Harasymiw, Bohdan. 2005. "Elections in Post-Communist Ukraine, 1994–2004: An Overview." *Canadian Slavonic Papers / Revue Canadienne Des Slavistes* 47 (3/4): 191–239.

Harmel, Robert, and Kenneth Janda. 1994. "An Integrated Theory of Party Goals and Party Change." *Journal of Theoretical Politics* 6 (3): 259–87.

Hazan, Reuven Y., and Gideon Rahat. 2006a. "Candidate Selection: Methods and Consequences." In *Handbook of Party Politics*, edited by Richard S. Katz and William Crotty. Thousand Oaks, CA: Sage Publications. Pp. 109–121.

———. 2006b. "The Influence of Candidate Selection Methods on Legislatures and Legislators: Theoretical Propositions, Methodological Suggestions and Empirical Evidence." *Journal of Legislative Studies* 12 (3/4): 366–85.

——. 2010. *Democracy within Parties: Candidate Selection Methods and Their Political Consequences*. New York: Oxford University Press.

Heckman, James J. 1976. "The Common Structure of Statistical Models of Truncation, Sample Selection and Limited Dependent Variables and a Simple Estimator for Such Models." *Annals of Economic and Social Measurement* 5 (4): 475–92.

Herron, Erik S. 2008. "The Parliamentary Election in Ukraine, September 2007." *Electoral Studies* 27 (3): 547–77.

——. 2009. *Elections and Democracy after Communism?* New York: Palgrave Macmillan.

——. 2014. "The Parliamentary Elections in Ukraine, October 2012." *Electoral Studies* 33 (March): 353–56.

——. 2018. "Electoral Systems in Context: Ukraine." In *Oxford Handbook of Electoral Systems*, edited by Erik S. Herron, Robert J. Pekkanen, and Matthew S. Shugart. New York: Oxford University Press. Pp. 903–20.

——. 2020. *Normalizing Corruption: Failures of Accountability in Ukraine*. Ann Arbor, Michigan: University of Michigan Press.

Herron, Erik S., Brian Fitzpatrick, and Maksym Palamarenko. 2019. "The Practice and Implications of Legislative Proxy Voting in Ukraine." *Post-Soviet Affairs* 35 (1): 41–62.

Herron, Erik S. and Misa Nishikawa. 2001. "Contamination Effects and the Number of Parties in Mixed-Superposition Electoral Systems." *Electoral Studies* 20: 63–86.

Herszenhorn, David M. 2013. "Putin Orders New System for Russian Parliamentary Elections." *New York Times*, January 2. Europe. www.nytimes.com.

Hesli, Vicki L. 2007. "The 2006 Parliamentary Election in Ukraine." *Electoral Studies* 26 (2): 507–11.

Holmes, Leslie. 2008. "Corruption and Organised Crime in Putin's Russia." *Europe-Asia Studies* 60 (6): 1011–31.

Holmes, Stephen. 1993. "Superpresidentialism and Its Problems." *East European Constitutional Review* 2: 123–26.

Howard, Marc Morjé, and Philip G. Roessler. 2006. "Liberalizing Electoral Outcomes in Competitive Authoritarian Regimes." *American Journal of Political Science* 50 (2): 365–81.

Huntington, Samuel P. 1968. *Political Order in Changing Societies*. New Haven, CT: Yale University Press.

——. 1991. "Democracy's Third Wave." *Journal of Democracy* 2 (2): 12–34.

Huskey, Eugene. 2005. "Putin as Patron: Cadres Policy in the Russian Transition." In *Leading Russia: Putin in Perspective, Essays in Honour of Archie Brown*, edited by Alex Pravda. New York: Oxford University Press. Pp. 161–78.

Hutcheson, Derek S. 2013. "Party Cartels beyond Western Europe: Evidence from Russia." *Party Politics* 19 (6): 907–24.

——. 2018. *Parliamentary Elections in Russia: A Quarter-Century of Multiparty Politics*. New York: Oxford University Press.

Ioffe, Julia. 2012. "The Master and Mikhail." *The New Yorker*, February 27, 2012. www.newyorker.com.

Ishiyama, John T. 1999. "The Communist Successor Parties and Party Organizational Development in Post-Communist Politics." *Political Research Quarterly* 52 (1): 87–112.

Ishiyama, John T., and Ryan Kennedy. 2001. "Superpresidentialism and Political Party Development in Russia, Ukraine, Armenia and Kyrgyzstan." *Europe-Asia Studies* 53 (8): 1177–91.

Ivanov, Vitalii. 2008. *Partiya Putina: Istoriya "Edinoi Rossii."* Moscow: Olma Media Group.

Jaffe, A., and R. Manning. 2001. "Russia, Energy and the West." *Survival* 43 (2): 133–52.

Javeline, Debra, and Vanessa A. Baird. 2011. "The Surprisingly Nonviolent Aftermath of the Beslan School Hostage Taking." *Problems of Post-Communism* 58 (4/5): 3–22.

Kahn, Jeffrey. 2001. "What Is the New Russian Federalism?" In *Contemporary Russian Politics: A Reader*, edited by Archie Brown. New York: Oxford University Press. Pp. 374–83.

———. 2002. *Federalism, Democratization, and the Rule of Law in Russia.* New York: Oxford University Press.

Kalandadze, Katya, and Mitchell A. Orenstein. 2009. "Electoral Protests and Democratization Beyond the Color Revolutions, Electoral Protests and Democratization Beyond the Color Revolutions." *Comparative Political Studies* 42 (11): 1403–25.

Karatnycky, Adrian. 2005. "Ukraine's Orange Revolution." *Foreign Affairs* 84: 35–52.

Katz, Richard S. 2001. "The Problem of Candidate Selection and Models of Party Democracy." *Party Politics* 7 (3): 277–96.

Kaya, Ruchan, and Michael Bernhard. 2013. "Are Elections Mechanisms of Authoritarian Stability or Democratization? Evidence from Postcommunist Eurasia." *Perspectives on Politics* 11 (3): 734–52.

Kitschelt, Herbert, Kirk A. Hawkins, Juan Pablo Luna, Guillermo Rosas, and Elizabeth J. Zechmeister. 2010. *Latin American Party Systems.* New York: Cambridge University Press.

Kitschelt, Herbert, Zdenka Mansfeldova, Radoslaw Markowski, and Gabor Toka. 1999. *Post-Communist Party Systems: Competition, Representation, and Inter-Party Cooperation.* New York: Cambridge University Press.

Klein, Aidan, and Bryon J. Moraski. 2020. "Incentives to Deliver: Authoritarian Rule, Proportional Representation, and Support for Russia's Ruling Party." *Journal of Elections, Public Opinion & Parties* 30 (4): 524–41.

Kline, Rex B. 2015. *Principles and Practice of Structural Equation Modeling, Fourth Edition.* New York: The Guilford Publications.

Klobucar, Thomas F., Arthur H. Miller, and Gwyn Erb. 2002. "The 1999 Ukrainian Presidential Election: Personalities, Ideology, Partisanship, and the Economy." *Slavic Review* 61 (2): 315–44.

Knutsen, Carl Henrik, Håvard Mokleiv Nygård, and Tore Wig. 2017. "Autocratic Elections: Stabilizing Tool or Force for Change?" *World Politics* 69 (1): 98–143.

Konitzer, Andrew. 2005. *Voting for Russia's Governors: Regional Elections and Accountability Under Yeltsin and Putin.* Baltimore, MD: Johns Hopkins University Press.

Kortukov, Dima. 2019. "The Politics of Electoral Reform in Ukraine." *Problems of Post-Communism* 67 (6): 488–99.

Koshkina, Sonya. 2015. *Maidan: Nerasskazannaya Istoriya.* Kyiv: Bright Star Publishing.

Kostadinova, Tatiana. 2002. "Do Mixed Electoral Systems Matter? A Cross-National Analysis of Their Effects in Eastern Europe." *Electoral Studies* 21 (1): 23–34.

Kozlovsky, Sergey. 2018. "World Cup Fails to Quell Russian Anger over Pension Reform." *BBC News.* 5 July. www.bbc.com.

"Krome Yushchenko, v deputaty vydvinuli ego plemyannika, brata i press-sekretarya." 2005. *Ukrainskaya Pravda.* December 3. www.pravda.com.ua.

Kreuzer, Marcus, and Vello Pettai. 2003. "Patterns of Political Instability: Affiliation Patterns of Politicians and Voters in Post-Communist Estonia, Latvia, and Lithuania." *Studies in Comparative International Development* 38 (2): 76–98.

Kryshtanovskaya, Ol'ga, and Stephen White. 2009. "The Sovietization of Russian Politics." *Post-Soviet Affairs* 25 (4): 283–09.

Kudelia, Serhiy. 2013. "If Tomorrow Comes: Power Balance and Time Horizons in Ukraine's Constitutional Politics." *Demokratizatsiya* 21 (2): 151–78.

———. 2014. "The House That Yanukovych Built." *Journal of Democracy* 25 (3): 19–34.

Kudelia, Serhiy, and Taras Kuzio. 2014. "Nothing Personal: Explaining the Rise and Decline of Political Machines in Ukraine." *Post-Soviet Affairs* 31 (3): 250–78.

Kunicova, Jana, and Thomas Frederick Remington. 2008. "Mandates, Parties and Dissent: Effect of Electoral Rules on Parliamentary Party Cohesion in the Russian State Duma, 1994–2003." *Party Politics* 14 (5): 555–74.

Kuzio, Taras. 2003. "The 2002 Parliamentary Elections in Ukraine: Democratization or Authoritarianism?" *Journal of Communist Studies and Transition Politics* 19 (2): 24–54.

———. 2005. "From Kuchma to Yushchenko Ukraine's 2004 Presidential Elections and the Orange Revolution." *Problems of Post-Communism* 52 (2): 29–44.

———. 2006. "The Orange Revolution at the Crossroads." *Demokratizatsiya* 14 (4): 477–93.

———. 2014. "Crime, Politics and Business in 1990s Ukraine." *Communist and Post-Communist Studies* 47 (2): 195–210.

Kynev, A. V., and A. E. Liubarev. 2011. *Partii i Vybory v Sovremennoi Rossii: Evoliutsiia i Devoliutsiia.* Moscow: Novoe Literaturnoe Obozrenie.

Lakeman, Enid. 1974. *How Democracies Vote: A Study of Electoral Systems.* London: Faber & Faber.

Langston, Joy. 2006. "Elite Ruptures: When Do Ruling Parties Split?" In *Electoral Authoritarianism: The Dynamics of Unfree Competition.* Boulder, CO: Lynne Rienner Publishers. Pp. 57–75.

Laver, Michael, and Norman Schofield. 1990. *Multiparty Government: The Politics of Coalition in Europe.* Ann Arbor, MI: University of Michigan Press.

Laver, Michael, and Kenneth A. Shepsle. 1996. *Making and Breaking Governments: Cabinets and Legislatures in Parliamentary Democracies.* New York: Cambridge University Press.

Laverty, Nicklaus. 2008. "Limited Choices: Russian Opposition Parties and the 2007 Duma Election." *Demokratizatsiya* 16(4): 363–81.

———. 2015. "The 'Party of Power' as a Type." *East European Politics* 31 (1): 71–87.

Levitsky, Steven. 1998. "Institutionalization and Peronism: The Concept, the Case and the Case for Unpacking the Concept." *Party Politics* 4 (1): 77–92.

Levitsky, Steven, and Lucan Way. 2002. "The Rise of Competitive Authoritarianism." *Journal of Democracy* 13 (2): 51–65.

———. 2010. *Competitive Authoritarianism: Hybrid Regimes After the Cold War*. New York: Cambridge University Press.

Lijphart, Arend. 1994. *Electoral Systems and Party Systems: A Study of Twenty-Seven Democracies, 1945–1990*. New York: Oxford University Press.

———. 2004. "Constitutional Design for Divided Societies." *Journal of Democracy* 15 (2): 96–109.

Lijphart, Arend, and Bernhard Grofman. 1984. "Choosing an Electoral System." In *Choosing an Electoral System: Issues and Alternatives*, edited by Arend Lijphart and Bernhard Grofman. New York: Praeger. Pp. 3–12.

Lindberg, Staffan I. 2009. "A Theory of Elections as a Mode of Transition." In *Democratization by Elections: A New Mode of Transition*, edited by Staffan I. Lindberg. Baltimore, MD: Johns Hopkins University Press. Pp. 314–41.

Linz, Juan J., and Alfred Stepan. 1996. *Problems of Democratic Transition and Consolidation: Southern Europe, South America, and Post-Communist Europe*. Baltimore, MD: Johns Hopkins University Press.

Lipset, Seymour Martin. 2000. "The Indispensability of Political Parties." *Journal of Democracy* 11 (1): 48–55.

"List of 'Snubbed Governors.'" 2007. *Russian Analytical Digest* 31: 11.

"Lone United Russia Deputy Defies Leadership on Pension Vote, Refuses Calls to Resign." 2018. *The Moscow Times*. July 27. http://themoscowtimes.com.

Luna, Juan Pablo, Rafael Piñeiro Rodríguez, Fernando Rosenblatt, and Gabriel Vommaro. 2021. "Political Parties, Diminished Subtypes, and Democracy." *Party Politics* 27 (2): 294–307.

Lundell, Krister. 2010. *The Origin of Electoral Systems in the Postwar Era: A Worldwide Approach*. New York: Routledge.

Luong, Pauline Jones. 2002. *Institutional Change and Political Continuity in Post-Soviet Central Asia: Power, Perceptions, and Pacts*. New York: Cambridge University Press.

Lupu, Noam, and Rachel Beatty Riedl. 2013. "Political Parties and Uncertainty in Developing Democracies." *Comparative Political Studies* 46 (11): 1339–65.

Lust-Okar, Ellen. 2006. "Elections under Authoritarianism: Preliminary Lessons from Jordan." *Democratization* 13 (3): 456–71.

Lust-Okar, Ellen, and Amaney Jamal. 2002. "Rulers and Rules: Reassessing Electoral Laws and Political Liberalization in the Middle East." *Comparative Political Studies* 35 (3): 337–70.

Lynch, Allen C. 2005. *How Russia is Not Ruled: Reflections of Russian Political Development*. New York: Cambridge University Press.

Lyubarev, Arkady. 2012. "An Evaluation of the Results of the Duma Elections." *Russian Analytical Digest* 108 (6): 2–5.

Magaloni, Beatriz. 2006. *Voting for Autocracy: Hegemonic Party Survival and Its Demise in Mexico*. New York: Cambridge University Press.

Magaloni, Beatriz, and Ruth Kricheli. 2010. "Political Order and One-Party Rule." *Annual Review of Political Science* 13: 123–43.

Magar, Eric. 2012. "Gubernatorial Coattails in Mexican Congressional Elections." *Journal of Politics* 74 (2): 383–99.

Mainwaring, Scott. 1999. *Rethinking Party Systems in the Third Wave of Democratization: The Case of Brazil*. Stanford, CA: Stanford University Press.

Mainwaring, Scott, and Timothy Scully. 1995. "Introduction: Party Systems in Latin America." In *Building Democratic Institutions: Party Systems in Latin America*, edited Scott Mainwaring and Timothy Scully. Stanford, CA: Stanford University Press. Pp. 1–34.

Mainwaring, Scott, and Mariano Torcal. 2006. "Party System Institutionalization and Party System Theory after the Third Wave of Democratization." In *Handbook of Party Politics*, edited by Richard S. Katz and William Crotty. Thousand Oaks, CA: Sage Publications. Pp. 204–27.

Mainwaring, Scott, and Edurne Zoco. 2007. "Political Sequences and the Stabilization of Interparty Competition: Electoral Volatility in Old and New Democracies." *Party Politics* 13 (2): 155–78.

Makarenko, Boris I. 2012. "The Post-Soviet Party of Power: United Russia in Comparative Context." *Russian Politics and Law* 50 (1): 54–83.

Maksimov, Andrei. 1999. "'Chistie' i 'Griaznie' Tekhnologii Vyborov (Rossiiskii Opyt). Moscow: Mordodey & Imagemakers.

Maksymiuk, Jan. 2007. "Ukraine: Political Class Misses Its Station." *Radio Free Europe / Radio Liberty*. June 13. www.rferl.org.

Manning, Carrie. 2005. "Assessing African Party Systems after the Third Wave." *Party Politics* 11 (6): 707–27.

March, Luke. 2009. "Managing Opposition in a Hybrid Regime: Just Russia and Parastatal Opposition." *Slavic Review* 68 (3): 504–27.

———. 2012. "The Russian Duma 'Opposition': No Drama Out of Crisis?" *East European Politics* 28 (3): 241–55.

Matsuzato, Kimitaka. 2004. "Authoritarian Transformations of the Mid-Volga National Republics: An Attempt at Macro-Regionology." *Journal of Communist Studies and Transition Politics* 20 (2): 98–123.

Mayhew, David R. 1974. *Congress: The Electoral Connection*. New Haven, CT: Yale University Press.

McAllister, Ian, and Stephen White. 2008. "'It's the Economy, Comrade!' Parties and Voters in the 2007 Russian Duma Election." *Europe-Asia Studies* 60 (6): 931–57.

McCoy, Jennifer L., and Jonathan Hartlyn. 2009. "The Relative Powerlessness of Elections in Latin America." In *Democratization by Elections: A New Mode of Transition*, edited by Staffan I. Lindberg. Baltimore: Johns Hopkins University Press. Pp. 47–76.

McFaul, Michael. 1992. "Russia's Emerging Political Parties." *Journal of Democracy* 3 (1): 25–40.

———. 2000. "One Step Forward, Two Steps Back." *Journal of Democracy* 11 (3): 19–33.

———. 2007. "Ukraine Imports Democracy: External Influences on the Orange Revolution." *International Security* 32 (2): 45–83.

McFaul, Michael, and Nikolai Petrov. 2004. "What the Elections Tell Us." *Journal of Democracy* 15 (3): 20–31.

McFaul, Michael, and Kathryn Stoner-Weiss. 2008. "Myth of the Authoritarian Model: How Putin's Crackdown Holds Russia Back." *Foreign Affairs* 87 (1): 68–84.

McFaul, Michael, and Richard Youngs. 2013. "Ukraine: External Actors and the Orange Revolution." In *Transitions to Democracy: A Comparative Perspective*, edited by Kathryn Stoner and Michael McFaul. Baltimore, MD: Johns Hopkins University Press. Pp. 120–43.

Meleshevich, Andrey A. 2007. *Party Systems in Post-Soviet Countries: A Comparative Study of Political Institutionalization in the Baltic States, Russia, and Ukraine*. New York: Palgrave Macmillan.

Miller, Arthur H., Gwyn Erb, William M. Reisinger, and Vicki L. Hesli. 2000. "Emerging Party Systems in Post-Soviet Societies: Fact or Fiction?" *Journal of Politics* 62 (2): 455–90.

Miller, Arthur H., and Thomas F. Klobucar. 2000. "The Development of Party Identification in Post-Soviet Societies." *American Journal of Political Science* 44 (4): 667–86.

Monitoring Zakonoproektov RF GD. https://lawmon.ru.

Monroe, Alan D. 1977. "Urbanism and Voter Turnout: A Note on Some Unexpected Findings." *American Journal of Political Science*, 21 (1): 71–78.

Moore, Barrington. 1966. *Social Origins of Dictatorship and Democracy: Lord and Peasant in the Making of the Modern World*. Boston, MA: Beacon Press.

Moraski, Bryon. 2006. "Mandating Party Development in the Russian Federation: Effects of the 2001 Party Law." *Journal of Elections, Public Opinion & Parties* 16 (3): 199–219.

———. 2007. "Electoral System Reform in Democracy's Grey Zone: Lessons from Putin's Russia." *Government and Opposition* 42 (4): 536–63.

———. 2015. "Closed-List Proportional Representation in Russia The Fates of Former District Deputies." *Party Politics* 21 (3): 381–92.

———. 2016. "Social Media, Kyiv's Euromaidan, and Demands for Sovereignty in Eastern Ukraine." In *Informational Politics, Protests, and Human Rights in the Digital Age*, edited by Mahmood Monshipouri. New York: Cambridge University Press. Pp. 127–50.

———. 2017. "Adapting to Closed-list Proportional Representation: Lessons from Ukraine." *Journal of Elections, Public Opinion & Parties* 27(2): 113–32.

Moraski, Bryon J., and William M. Reisinger. 2007. "Eroding Democracy: Federal Intervention in Russia's Gubernatorial Elections." *Democratization* 14 (4): 603–21.

Morgenstern, Scott. 2003. *Patterns of Legislative Politics: Roll-Call Voting in Latin America and the United States*. New York: Cambridge University Press.

Morlino, Leonardo. 1998. *Democracy between Consolidation and Crisis: Parties, Groups, and Citizens in Southern Europe*. New York: Oxford University Press.

Moser, Robert G. 1995. "The Impact of the Electoral System on Post-Communist Party Development: The Case of the 1993 Russian Parliamentary Elections." *Electoral Studies* 14 (4): 377–98.

———. 1997. "The Impact of Parliamentary Electoral Systems in Russia." *Post-Soviet Affairs* 13 (3): 284–302.

———. 2001. *Unexpected Outcomes: Electoral Systems, Political Parties, and Representation in Russia*. Pittsburgh, PA: University of Pittsburgh Press.

Moser, Robert G., and Ethan Scheiner. 2004. "Mixed Electoral Systems and Electoral System Effects: Controlled Comparison and Cross-National Analysis." *Electoral Studies* 23 (4): 575–99.

———. 2012. *Electoral Systems and Political Context: How the Effects of Rules Vary Across New and Established Democracies*. New York: Cambridge University Press.

Motyl, Alexander J. 2010. "Ukrainian Blues: Yanukovych's Rise, Democracy's Fall." *Foreign Affairs* 89 (4): 125–36.

Mozaffar, Shaheen, and James R. Scarritt. 2005. "The Puzzle of African Party Systems." *Party Politics* 11 (4): 399–421.

Myagkov, Mikhail, Peter C. Ordeshook, and Dimitri Shakin. 2009. *The Forensics of Election Fraud: Russia and Ukraine*. New York: Cambridge University Press.

Niemi, Richard G., Bernard Grofman, Carl Carlucci, and Thomas Hofeller. 1990. "Measuring Compactness and the Role of a Compactness Standard in a Test for Partisan and Racial Gerrymandering." *Journal of Politics* 52 (4): 1155–81.

Nisnevich, Yulii Anatol'evich. 2014. *Elektoral'naya Korruptsiya v Rossii: Politiko-Pravovoi Analiz Federal'nykh Izbiratel'nykh Kampanii v 2003–2012 Godakh*. Moscow: Fond "Liberal'naya Missiya."

Nohlen, Dieter. 1984. "Changes and Choices in Electoral Systems." In *Choosing an Electoral System: Issues and Alternatives*, edited by Arend Lijphart and Bernhard Grofman. New York: Praeger. Pp. 217–24.

Norris, Pippa. 2004. *Electoral Engineering: Voting Rules and Political Behavior*. New York: Cambridge University Press.

Norris, Pippa, and Joni Lovenduski. 1993. "'If Only More Candidates Came Forward': Supply-Side Explanations of Candidate Selection in Britain." *British Journal of Political Science* 23 (3): 373–408.

———. 1995. *Political Recruitment: Gender, Race and Class in the British Parliament*. Cambridge University Press.

Official Web Portal of the Verkhovna Rada of Ukraine. www.rada.gov.ua.

Official Website of the Central Election Commission of the Russian Federation. www.cikrf.ru.

Official Website of the State Duma of the Federal Assembly of the Russian Federation. http://duma.gov.ru.

Official Website of Ukraine's Central Election Commission. www.cvk.gov.ua.

Ofitsiina Ukraina S'ogodni. http://dovidka.com.ua.

Olivella, Santiago, and Margit Tavits. 2014. "Legislative Effects of Electoral Mandates." *British Journal of Political Science* 44 (2): 301–21.

Oracheva, Oksana. 2009. "Unification as a Political Project: The Case of Permskii Krai." In *Federalism and Local Politics in Russia*, edited by Cameron Ross and Adrian Campbell. New York: Routledge. Pp. 82–105.

Oversloot, Hans, and Ruben Verheul. 2006. "Managing Democracy: Political Parties and the State in Russia." *Journal of Communist Studies and Transition Politics* 22 (September): 383–405.

Özbudun, Ergun. 1970. *Party Cohesion in Western Democracies: A Causal Analysis.* Thousand Oaks, CA: Sage Publications.

Pain, Emil. 2011. "The Political Regime in Russia in the 2000s: Special Features, Inherited and Acquired." *Russian Politics and Law* 49 (3): 7–28.

Panebianco, Angelo. 1988. *Political Parties: Organization and Power.* Cambridge University Press.

Panov, Petr, and Cameron Ross. 2013. "Sub-national Elections in Russia: Variations in United Russia's Domination of Regional Assemblies." *Europe-Asia Studies* 65 (4): 737–52.

"Parliamentary Elections in the Republic of Moldova: Statement by Pre-electoral Delegation of Europe." 2019. Parliamentary Assembly of the Council of Europe. January 31. http://assembly.coe.int.

"Partiya Regionov." n.d. *Ukraine Elections.* http://ukraine-elections.com.ua.

Petrov, Nikolai, and Aleksei Titkov. 2013. *Reiting Demokratichnosti Regionov Moskovskogo Tsentra Karnegi: 10 Let v Stroyu.* Moscow: Carnegie Center. http://carnegieendowment.org.

Petrov, Nikolay. 2007. "The Faces of United Russia." *Moscow Times,* October 23. www.carnegie.ru.

Pharr, Susan J., Robert D. Putnam, and Russell J. Dalton. 2000. "A Quarter-Century of Declining Confidence." *Journal of Democracy* 11 (2): 5–25.

Pipes, Richard. 1997. *The Formation of the Soviet Union: Communism and Nationalism, 1917–1923.* Cambridge, MA: Harvard University Press.

Piskovii, Vladimir. 2002 "Traurnye Somneniya. Povodom Dlya Nikh Stala Skoropostizhnaya Smert' Narodnogo Deputata Olega Oleksenko." *Zerkalo Nedeli.* July 26. http://gazeta.zn.ua.

Polity Project. www.systemicpeace.org/polityproject.html.

Poole, Keith T., and Howard Rosenthal. 1985. "A Spatial Model for Legislative Roll Call Analysis." *American Journal of Political Science* 29 (2): 357–84.

Portnov, Andriy. 2014. "The Dynamics of the Ukrainian Eurorevolutions." *Religion & Society in East and West* 42: 9–12.

"Poslanie Prezidenta Federal'nomu Sobraniyu." 2011. *Prezident Rossii.* December 22. www.kremlin.ru.

Powell, G. Bingham. 2000. *Elections as Instruments of Democracy: Majoritarian and Proportional Visions.* New Haven, CT: Yale University Press.

———. 2009. "The Ideological Congruence Controversy: The Impact of Alternative Measures, Data, and Time Periods on the Effects of Election Rules." *Comparative Political Studies* 42 (12): 1475–97.

Pravda, Alex. 1978. "Elections in Communist Party States." In *Elections Without Choice*, edited by Guy Hermet, Richard Rose and Alain Rouquie. London: The Macmillan Press. Pp. 169–95.

"Protesters Challenge Pension Reform as Russian Lawmakers Approve Bill in First Reading." 2018. *Radio Free Europe/Radio Liberty*. July 19. www.rferl.org.

Rae, Douglas W. 1967. *The Political Consequences of Electoral Laws*. New Haven, CT: Yale University Press.

Rahat, Gideon, and Reuven Y. Hazan. 2001. "Candidate Selection Methods: An Analytical Framework." *Party Politics* 7 (3): 297–322.

Randall, Vicky, and Lars Svåsand. 2002. "Party Institutionalization in New Democracies." *Party Politics* 8 (1): 5–29.

Ranney, Austin. 1981. "Candidate Selection." In *Democracy at the Polls*, edited by Austin David Butler, Howard R. Penniman, and Austin Ranney. Washington, DC: American Enterprise Institute. Pp. 75–106.

Reisinger, William M., and Bryon J. Moraski. 2010. "Regional Changes and Changing Regional Relations with the Center." In *The Politics of Sub-national Authoritarianism in Russia*, edited by Vladimir Gel'man and Cameron Ross. Aldershot: Ashgate. Pp. 67–84.

———. 2013. "Deference or Governance? A Survival Analysis of Russia's Governors under Presidential Control." In *Russia Beyond the Kremlin: Comparative Subnational Politics*, edited by William Reisinger. New York: Routledge. Pp. 40–62.

———. 2017. *The Regional Roots of Russia's Political Regime*. Ann Arbor, MI: University of Michigan Press.

Reisinger, William M., Marina Zaloznaya, and Vicki L. Hesli Claypool. 2017. "Does Everyday Corruption Affect How Russians View Their Political Leadership?" *Post-Soviet Affairs* 33 (4): 255–75.

Remington, Thomas F. 2000. "The Evolution of Executive-Legislative Relations in Russia since 1993." *Slavic Review* 59 (3): 499–520.

———. 2006. "Presidential Support in the Russian State Duma." *Legislative Studies Quarterly* 31 (1): 5–32.

———. 2011. *The Politics of Inequality in Russia*. New York: Cambridge University Press.

Remington, Thomas F., and Steven S. Smith. 1996. "Political Goals, Institutional Context, and the Choice of an Electoral System: The Russian Parliamentary Election Law." *American Journal of Political Science* 40 (4): 1253–79.

Remmer, Karen L. 2008. "The Politics of Institutional Change: Electoral Reform in Latin America." *Party Politics* 14 (1): 5–30.

Reuter, Ora John. 2010. "The Politics of Dominant Party Formation: United Russia and Russia's Governors." *Europe-Asia Studies* 62 (2): 293–327.

———. 2016. "2016 State Duma Elections: United Russia after 15 Years." *Russian Analytical Digest* 189 (September 29): 2–6.

———. 2017. *The Origins of Dominant Parties: Building Authoritarian Institutions in Post-Soviet Russia*. New York: Cambridge University Press.

Reuter, Ora John, and Thomas F. Remington. 2009. "Dominant Party Regimes and the Commitment Problem: The Case of United Russia." *Comparative Political Studies* 42 (4): 501–26.

Reuter, Ora John, and Graeme B. Robertson. 2012. "Subnational Appointments in Authoritarian Regimes: Evidence from Russian Gubernatorial Appointments." *Journal of Politics* 74 (4): 1023–37.

———. 2015. "Legislatures, Cooptation, and Social Protest in Contemporary Authoritarian Regimes." *Journal of Politics* 77 (1): 235–48.

Reuter, Ora John, and David Szakonyi. 2019. "Elite Defection under Autocracy: Evidence from Russia." *American Political Science Review* 113 (2): 552–68.

———. 2021. "Electoral Manipulation and Regime Support: Survey Evidence from Russia." *World Politics* 73 (2): 275–314.

Reuter, Ora John, and Rostislav Turovsky. 2014. "Dominant Party Rule and Legislative Leadership in Authoritarian Regimes." Party Politics 20 (5): 663–74.

Reynolds, Andrew. 1995. "The Case for Proportionality." *Journal of Democracy* 6 (4): 117–24.

———. 1999. "Women in the Legislatures and Executives of the World: Knocking at the Highest Glass Ceiling." *World Politics* 51 (4): 547–72.

"Rinat Akhmetov budet ballotirovat'sya v parlament po spisku partii regionov." 2005. *Fakty i Kommentarii*. November 29. http://fakty.ua.

Rivera, Mauricio. 2017. "Authoritarian Institutions and State Repression: The Divergent Effects of Legislatures and Opposition Parties on Personal Integrity Rights." *Journal of Conflict Resolution* 61 (10): 2183–207.

Roberts, Kenneth M., and Erik Wibbels. 1999. "Party Systems and Electoral Volatility in Latin America: A Test of Economic, Institutional, and Structural Explanations." *American Political Science Review* 93 (3): 575–90.

Roberts, Sean P. 2012a. *Putin's United Russia Party*. New York: Routledge.

———. 2012b. "United Russia and the Dominant-Party Framework: Understanding the Russian Party of Power in Comparative Perspective." *East European Politics* 28 (3): 225–40.

Robinson, Neil. 2007. "The Political Is Personal: Corruption, Clientelism, Patronage, Informal Practices and the Dynamics of Post-Communism." *Europe-Asia Studies* 59 (7): 1217–24.

———. 2012. "Institutional Factors and Russian Political Parties: The Changing Needs of Regime Consolidation in a Neo-patrimonial System." *East European Politics* 28 (3): 298–309.

———. 2017. "Russian Neo-patrimonialism and Putin's 'Cultural Turn.'" *Europe-Asia Studies* 69 (2): 348–66.

Rodden, Jonathan, and Erik Wibbels. 2011. "Dual Accountability and the Nationalization of Party Competition: Evidence from Four Federations." *Party Politics* 17 (5): 629–53.

Rose, Richard. 2000. "How Floating Parties Frustrate Democratic Accountability: A Supply-Side View of Russia's Elections." *East European Constitutional Review* 9: 53–59.

Rose, Richard, and William Mishler. 2009. "How Do Electors Respond to an 'Unfair' Election? The Experience of Russians." *Post-Soviet Affairs* 25 (2): 118–36.

Ross, Cameron. 2005. "Federalism and Electoral Authoritarianism under Putin." *Demokratizatsiya* 13 (3): 347–71.

——. 2011. "Regional Elections and Electoral Authoritarianism in Russia." *Europe-Asia Studies* 63 (4): 641–61.

Rossiiskii Professional'nii Portal o Lobbizme i GR. http://lobbying.ru.

Rule, Wilma. 1987. "Electoral Systems, Contextual Factors and Women's Opportunity for Election to Parliament in Twenty-Three Democracies." *Western Political Quarterly* 40 (3): 477–98.

Russian Census 2002. "Vserossiiskaya Perepis' Naseleniya 2002 Goda." www.perepis2002.ru.

Russian Census 2010. "Vserossiiskaya Perepis' Naseleniya 2010." www.perepis-2010.ru.

Russian Federal State Statistics Agency. *Regiony Rossii: Informatsionno-Statisticheskii Sbornik.* Moscow: Gosudarstvennii Komitet Rossiiskoi Federatsii Po Statistike. (Various years.)

Rutland, Peter. 2008. "Russia as an Energy Superpower." *New Political Economy* 13 (2): 203–10.

"S"ezd 'Edinoi Rossii' Utverdil Federal'nyi Spisok Partii." 2007. *Lenta.* October 2. https://lenta.ru.

Saikkonen, Inga A.-L. 2016. "Variation in Subnational Electoral Authoritarianism: Evidence from the Russian Federation." *Democratization* 23 (3): 437–58.

Sakwa, Richard. 2011. *The Crisis of Russian Democracy: The Dual State, Factionalism and the Medvedev Succession.* New York: Cambridge University Press.

——. 2012. "Party and Power: Between Representation and Mobilisation in Contemporary Russia." *East European Politics* 28 (3): 310–27.

——. 2016. *Frontline Ukraine: Crisis in the Borderlands.* London: I.B. Tauris & Co.

Samuels, David J. 2000. "The Gubernatorial Coattails Effect: Federalism and Congressional Elections in Brazil." *Journal of Politics* 62 (1): 240–53.

Samuels, David, and Richard Snyder. 2001. "The Value of a Vote: Malapportionment in Comparative Perspective." *British Journal of Political Science* 31(4): 651–71.

Sartori, Giovanni. 2005. *Parties and Party Systems: A Framework for Analysis.* Colchester, UK: ECPR Press.

Schedler, Andreas. 1995. "Under- and Overinstitutionalization: Some Ideal Typical Propositions Concerning Old and New Party Systems." University of Notre Dame, Kellogg Institute for International Studies Working Paper 213.

———. 2002. "The Menu of Manipulation." *Journal of Democracy* 13 (2): 36–50.

———. 2006. "The Logic of Electoral Authoritarianism." In *Electoral Authoritarianism: The Dynamics of Unfree Competition*, edited by Andreas Schedler. Boulder, CO: Lynne Rienner Publishers. Pp. 1–23.

———. 2013. *The Politics of Uncertainty: Sustaining and Subverting Electoral Authoritarianism*. New York: Oxford University Press.

Schofield, Norman, and Itai Sened. 2006. *Multiparty Democracy: Elections and Legislative Politics*. New York: Cambridge University Press.

Sedelius, Thomas, and Olga Mashtaler. 2013. "Two Decades of Semi-presidentialism: Issues of Intra-Executive Conflict in Central and Eastern Europe 1991–2011." *East European Politics* 29 (2): 109–34.

Seeberg, Merete Bech. 2021 "How State Capacity Helps Autocrats Win Elections." *British Journal of Political Science*, 51 (2): 541–58.

Semenova, Elena. 2012. "Patterns of Parliamentary Representation and Careers in Ukraine: 1990–2007." *East European Politics & Societies* 26 (3): 538–60.

Sharafutdinova, Gulnaz. 2010. "Subnational Governance in Russia: How Putin Changed the Contract with His Agents and the Problems It Created for Medvedev." *Publius: The Journal of Federalism* 40 (4): 672–96.

Shevtsova, Lilia. 2014. "The Russia Factor." *Journal of Democracy* 25 (3): 74–82.

Shore, Marci. 2018. *The Ukrainian Night: An Intimate History of Revolution*. New Haven, CT: Yale University Press.

Shugart, Matthew Soberg, and John M. Carey. 1992. *Presidents and Assemblies: Constitutional Design and Electoral Dynamics*. New York: Cambridge University Press.

Shugart, Matthew Soberg, and Martin P. Wattenberg. 2001a. "Conclusion: Are Mixed-Member Systems the Best of Both Worlds?" In *Mixed-Member Electoral Systems: The Best of Both Worlds?*, edited by Matthew Soberg Shugart and Martin P. Wattenberg. New York: Oxford University Press. Pp. 571–96.

———. 2001b. "Mixed-Member Electoral Systems: A Definition and Typology." In *Mixed-Member Electoral Systems: The Best of Both Worlds?*, edited by Matthew Soberg Shugart and Martin P. Wattenberg. New York: Oxford University Press. Pp. 9–24.

Shveda, Yuriy. 2014. "The Revolution of Dignity in the Context of Social Theory of Revolutions." *Religion & Society in East and West* 42: 20–22.

Shvetsova, Olga. 2003. "Endogenous Selection of Institutions and Their Exogenous Effects." *Constitutional Political Economy* 14 (3): 191–212.

Sieberer, Ulrich. 2010. "Behavioral Consequences of Mixed Electoral Systems: Deviating Voting Behavior of District and List MPs in the German Bundestag." *Electoral Studies* 29 (3): 484–96.

Skocpol, Theda. 1979. *States and Social Revolutions: A Comparative Analysis of France, Russia, and China*. New York: Cambridge University Press.

Slider, Darrell. 2001. "Russia's Governors and Party Formation." In *Contemporary Russian Politics: A Reader*, edited by Archie Brown. New York: Oxford University Press. Pp. 224–34.

Smith, Benjamin. 2005. "Life of the Party: The Origins of Regime Breakdown and Persistence under Single-Party Rule." *World Politics* 57 (3): 421–51.

Smyth, Regina. 2006. *Candidate Strategies and Electoral Competition in the Russian Federation: Democracy without Foundation.* New York: Cambridge University Press.

Smyth, Regina, Anna Lowry, and Brandon Wilkening. 2007. "Engineering Victory: Institutional Reform, Informal Institutions, and the Formation of a Hegemonic Party Regime in the Russian Federation." *Post-Soviet Affairs* 23 (2): 118–37.

Snyder, Richard, and David Samuels. 2001. "Devaluing the Vote in Latin America." *Journal of Democracy* 12 (1): 146–59.

Solomon Jr., Peter H., and Todd S. Foglesong. 2000. "The Two Faces of Crime in Post-Soviet Ukraine." *East European Constitutional Review* 9: 72–76.

Stacher, Joshua. 2012. *Adaptable Autocrats: Regime Power in Egypt and Syria.* Stanford, CA: Stanford University Press.

"Stenograma plenarnoho zasidannya 20 Kvitnya 2004." Official Web Portal of the Verkhovna Rada of Ukraine. www.rada.gov.ua.

Stepan, Alfred. 2000. "Russian Federalism in Comparative Perspective." *Post-Soviet Affairs* 16 (2): 133–76.

Stratmann, Thomas, and Martin Baur. 2002. "Plurality Rule, Proportional Representation, and the German Bundestag: How Incentives to Pork-Barrel Differ across Electoral Systems." *American Journal of Political Science* 46 (3): 506–14.

Stroh, Alexander. 2010. "Electoral Rules of the Authoritarian Game: Undemocratic Effects of Proportional Representation in Rwanda." *Journal of Eastern African Studies* 4 (1): 1–19.

Studlar, Donley T., and Ian McAllister. 1991. "Political Recruitment to the Australian Legislature: Toward an Explanation of Women's Electoral Disadvantages." *Western Political Quarterly* 44 (2): 467–85.

Svolik, Milan W. 2012. *The Politics of Authoritarian Rule.* New York: Cambridge University Press.

"Svyatash Dmitrii." n.d. *LIGA.* https://file.liga.net.

Taagepera, Rein, and Matthew Soberg Shugart. 1989. *Seats and Votes: The Effects and Determinants of Electoral Systems.* New Haven, CT: Yale University Press.

Tavits, Margit. 2005. "The Development of Stable Party Support: Electoral Dynamics in Post-Communist Europe." *American Journal of Political Science* 49 (2): 283–98.

———. 2008. "On the Linkage between Electoral Volatility and Party System Instability in Central and Eastern Europe." *European Journal of Political Research* 47 (5): 537–55.

———. 2009. "The Making of Mavericks Local Loyalties and Party Defection." *Comparative Political Studies* 42 (6): 793–815.

Teorell, Jan, Michael Coppedge, Svend-Erik Skaaning, and Staffan I. Lindberg. 2016. "Measuring Electoral Democracy with V-Dem Data: Introducing a New Polyarchy Index." V-Dem Working Papers 2016:15. Gothenburg, Sweden: V-Dem Institute.

Thames, Frank C. 2007a. "Searching for the Electoral Connection: Parliamentary Party Switching in the Ukrainian Rada, 1998–2002." *Legislative Studies Quarterly* 32 (2): 223–56.

———. 2007b. "Discipline and Party Institutionalization in Post-Soviet Legislatures." *Party Politics* 13 (4): 456–77.

———. 2016. "Electoral Rules and Legislative Parties in the Ukrainian Rada." *Legislative Studies Quarterly* 41 (1): 35–59.

———. 2017. "The Legislative Logic of Electoral Reform in Ukraine." *Europe-Asia Studies* 69 (4): 614–41.

Treisman, Daniel. 2010. "Is Russia Cursed by Oil?" *Journal of International Affairs* 63 (2): 85–102.

Tuathail, Gearóid Ó. 2009. "Placing Blame: Making Sense of Beslan." *Political Geography* 28 (1): 4–15.

Tucker, Joshua A. 2006. *Regional Economic Voting: Russia, Poland, Hungary, Slovakia, and the Czech Republic, 1990–1999*. New York: Cambridge University Press.

———. 2007. "Enough! Electoral Fraud, Collective Action Problems, and Post-Communist Colored Revolutions." *Perspectives on Politics* 5 (3): 535–51.

"Turmanov, Viktor Ivanovich—Dos'e." n.d. *Dosye*. https://dosye.info.

Turovskii, Rostislav F. 2010. "How Russian Governors Are Appointed." *Russian Politics & Law* 48 (1): 58–79.

Turovsky, Rostislav. 2011. "Party Systems in Post-Soviet States: The Shaping of Political Competition." *Perspectives on European Politics and Society* 12 (2): 197–213.

"Ukraine, Freedom in the World 2011." Freedom House. https://freedomhouse.org.

"V bloke Yushchenko budet shestero." 2005. *Ukrainskaya Pravda*. December 3. www.pravda.com.ua.

Van de Walle, Nicolas. 2003. "Presidentialism and Clientelism in Africa's Emerging Party Systems." *Journal of Modern African Studies* 41 (2): 297–321.

Van Zon, Hans. 2008. *Russia's Development Problem: The Cult of Power*. New York: Palgrave-Macmillan.

"Vasil'ev Vladimir Alekseevich—Biografiya." n.d. *Depdela*. www.depdela.ru.

"Venice Commission Criticises Changes to Electoral System." 2017. *The Economist Intelligence Unit*. June 26. http://country.eiu.com.

"Vladimir Putin vystupil po voprosam gosudarstvennogo upravleniya i ukrepleniya sistemy bezopasnosti strany." 2014. *Rossiiskaya Gazeta*. September 14. https://rg.ru.

Von Gall, Caroline, and Laura Jäckel. 2020. "The 2020 Russian Constitutional Reform." *Russian Analytical Digest* 250 (9): 2–5.

Wagner, Alexander F., Friedrich Schneider, and Martin Halla. 2009. "The Quality of Institutions and Satisfaction with Democracy in Western Europe: A Panel Analysis." *European Journal of Political Economy* 25 (1): 30–41.

Warren, Mark E. 1999. *Democracy and Trust*. New York: Cambridge University Press.

Way, Lucan A. 2005a. "Authoritarian State Building and the Sources of Regime Competitiveness in the Fourth Wave: The Cases of Belarus, Moldova, Russia, and Ukraine." *World Politics* 57: 231–61.

———. 2005b. "Ukraine's Orange Revolution: Kuchma's Failed Authoritarianism." *Journal of Democracy* 16 (2): 131–45.

———. 2006. "Authoritarian Failure: How Does State Weakness Strengthen Electoral Competition?" In *Electoral Authoritarianism: The Dynamics of Unfree Competition*, edited by Andreas Schedler. Boulder, CO: Lynne Rienner Publishers. Pp. 167–80.

———. 2016. *Pluralism by Default: Weak Autocrats and the Rise of Competitive Politics*. Baltimore, MD: Johns Hopkins University Press.

Weghorst, Keith R., and Michael Bernhard. 2014. "From Formlessness to Structure? The Institutionalization of Competitive Party Systems in Africa." *Comparative Political Studies* 47 (12): 1707–37.

Weiner, Myron, and Joseph La Palombara. 1966. "The Impact of Parties on Political Development." In *Political Parties and Political Development*, edited by Joseph La Palombara and Myron Weiner. Princeton, NJ: Princeton University Press. Pp. 3–42.

White, John Kenneth. 2006. "What Is a Political Party?" In Handbook of Party Politics, edited by Richard S. Katz and William Crotty. Thousand Oaks, CA: Sage Publications. Pp. 5–15.

White, Stephen, and Ol'ga Kryshtanovskaya. 2011. "Changing the Russian Electoral System: Inside the Black Box." *Europe-Asia Studies* 63 (4): 557–78.

White, Stephen, and Ian McAllister. 2003. "Putin and His Supporters." *Europe-Asia Studies* 55 (3): 383–99.

Whitmore, Sarah. 2004. *State Building in Ukraine: The Ukrainian Parliament, 1990-2003*. New York: Routledge.

———. 2010. "Parliamentary Oversight in Putin's Neo-patrimonial State: Watchdogs or Show-Dogs?" *Europe-Asia Studies* 62 (6): 999–1025.

Wilson, Andrew. 2002. "Ukraine's 2002 Elections: Less Fraud, More Virtuality." East European Constitutional Review 11: 91–98.

———. 2005. *Ukraine's Orange Revolution*. New Haven, CT: Yale University Press.

Wilson, Kenneth. 2006. "Party-System Development under Putin." *Post-Soviet Affairs* 22 (4): 314–48.

———. 2016. "How Increased Competition Can Strengthen Electoral Authoritarianism: Party-System Pluralization in Russia." *Problems of Post-Communism* 63 (4): 199–209.

Wolowski, Pawel. 2008. "Ukrainian Politics after the Orange Revolution—How Far from Democratic Consolidation?" In *Ukraine: Quo Vadis?*, edited by Sabine Fischer. Paris: European Union Institute for Security Studies. Pp. 25–53.

Wright, Joseph. 2008. "Do Authoritarian Institutions Constrain? How Legislatures Affect Economic Growth and Investment." *American Journal of Political Science* 52 (2): 322–43.

Wright, Joseph, and Abel Escribà-Folch. 2012. "Authoritarian Institutions and Regime Survival: Transitions to Democracy and Subsequent Autocracy." *British Journal of Political Science* 42 (2): 283–309.

"Yanukovych ne boitsya Akhmetova i priznalsya, kto privel Piskuna." 2005. *Ukrainskaya Pravda*. December 3. www.pravda.com.ua.

Yargomskaia, Nataliia B. 1999. "Izbiratel'naia Sistema i Uroven' Partiinoi Fragmentatsii v Rossii." *POLIS: Politicheskie Issledovaniia* 4: 122–29.

"Zaginuv Narodnii Deputat Yurii Orobets.'" 2006. *UNIAN Information Agency*. October 16. www.unian.ua.

Zhdanov, Igor. 2002. "Corruption in Ukraine: Essence, Scale, and Influence." *Connections* 1 (2): 33–50.

"Zhukov, Aleksandr." n.d. *Lenta*. https://lenta.ru.

Zielinski, Jakub, Kazimierz M. Slomczynski, and Goldie Shabad. 2005. "Electoral Control in New Democracies: The Perverse Incentives of Fluid Party Systems." *World Politics* 57 (3): 365–95.

Zimmer, Kerstin, and Olexiy Haran. 2008. "Unfriendly Takeover: Successor Parties in Ukraine." *Communist and Post-Communist Studies* 41 (4): 541–61.

Zudin, Aleksei. 1999. "Oligarkhiia kak Politicheskaia Problema Rossiskogo Post Kommunizma." *Obshchestvennie Nauki I Sovremennost'* 1: 45–65.

"Zvarich Roman." n.d. *Informational Agency LIGA BusinessInform*. https://file.liga.net.

INDEX

Page numbers in italic indicate figures and tables.

ABOUT THE AUTHOR

Bryon Moraski is Associate Professor of Political Science at the University of Florida. He is the author of *Elections by Design: Parties and Patronage in Russia's Regions* and coauthor of *The Regional Roots of Russia's Political Regime* (with William Reisinger). From January through May 2014, he was a Fulbright scholar in Kyiv, Ukraine.